COSMIC ASCENSION:

Your Cosmic Map Home

Joshua David Stone, Ph.D.

THE EASY-TO-READ ENCYCLOPEDIA
of the SPIRITUAL PATH
✦ Volume VI ✦

Published by
Light Technology Publishing

Cover design by
Fay Richards

ISBN 0-929385-99-3

 Published by
Light Technology Publishing
P.O. Box 1526
Sedona, AZ 86339
(800) 450-0985

Printed by
MISSION POSSIBLE
Commercial Printing
P.O. Box 1495
Sedona, AZ 86339

Dedication

This book is dedicated to my planetary, solar, galactic and universal teachers Djwhal Khul, Lord Maitreya and Lord Melchizedek, whose guidance, information and love have been the inspiration for this book.

Namasté.

1) INSTall
2) ActivaTe
3) Actualize

Contents

Introduction

Since writing my book *Beyond Ascension*, I have received a great deal more clarification and refinement in my understanding of the process of cosmic ascension. I use the word "cosmic" ascension as differentiated from the understanding of planetary ascension. Literally almost all the books on the planet on the subject of ascension are written about planetary ascension, which is wonderful. However, because of the extraordinary times in which we now live, in terms of Earth's history, there is a new opening and potentiality to also begin one's cosmic ascension process.

This has never really been available. It must be understood, as Vywamus has said, that in completing our planetary ascension we are no more than one-tenth of the way up a ten-inch ruler in terms of our cosmic ascension process. This includes most of the ascended masters. We on Earth who are working to complete our seven levels of initiation must remember that there are 352 levels of initiation to return to the godhead, or Father-Mother God, at the top of creation. Most of the ascended masters of the entire Spiritual Hierarchy are not beyond the twelfth initiation. This is not a criticism, just a simple statement of fact.

The question is, "What lies beyond the next nine-tenths of the ruler, and how do we achieve our cosmic ascension as well as our planetary ascension (which is no small feat in and of itself)?" It is for this purpose that I have been guided to write this book.

Channeled Introduction from Melchizedek, the Universal Logos

With the utmost of love do I welcome you to the pages of this book of wisdom revealed. The first glimpse of the cosmos I wish to give you is the knowledge of the advancement of planet Earth herself, which allows for the connection between you who dwell upon her soil and that of one such as myself, the Logos Universal, to join in holy communion—one with the other. This is a blessing for us both, for it means life is evolving as it should and each of you are stepping ever more fully into your divine heritage as cocreators with God. Welcome to these words, oh ye children of the most high, and rejoice that I and a vast array of cosmic beings can now come unto you, as with your ascension process, we may step down, descend our vibratory heights. From our vastness we can take familiar form within your mind's eye and speak unto you of great and glorious things and help to guide, ease and enlighten your pathway—your own pathway into the cosmos. It is thus with the utmost of love and wisdom revealed that I welcome you to the journey through the cosmos contained within these pages.

Who I am in the vast reaches of the cosmos is in truth beyond comprehension, and yet more and more of my very self is able to be revealed. I am often called Father, divine Father, and this in truth reveals a great and most esoteric aspect of my beingness. You and your world and indeed the many systems of worlds that are evolving within the universe I embody are of my seed and bear my unique imprint. Like the ideal father I stand in unconditional love of my children, taking unbounded joy in your growth and evolution and awaiting every opportunity to give forth the light of my wisdom. For many eons have I awaited the opportunity to feed you, my hungry ones, on the light/wisdom that I embody. Yet patiently I have waited, contacting only those few who had grown to a point where they could conceive me and always working within for greater limitations than I now am.

I welcome you again into my presence, or rather into the greater awareness of my presence; forever have we been and are one. I enfold you in the arms of love and light that upon reading the forthcoming pages you may feel safe and protected by the very light/wisdom revealed therein, and know that you can invoke me at any time to further your understanding of cosmic design.

It has been taught and revealed that upon all planes of existence there are various offices held, or job positions, and more accurately stated, divine function and specific puzzlepieces. There is always a hierarchical nature

that exists within every kingdom that leads from the confines of one kingdom into the freedom of the next, leading from realm to realm, plane to
plane, dimension to dimension into and unto that which you call godhead
itself. To repeat, the time is *now*, when so many of you are stepping upward
into your hierarchical positions, which enables many of us to reach downward into your world, or more accurately stated, for those of us from our
Cosmically expansive and awakened state to connect with those of you who
are now expanding, now awakening. It is really the process of the more
awakened, lighted, love/wisdom unfolded and all-inclusive aspects of the
whole reaching to the less-awakened part of the whole, for as unique and diverse as our cosmic puzzlepieces can be, the nature of God, of cosmos itself,
is based on oneness and unity . . . and so I come to you as Father.

It is my intent that you know me thus and thus take succor from my
love, strength, light and wisdom revealed. "Ask and it shall be given you"
[Matt. 7:7]. So I ask that you call upon me as father and request of me the
continuously unfolding of divine wisdom within you, for it is with the light
of that wisdom that I seek to see you fed. The great paradox is that as within
all areas of the greater cosmology, beings such as myself at once enfold you
within our divine selves, as we and I are part and parcel of each and every
one of you. Yet likewise do we, do I, transcend you, having established ourselves in the vastness of the great whole to which you aspire. The subject of
cosmic ascension is so vast that the mind of man reels, and this is not what
we seek. The fact that this book was brought into physical manifestation is
testament to that, for what is now desired is that your brain cells and nervous systems are expanded in such a manner that what you know, have become and have been awakened to in the higher realms may be accessed
upon the dense physical and that which has hitherto been secret or incomprehensible may now be revealed. The best way to do this, in studying the
material presented herein as well as in your private meditation, is to allow
for the heart/mind, intuition/brain, word and the silence to function as one.
It is in that space where these aspects are allowed to conjoin and blend that
comprehension and realization of the wisdom word can best flourish.

With this in mind, I ask for your attention upon another great matter.
This subject embraces both the planetary world on which you dwell and
the cosmic/universal realm from which I attempt to communicate. To
many of you the masculine/feminine principles of life are a most delicate
subject. To both me and the cosmic masters it is a fact of cosmic manifestation itself. Therefore there is a specific aspect of my work that I need
you to ponder and know also as an aspect of yourself. As on Earth the yin
and yang, masculine and feminine, function as a whole, so it is with the
universe. While at once abiding in total unity with me and yet retaining
her own individuality, know that the divine Mother aspect, the yin es-

sence, is ever interwoven with me and my work, even as the divine Mother aspect is part of each and every one of you in varying degrees. Beingness and substance, light and the form that light takes, could not be without the divine feminine principle. When I speak thus as a stepped-down aspect of the Universal Logos, know that words cannot but hint at a great and vast universal truth. And yet also can they be understood by following the axiom "as above so below." Each of you, my children, is diligently working to balance the feminine and masculine energies within you. Even so, I, in eons incomprehensible, have done this and divine Mother Herself carries the mantle of balanced yin and yang—as do all who have achieved cosmic ascension. The fact remains that the truth of the puzzlepiece traverses the universe and She, who is Mother Divine, finds her point of balance more on the yin and embodies the feminine principle, even as it is Her cosmic function to put that principle forth. I, balanced in myself, embody more of the yang principle and it is my divine function to put that forth.

We seek you to keep this in the fore of your awareness, for the Father I Am functions in unity with the divine Mother, which is an important truth to ponder (although more will be said elsewhere on the subject). Take this truth into your heart/mind however, for when I speak of universal function it is my intention that you know how vital the point of interconnectiveness is—even upon universal levels, where naught but oneness abides. The ultimate paradox is that were you to call me, Melchizedek, divine Father/Mother, that would also be truth. What I seek to impart is simply that on every level, that which is one and complete within itself is likewise interconnected with other aspects that are also complete. For those who wish to look at me through this paradigm, I embrace you as your father and mother, and this pleases me as well. See me then in the "light" you so choose, for in essence, what I am *is light.*

Having said this I shall move on by reminding you again that you are my children and I will feed you well with the bread of light, which is another word for wisdom. In truth those of you who have been inwardly awake have long known who you are and have long recognized one another, even though your outer mind was but dimly aware. Some who recognized me were there throughout your planetary history, who paid homage to who I Am and to one another and consciously and together did we traverse and expand upon wings of light into the realms of light. These people were known as the priests and priestesses, the hierophants, the disciples and initiates of the Order of Melchizedek. And although they used not the term "Universal Logos" and might have known me in my various guises, they knew the truth of the one and drank of the light/wisdom that I am and have spoken and written the word of truth. Those of you in later times, now in the awakening times, have deeply traced your heritage—be it through the scattered and sparse written word, the later written revelations or in the silence of meditation—and finally does the light begin to blaze within the heart/mind, soul/monad of those of you who know yourselves as Melchizedeks.

So you are, my beloved children, who read these words and the words contained within this most rare and precious book, Melchizedeks. Let your hearts, minds, soul and monads come likewise ablaze as you eat and drink into your lightselves the wondrous light contained in the pages herein. So shall your light quotient quickly grow—how could it be otherwise when the light of wisdom is that with which you are gaining sustenance and nourishment? Let this book thus nourish you, let it be a portal from the finite into the infinite. Come ye forward with me, you Melchizedeks who are of my very self, and study the wisdom that has taken root upon the plane of matter and blossom with it and with me into the realms that are the source of wisdom itself. Light and wisdom are one, which melds with love in perfect balance. Come ye forth into that perfect blending and let your minds blaze into the hitherto uncharted realms of cosmic ascension. And in thus doing, remember, we are and ever have been one, Melchizedek.

1

What Is Cosmic Ascension?

The best way to understand cosmic ascension is to compare it with planetary ascension. Was it not Thoth/Hermes who stated in the Hermetic law, "As within, so without; as above, so below"? To understand all of creation all one really has to do is to look at the atom. We will be applying this same principle here on the subject of ascension. The following chart is very similar to the cosmic map in my book *Beyond Ascension*, with a few more additions I have received since writing that book.

Now, let us begin first with the understanding of initiations. The keys to understanding the planetary and cosmic ascension process are: initiations, light quotient, the monad, the soul, the chakras and the bodies.

The Initiations

To achieve planetary ascension one must complete the seven levels of initiations. Planetary ascension begins when one takes the sixth initiation and is completed when one completes the seventh initiation. Liberation from the wheel of rebirth is not attained until one takes the beginning of the seventh initiation.

It must be understood that ascension occurs when you receive the rod of initiation from Sanat Kumara, however it is also a process. The sixth initiation is considered the ascension initiation, however again it must be remembered that there are seven sublevels between each initiation and those all must be completed before each major initiation is complete.

There are some people who use the twelve-initiation system. Here again I state that the twelve initiations in Brian Grattan's system are exactly the same as the complete seven levels of initiations. That system is using the concept of three sublevels for initiations six and seven. Either system can be used. I personally have been guided by Djwhal Khul, Lord Maitreya and Melchizedek to use the seven levels of initiations with the seven sublevels system between each initiation.

There is also a major misconception among some lightworkers in believing that they can take initiations beyond the seventh initiation or twelfth initiation in the other system, and I am here to tell you that this is illusion. I mean no judgment in saying this, but it just isn't true and this is one thing about which I am absolutely positive.

One can still continue to grow spiritually after the seven levels of initiation, build the light quotient, anchor dimensions, anchor chakras, anchor bodies. However, one cannot take any more initiations beyond this while still retaining a physical vehicle. The belief otherwise is a manifestation of the negative ego, which we all—and I mean *all*—need to constantly be vigilant against.

Cosmic Initiations

As stated, seven levels of initiation complete our planetary ascension. In order to complete our cosmic ascension we must complete 352 levels of initiation to return to the godhead, Source, Father-Mother God. Each initiation is an expansion of consciousness and increase in frequency and light. There is no skipping steps. We must serve and prove ourselves worthy at each level (planetary, solar, galactic, universal, multiuniversal, cosmic). Each level must be stabilized and raised before one is allowed to enter the next level.

When I refer here to the multiuniversal level, I am referring to the forty-three christed universes that make up the Source of our Cosmic Day. One could break the ascension process down into these six smaller ascension divisions. First planetary ascension, then solar ascension, then galactic ascension, then universal ascension, then multiuniversal ascension, then cosmic ascension. For the purposes of this book however I am just breaking the ascension process into planetary versus cosmic ascension, which embodies the final five in that list. These divisions are an extremely helpful conceptual tool.

This is how Melchizedek, the Universal Logos, has broken down the process for our core group. On the right side of the cosmic map you can see the planetary initiations on the bottom and as you move up on the map, you can see the cosmic initiations moving up to the number 352.

Planetary Light-Quotient Ascension Process

The next key principle we will focus on in understanding planetary versus cosmic ascension is the issue of light quotient. This is one of the key

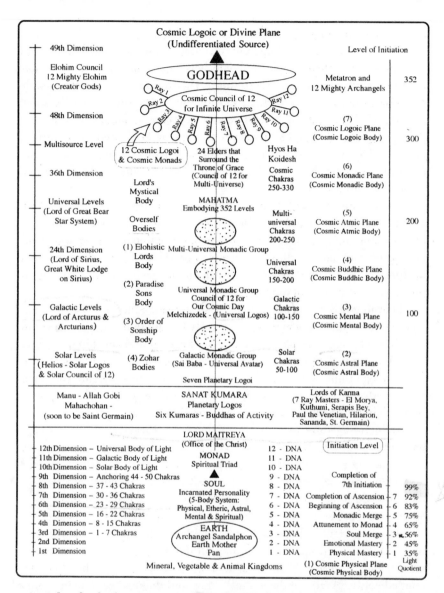

	Cosmic Logoic or Divine Plane (Undifferentiated Source)	Level of Initiation
49th Dimension	▲	
Elohim Council 12 Mighty Elohim (Creator Gods)	GODHEAD	Metatron and 12 Mighty Archangels — 352
	Ray 1 ... Ray 12 Cosmic Council of 12 for Infinite Universe	
48th Dimension	Ray 2 ... Ray 11 Ray 3 ... Ray 10 Ray 4 Ray 5 Ray 6 Ray 7 Ray 8 Ray 9	(7) Cosmic Logoic Plane (Cosmic Logoic Body) — 300
Multisource Level	12 Cosmic Logoi & Cosmic Monads	24 Elders that Surround the Throne of Grace (Council of 12 for Multi-Universe)	Hyos Ha Koidesh Cosmic Chakras 250-330	(6) Cosmic Monadic Plane (Cosmic Monadic Body)
36th Dimension	Lord's Mystical Body		
Universal Levels (Lord of Great Bear Star System)	Overself Bodies	MAHATMA Embodying 352 Levels	Multi-universal Chakras 200-250	(5) Cosmic Atmic Plane (Cosmic Atmic Body) — 200
24th Dimension (Lord of Sirius, Great White Lodge on Sirius)	(1) Elohistic Lords Body	Multi-Universal Monadic Group	Universal Chakras 150-200	(4) Cosmic Buddhic Plane (Cosmic Buddhic Body)
	(2) Paradise Sons Body	Universal Monadic Group Council of 12 for Our Cosmic Day		
Galactic Levels (Lord of Arcturus & Arcturians)	(3) Order of Sonship Body	Melchizedek - (Universal Logos)	Galactic Chakras 100-150	(3) Cosmic Mental Plane (Cosmic Mental Body) — 100
Solar Levels (Helios - Solar Logos & Solar Council of 12)	(4) Zohar Bodies	Galactic Monadic Group (Sai Baba - Universal Avatar)	Solar Chakras 50-100	(2) Cosmic Astral Plane (Cosmic Astral Body)
		Seven Planetary Logoi		
Manu - Allah Gobi Mahachohan - (soon to be Saint Germain)	SANAT KUMARA Planetary Logos Six Kumaras - Buddhas of Activity	Lords of Karma (7 Ray Masters - El Morya, Kuthumi, Serapis Bey, Paul the Venetian, Hilarion, Sananda, St. Germain)

	LORD MAITREYA (Office of the Christ)		Initiation Level	
12th Dimension – Universal Body of Light		12 - DNA		
11th Dimension – Galactic Body of Light	MONAD	11 - DNA		
10th Dimension – Solar Body of Light	Spiritual Triad	10 - DNA		
9th Dimension – Anchoring 44 - 50 Chakras	▲	9 - DNA	Completion of	
8th Dimension – 37 - 43 Chakras	SOUL	8 - DNA	7th Initiation	99%
7th Dimension – 30 - 36 Chakras	Incarnated Personality (5-Body System:	7 - DNA	Completion of Ascension	7 — 92%
6th Dimension – 23 - 29 Chakras	Physical, Etheric, Astral,	6 - DNA	Beginning of Ascension	6 — 83%
5th Dimension – 16 - 22 Chakras	Mental & Spiritual)	5 - DNA	Monadic Merge	5 — 75%
4th Dimension – 8 - 15 Chakras		4 - DNA	Attunement to Monad	4 — 65%
3rd Dimension – 1 - 7 Chakras	EARTH	3 - DNA	Soul Merge	3 — 56%
2nd Dimension	Archangel Sandalphon Earth Mother	2 - DNA	Emotional Mastery	2 — 45%
1st Dimension	Pan	1 - DNA	Physical Mastery	1 — 35%
	Mineral, Vegetable & Animal Kingdoms		(1) Cosmic Physical Plane (Cosmic Physical Body)	Light Quotient

principles for both processes. To achieve planetary ascension one must stabilize his/her light quotient between 80 to 83%, to take the beginning of the sixth initiation. At the seventh initiation one must stabilize the 92% light-quotient level. To complete the seven levels of initiation one must stabilize the 99% light-quotient level.

The term "stabilization" is extremely important here. Many people (by themselves or more often in a group setting) have on occasion achieved a very high-level meditation or light experience. The problem is that they are not able to hold the light. It quickly dissipates and more often than not, they are not able to get back to that level for a long time.

This brings up a very important question: How does one stabilize the light quotient? Most people fluctuate between as much as three or four light-quotient points at any given time. This becomes even more complicated because they even fluctuate at different levels within their five-body system. Their mental body might be at 90%; their emotional body at 84%; their physical body at 82%; their etheric body at 86%; and their spiritual body at 92%. This is why to achieve true self-realization one must become a master on all levels. I usually break this down to the spiritual, the psychological and the physical.

The key question still being, how does one stabilize the light quotient? This is a complicated and multifaceted issue. The first and most important key is maintaining mastery over your mental, emotional, etheric and physical bodies, and most of all, your negative ego. Many lightworkers are great meditators. However, they are very weak on the emotional or psychological level, which drains light quotient.

 Learning to develop evenmindedness and being the cause of your reality at all times and not a victim is extremely helpful in this process. A combination of eating well, physical exercise, fresh air and sunshine is helpful in maintaining light-quotient levels. Learning to live a life as free of negative-ego thinking as possible is a super key. Spiritualizing your emotional body, so your emotions are programmed by your soul and monad rather than the negative ego is another correlating key.

Maintaining your focus on the mighty I Am Presence at all times and not letting your attention follow the course of the lower self is another key. Spiritualizing your sexual habits and practicing the course of moderation is also a key. Another important focus is positive thinking, optimism, keeping the mind thinking about, affirming and chanting the nature of God—in other words, not being idle, for an idle mind is the "devil's workshop."

Also important is daily meditation practice. Making your life a meditation and doing light-quotient building all day long as I have suggested in my *Beyond Ascension* book is another key. Meditating with other like-minded souls, practicing love at all times and dedicating your life to the service of humanity are also keys. If possible, never allow your consciousness to leave attunement with your soul and monad. This is practicing what Djwhal Khul calls "keeping your mind steady in the light."

Other keys include: remaining in joy and inner peace at all times or as much as possible; being unceasing in your quest for planetary and cosmic ascension; and not wasting a single moment or piece of energy. Be balanced in all things and take time to have fun and enjoyment also. These are a number of ideas I personally have found useful in learning to stabilize my own light quotient.

I return now to my original theme, involving the need to ultimately stabilize the 99% light quotient. This correlates with completing the seven levels of initiation, the anchoring and activation of one's fifty chakras and the anchoring and activation of the first nine bodies, all of which I will speak in depth about as the chapter progresses.

The Cosmic Light-Quotient Ascension Process

It must be understood that the 99% light-quotient level in the planetary system is nothing more than 10% light quotient on the cosmic light-quotient scale. Remember what Vywamus said about planetary ascension being only one-tenth up a ten-inch ruler. Well, there it is.

As of writing this chapter our core group has just about stabilized our 99% light-quotient level. We have anchored and activated our fifty chakras, anchored and activated up through our ninth body and of course completed our seven levels of initiation. In doing this we are just now in the process of beginning our cosmic ascension process, which is why the writing of this book is very meaningful and pertinent to me.

The cosmic ascension process is much slower because of the incredible vastness of the infinite universe and the incredible increase in voltage we are dealing with on the cosmic levels. Our core group is now in the process of switching over to the cosmic light-quotient scale. We are now moving from 99% to 10%—rather humbling isn't it!

The two highest spiritual beings on the planet are Lord Maitreya and Sai Baba. Lord Maitreya is a galactic avatar and Sai Baba is a universal avatar. Lord Maitreya, who is the teacher of Jesus, Kuthumi, Saint Germain and all the ascended masters we revere, anchors 10% of the full cosmic Christ energy in the infinite universe on this planet. Cosmic Christ energy is a little above in frequency that which might be considered pure light quotient. Sai Baba anchors on this planet 31% of the cosmic Christ energy. Look how far even they have to go, and these are by far the most advanced beings on the planet.

To achieve cosmic ascension one must build his/her light quotient up to the 100% level on the cosmic light-quotient scale. When we first asked the masters about this they seemed to indicate that there was some kind of limit for us. However, in more recent times they have told us that there was not a limit and we could raise our light quotient as high as we are able during this incarnation. This was interesting to me, for I knew we had to stop our initiations at the completion of our seventh. However, light-quotient raising has no limits.

Why has cosmic ascension not been focused on in the past? Cosmic ascension has not been focused on in the past because, for one, humanity was not at the level to even complete planetary ascension, let alone cosmic ascension. Look at the most-revered masters: Djwhal Khul completed his ascension in this century, as did Jesus; El Morya completed his in the 1800s, as did Kuthumi; and Saint Germain did so in the 1700s or 1800s. Even the most advanced beings we know of have done it rather recently themselves.

The second reason is that most people who have ascended in the past have left their bodies shortly after taking the sixth initiation. This is what Djwhal Khul, Jesus, Kuthumi and El Morya did. Saint Germain was an exception. Even Sai Baba left his body; however, he is unique in that he is doing a triple-avatar incarnation. The point here is that this push for lightworkers to remain on the Earth after taking their ascension is a new push by the Spiritual Hierarchy. In the past it was just the opposite—no one remained on the Earth to even consider such an option.

The third reason why cosmic ascension has not been done before is because it was not really possible until the Harmonic Convergence, when the Earth moved into the fourth dimension. It was also at this time that the galactic core opened up to the Earth for the first time. The year 1988 was the first time the Mahatma, or avatar of synthesis, first became physically anchored on the Earth.

Part of this is tied up with the ending of the Piscean Age and the beginning of the Aquarian Age. This is also related to the window of mass ascension that we have entered from 1995 to the year 2000, which has been spoken of by Vywamus.

Other factors include the fact that the Earth has moved into the fifth dimension as of December 12, 1994, and the incredible acceleration of lightworkers around the planet. Other reasons are: the end of Communism in the Soviet Union and East Germany; the descent of Sai Baba and Lord Maitreya on Earth and the externalization of the Spiritual Hierarchy; the greater involvement of Buddha again in Earth's evolution; the much greater involvement of Melchizedek, the Universal Logos, and the reawakening of the Order of Melchizedek on Earth again.

The greater involvement of the archangels and angels has also furthered the process. The fact that we are now in the process of experiencing for the first time on Earth the inbreath and outbreath of Brahma, as I spoke of in my first book, *The Complete Ascension Manual*, is another factor. The fact that Melchizedek closed down ten universes in 1988 as the Source of our Cosmic Day, which now leaves our Cosmic Day with forty-three christed universes, had an extraordinary impact as well. (For a more detailed account of this read *Beyond Ascension*.)

Another driving force has been the dissemination of certain revelatory material on Earth this century including: the Alice Bailey books, Tibetan Foundation material, theosophical movements, *A Course in Miracles*, *The Keys of Enoch*, life and teaching of the masters of the Far East and *The "I*

AM" Discourses. The enormous influx of channeled material includes the works of Edgar Cayce and Earlyne Chaney, Vywamus' books through Janet McClure, the messages of Yogananda and Sai Baba and extraterrestrial involvement and channelings.

All of these and much more have facilitated an enormous expansion and acceleration in consciousness. In more recent times another factor is the newly developing ascension movement, which is gaining momentum with each passing day.

Except for these most recent times there were very few masters who were achieving these levels of initiation, and they were doing it in very small groups living in the Himalayas. The evolutionary process is now completely different; that which took a whole lifetime or fourteen years is now taking one year. The truth is, it is much easier now than it was in the past. This is also why the advanced abilities that we have correlated with achieving our ascension are much slower to develop.

Masters in the past had twenty-five years or a whole lifetime to process one initiation and develop the corresponding abilities. By the grace of God I actually went through the major initiations in a year and a half. This is one of the great blessings of the times we live in—and also one of its dangers. The danger being that the lightworkers are spiritually evolving as a whole much quicker than they are in terms of their emotional and/or psychological makeup.

Initiations have more to do with spiritual evolution than they do with psychological evolution, which came as a total shock to me. For this reason you will find people who are taking their higher levels of initiation, but are not necessarily clear of their negative ego or in control of their emotional body.

One can complete his/her seven levels of initiation and still be rather unclear in some aspects of personality. We can all be very grateful that it is much easier than it was in the past. Melchizedek has told me, however, that the ring-pass-not on this issue is cosmic ascension. People will not be allowed to move into the solar, galactic and universal levels without getting greater control over the negative ego and the emotional and psychological self.

For the first time in the history of the Earth, which is now over 3.1 billion years, we have the opportunity to actually begin working on our cosmic ascension while still physically incarnate.

The Soul and the Monad in the Ascension Process

Planetary ascension can be understood most clearly by recognizing that the ascension can be defined as the merger of the monad (mighty I Am Presence), the soul (higher self, or oversoul) and the personality (soul extension, or human being on Earth). When these three facets of your being merge and become one, you have ascended, you have become one with the mighty I Am Presence, or monad, on Earth, one with the Atma, or eternal self. At the beginning of the sixth initiation you have accomplished this at the 83% level. At the completion of the seventh initiation you have accomplished this at 99%. The third initiation is the merger with the soul. The fifth initiation begins the process of merger with the monad, or I Am Presence. I use both terms here to synthesize the teachings of Saint Germain, Kuthumi and Djwhal Khul.

The Cosmic Monad and the Cosmic Soul

Let us now extrapolate to the cosmic level. As within, so without; as above, so below. Cosmic ascension is the merger with the cosmic monad or the cosmic mighty I Am Presence. Planetary ascension is movement into the seventh, or logoic, plane of consciousness on the cosmic physical plane. Cosmic ascension is full merger and completion of the cosmic logoic, or cosmic seventh plane. We are speaking here of the difference between the planetary logoic plane and the cosmic logoic plane.

Seven Planetary Planes	Seven Cosmic Planes
Physical	Cosmic physical
Astral	Cosmic astral
Mental	Cosmic mental
Buddhic	Cosmic buddhic
Atmic	Cosmic atmic
Monadic	Cosmic monadic
Logoic	Cosmic logoic

The completion of the seven planetary planes is the completion of just the first cosmic plane called the cosmic physical plane. None of us have even entered the other six cosmic planes. The choice of which of the seven paths to higher evolution you choose will determine which of these cosmic planes you will work in on your path of cosmic evolution.

The Seven Paths of Evolution
Path of Earth service
Path of magnetic work
Path of training to become a Planetary Logos
Path to Sirius
Ray path
Path on which our Solar Logos is found
Path of absolute Sonship

(For more information on these paths, read *Beyond Ascension* and *The Complete Ascension Manual.*)

In planetary ascension the soul, or higher self, is the intermediary between the personality on Earth and the monad, or mighty I Am Presence. In cosmic ascension the Mahatma might be considered the intermediary between God and His evolving sons and daughters of God. The Mahatma, or Avatar of Synthesis, is a group-consciousness being that embodies all 352 levels of the godhead.

Planetary and Cosmic Trinity

Planetary Ascension	Cosmic Ascension
Monad	God and cosmic monad
Soul	Mahatma
Personality	Planetary ascended master

The Mahatma, being the intermediary for God, could also be broken down even further. Speaking for myself personally, a second intermediary is my "cosmic ascension lineage." In my case it is Djwhal Khul on the planetary and solar level, Lord Maitreya on the galactic level and Melchizedek on the universal level. Melchizedek is the Universal Logos and is not only the being who is the president of the entire universe but also the president of the forty-three universes for our Cosmic Day. So he is the head of the multiuniversal level for our Cosmic Day. To realize the vastness of God there are infinite numbers of sources for Cosmic Days throughout God's infinite universe.

In terms of this discussion of ascension lineage I am not one hundred percent positive about this, however I think most lightworkers on Earth will share Lord Maitreya and Melchizedek with me—given the fact that Lord Maitreya is the head of the entire Spiritual Hierarchy, runs seven planetary ashrams and is the teacher for all seven chohans.

Melchizedek, on even a higher level, is the teacher for all lightworkers for not only our planet but our entire universe. Melchizedek is the grand master of all masters for our universe. There are some people who believe that there is only an Order of Melchizedek and not a person who runs that order. This is not true. I know this for a fact, for I have had literally hundreds of conversations with him and he is very much alive and well.

I consider my personal contact with him as the single greatest blessing of my entire lifetime and probably all my lifetimes. What our core group and I have learned from him has been absolutely mind-boggling. In his cosmic ascension process he is between the fifth and seventh cosmic plane. He is very close now to completing his cosmic ascension and the other nine-tenths of the ruler, which we have not even begun.

Cosmic Monads

My understanding at this time is that there are twelve cosmic monads that have a relationship to the Cosmic Council of Twelve at the 352d level of the godhead. Ultimately, we each come from one of these cosmic monads. I have outlined this on the cosmic map on the top of the page in the center. So just as each of us on the planetary level has a ray that makes up our planetary monad, we each also stem from a ray that makes up our cosmic monad. God and the cosmic ascension is the full merger with the cosmic monad and 352 levels of the Mahatma and the evolving ascended masters.

Planetary Chakras

One of the revolutionary pieces of information that has been revealed to us, which I don't think has ever been revealed in written form before, is the understanding that we don't have seven chakras, or twelve chakras, but in actuality, fifty major chakras. I am not talking about minor chakras here.

The seven-chakra system was appropriate when Earth was still in the third dimension. When Earth moved into the fourth dimension, the twelve-chakra system became very prevalent. As the Earth and the advanced initiates on the planet moved toward the fifth dimension, which is ascension, Vywamus channeled that we had twenty-two chakras not twelve. There are seven in the third dimension, seven more in the fourth dimension and an additional seven in the fifth dimension. Do you see that there is a chakra grid of seven for each dimension?

As the disciples and initiates on Earth evolve, the chakras begin to descend. At whatever level you are, you want to bring in the next higher chakra grid from above you. The twelve-chakra system is nothing more than a fourth-dimensional system. When you ascend, your sixteenth chakra becomes anchored into the crown. The fifteenth chakra becomes anchored in your third eye, your fourteenth chakra in your throat and so on, moving downward.

This is at the beginning of the sixth initiation. Once you take your sixth initiation, you want to begin anchoring in the full fifth-dimensional chakra grid. When that has been anchored and activated, then you want to bring in the sixth-dimensional chakra grid, that is chakras 23 through 29. When that is fully installed and activated, then you bring in the seventh-dimensional chakra grid—chakras 30 through 36. Then comes the eighth-dimensional chakra grid, chakras 37 through 43. Next is the ninth-dimensional grid of chakras 44 through 50. The ninth dimension is the full completion of the planetary chakra system.

In truth, this is far beyond our normal understanding of the ascension process, for ascension is considered the fifth dimension. By anchoring and activating these higher chakra grids and anchoring chakra 50 in the crown, chakra 49 in the third eye and chakra 48 in the throat, you are tapping into the ninth dimension.

Melchizedek has told us that there are forty-nine dimensions to be anchored to achieve cosmic ascension. The sixth initiation is the movement into the fifth dimension; the seventh initiation is movement into the sixth dimension. Even though one has to stop taking initiations at seven while still incarnated, one can continue to anchor and activate chakra grids, which gives humanity access to and grounding of dimensional frequencies.

What I present here is an incredible key to speeding up your spiritual evolution. For more information read *Beyond Ascension, Soul Psychology* and *The Complete Ascension Manual*. More will also be given later in this book. As of writing this chapter our core group has installed and activated chakra 50 in our crown, which leads me to the next lesson in understanding cosmic ascension.

Installation, Activation and Actualization

These three words play a crucial part in understanding both planetary and cosmic ascension. The first step in the process of anchoring the higher-dimensional chakra grids is requesting to your own mighty I Am Presence and the masters you work with to install the higher chakras. The second step, once they are installed by the masters and woven into your being, is to then work to activate them. It is working over time with the masters, love, service and meditation that achieves this goal. The final step, which is the final and hardest step, is to actualize the chakras.

This is the key to understanding why many who have achieved their ascension have not developed their advanced ascension master abilities. I will use myself as an example. I have currently installed and activated my fifty chakras, seven levels of initiation, 99% light quotient and twelve strands of DNA, merged with monad and soul at 99% level and installed and activated up through my ninth body.

So I have installed and activated across the board up through the ninth level, except for initiations, which must stop at completion of the seventh. Even though I have done this I still haven't developed the ability to teleport, dematerialize or materialize things, turn water into wine or raise the dead. These more advanced ascended master abilities come with this final third stage, which is the actualization of these advanced chakra grids.

I have completed two-thirds of the process and am currently working on this final stage of actualizing my advanced ascended master abilities while working on my cosmic ascension process. Both are being worked on simultaneously. Cosmic installations and activations can be continued while actualization of the full fifty chakras is taking place. The added cosmic installations and activations will add to and help the full cosmic actualization process in terms of advanced ascended-master abilities.

Some of these abilities are not required, such as teleportation or physical immortality. Sai Baba doesn't choose to manifest physical immortality, however he could if he wanted to use his energy that way. Everything is just energy and each person has to choose how he/she wants to use his energy given his mission. Some might choose to live on light instead of physical food; however, some will choose to eat food and have no desire, purpose or inclination to demonstrate this lesson. It is all how you want to use your energy. This now brings us to the understanding of the cosmic chakras.

Cosmic Chakras and the Ascension Process

The newest information that Melchizedek has shared with us is that there are actually 330 chakras that must be anchored and activated to take one back to the godhead. The fifty chakras are again what might be considered the planetary chakras. What we have been told (which is absolutely fascinating) is that there are also:

50 solar chakras
50 galactic chakras
50 universal chakras
50 multiuniversal chakras
80 cosmic chakras.

If you add all of these chakras up, you get 330. The extraordinary thing is that Melchizedek has told us that it is potentially possible to install and activate these cosmic chakras. What we have been told is that the installation and activation of the tenth, eleventh and twelfth bodies, which are the solar, galactic and universal bodies, correlate with the installation and activation of the first two hundred chakras.

Melchizedek said that this cannot even be considered until one has completed the seven levels of initiation, achieved the 99% light quotient, anchored and activated the fifty chakras, fully merged with his/her planetary soul and monad, installed and activated the first nine bodies and anchored the twelve strands of DNA into her etheric body. Therefore don't even consider asking for these things until this level is accomplished.

Every person who is now reading this book is fully capable of achieving these things in this embodiment if he/she applies the lessons given in my books and others like them in a focused, systematic, disciplined and one hundred percent-committed fashion, dedicating his life solely to unconditional love, egolessness and service of humanity. Again I am here to say that the extraordinary times we live in and the fact that we are in a five-year window for mass ascension makes this uniquely possible. So take advantage of it and "be about the Father's business."

Our core group has just recently accomplished these goals and demonstrated the willingness and abilities to dedicate our lives solely to planetary world service, which is a key. We have been told by Melchizedek, by the grace of God, that it will take (if all goes according to plans) five years for us to anchor and activate our solar, galactic and universal bodies and install and activate our two hundred chakras. This time period happens to be from 1995 to the year 2000, which is the window for mass ascension.

I share this with you not to be egotistical but to demonstrate that it is potentially possible. Certain cosmic dispensations are now being given that have never been given to the Earth before. I will emphasize here that to be allowed to anchor cosmic energies such as these one must be of the absolute highest focus, commitment, self-mastery, self-discipline, integrity, egolessness, unconditional love and commitment to service. I also warn you that when much is given by the masters, much is expected. I warn you now, if you are not willing to give yourself totally (and I mean *totally*) to God, service and your spiritual path, don't even consider invoking such energies.

This book and teachings are for the most advanced initiates and spiritual leadership group on this planet. It is meant to be read by all lightworkers to give them a cosmic map for future potentialities, and to inspire them to take the "hero's journey" at a level of focus and commitment that they might not have considered yet.

I share this information with you to tell you these things can be done and to tell you that I am not exceptional—and I really mean this. I very much consider myself an average Joe. I like to go to movies, have my favorite TV shows, like to converse with your everyday person I meet in the market or bank, live in Los Angeles and enjoy a good sports event on television occasionally. If you would meet me I would be like your neighbor next door.

I share my process with you to tell you if I can do it, anybody can. As God is my witness, I totally mean this. There is one thing, however, that I feel is exceptional about myself and that is the level of intense focus, commitment and self-discipline that I am willing to manifest in my quest of service to humanity, of God-realization and of cosmic ascension.

Djwhal Khul spoke of this in the Alice Bailey books, that sometimes the average man goes much further than the genius because of his greater commitment. I am very much the average man. My commitment every moment of my life is complete and has been for a very long time. That is how I have reached the point where I am. I share this with you to show that it doesn't take extraordinary psychic powers to achieve these things or being the best channel on the planet or special past lives or really any advanced abilities at all. It just takes one thing, which was summed up by the Master Jesus with the following statements: "Love the Lord thy God with all thine heart, and with all thy soul, and with all thy might" [Deut. 6:5] and "Love thy neighbor as thyself" [Lev. 19:18].

Yogananda said it all when he said, "If you truly want God, you must want Him like a drowning man wants air." If you love and are willing to strive for God and service of humanity that much, you will find Him. It is all up to your commitment. Do you want God, or do you want your ego (materialistic path)? If you truly want God then choose Him one hundred percent and never look back.

Apply the principles, meditations and instructions in these books and you can achieve your planetary ascension in an enormously short period of time and can then begin your cosmic ascension process. I personally am not a procrastinator. My motto is, "Why put off what I can get done now?" This path is not for the faint of heart. It is for those who are really ready to claim their personal power one hundred percent in the service of love of humanity, God and the masters. Take advantage of these extraordinary times we live in. You will never have a better opportunity than you have right now.

In review, cosmic ascension is the anchoring, activation and actualization of our 330th chakra in our crown. This can be seen on my newly revised cosmic map diagram [p. 13]. Can you imagine what it would be like to anchor and activate your 200th chakra in your crown and to install and activate your solar, galactic and universal bodies? If we can potentially do it in five years after completing our planetary ascension, so can you—even if it took ten years. This is nothing compared to the magnitude of energies we are talking about.

Melchizedek told us that the key to teleporting was the anchoring and activation of our universal body, which is the twelfth body and 200th chakra activation. Would you really rather invest your time and energy on overidentification with matter, or experience these sublime energies of God on Earth? It must also be stated here that even though we are allowed to install and activate these cosmic chakras and cosmic bodies, in truth we are only tapping into an aspect of their full power. Our initiation level limits the amount we can access.

Sai Baba, who is a universal avatar and who is operating out of these higher levels of initiation, is an example of what can be done on Earth when actualization and higher initiations have been attained. (Read *The Complete Ascension Manual* for more information about Sai Baba.) Even though our installation and activation won't be at the level of a Sai Baba, I am sure it will be amazing and this is available to every person reading this book, for God loves all His sons and daughters equally.

The question is not really what God will allow you but rather what you will allow yourself in terms of how you spend your time and energy this lifetime. The completion of planetary ascension is much like going to earthly school or earthly college. There are certain classes and units that must be achieved. The same is true of spiritual school. There are a certain number of light-quotient units to be achieved, chakras and bodies to install and activate and initiations to pass.

These books give you simple, easy-to-understand and fun tools for easily accomplishing these goals. In truth it is all very systematic. The problem we have had in the past is that we haven't had the tools and simple understanding of the process. Now we do, so it really is not that hard to achieve.

In my earlier life I never thought in a million years that I would achieve my ascension. I thought it was some mystical, insurmountable, unattainable goal. At forty-two years old I have not only achieved it but am helping others find the path to cosmic ascension. In my books I have shared with you exactly how I did it. I have literally given you everything.

I went through three major initiations in a year and a half. Apply what I did and you can potentially achieve the same thing. I have studied pretty much everything, and I honestly don't believe there is a faster path on the planet than working with the masters and with this level of ascension work.

There is one more reason I have chosen to share some of my personal experiences in this planetary and cosmic ascension process. This last reason is to give you, my reader, a timetable and perspective on how long it will take to achieve these things. In my personal opinion this is of invaluable importance. For example, if I tell you now that you can complete your major initiations in approximately one or two years, that is of incredible value. I know it would be for me. It gives me a perspective on the whole process and a short-term goal to strive for.

The masters have, by the grace of God, given us timetables to work with. Now the fact is that usually we have cut their predictions in half, and of course they are pleased with this. Just the fact that they gave us these timetables was incredibly helpful. It was also inspiring and hopeful to know that it was within our potential goals in such a relatively short period of time.

Now I realize not everyone has direct access to the masters. So as I am writing I am attempting to be an intermediary and am speaking in general terms of that which is available to the general high-level initiate. When I tell you that we have been told it would take five to ten years to integrate the solar, galactic and universal levels, I share this to give you a goal to strive toward.

Again, realize masters, in the not-too-distant past, took whole lifetimes to achieve one initiation. In a sense I am dangling a carrot before you to motivate you and inspire you to be about the Father's/Mother's business.

I think you can appreciate the great value of having this kind of timetable and see that what has been made available to our core group is available to you also. Sometimes I have debated within myself whether to put my personal experiences in the book because I didn't want it to sound like I was tooting my own horn. But I think it is helpful to know that someone is actually doing these things and not just theoretically talking about abstruse esoteric concepts. These concepts I speak of are living, breathing experiences in our lives.

I also want to explain here how the number of 330 cosmic chakras was derived. When we first asked Melchizedek about this, out of the blue he said 300 chakras to take one to the top of creation. He was speaking in basic, general terms. That statement turned out to be more accurate than I first thought.

When I went for my "ascension walk" one day, it came to me, probably from Melchizedek, that this could be exactly figured by just multiplying the seven chakras that make up each dimensional grid by the forty-nine dimensions. If you multiply 49 by 7 you get the number 344. One must take into account, however, that the chakras begin in the third dimension, not in the first two dimensions. To get the exact number of chakras, one then has to subtract 14 from 344, which equals 330.

I asked Melchizedek if I was accurate in following this line of thought. He said I was and that his first figure was a generalized figure that was amazingly accurate, for he could have said any number in the universe and I would have accepted it. His guidance got a double-confirmation by working out the mathematics of the rest of the cosmology we had previously been given.

We have now anchored and activated nine dimensional grids. We have forty more to install, activate and actualize to return to the godhead. The thing that I like about this process now is that I am starting to get the hang of how it works and what I need to do, which makes it much quicker. I see now that I will be using the same principles I used to achieve my planetary ascension to achieve my cosmic ascension, even when I leave this physical vehicle (or transfigure it).

One other interesting thing I discussed with Melchizedek is how light-quotient levels correlate with the solar, galactic and universal completion. He wouldn't give me exact information today when I asked him. It is interesting how these things work. Sometimes information comes through at certain times and not at others. I know a lot of times the masters don't give us information until we are ready to utilize it.

I intuitively suggested to Melchizedek that planetary completion was at 10% on the cosmic light-quotient scale. Solar completion was at the 30% level, universal completion around the 40% cosmic light-quotient scale and multiuniversal at around 60%. I asked Melchizedek if I was on the right track with these figures and he said I was and that he would give us more detailed figures at a later time.

The one point that Melchizedek did say, which I hadn't taken into consideration, was the fact that our solar installation and activation would be a different light quotient than Sai Baba's solar figure would be. Remember, we as seventh-degree initiates are only accessing a small portion of these levels, whereas Sai Baba being an avatar (God-realized at birth and coming in at the universal level) would have different solar, galactic and universal completion numbers.

The other thing that it is important to realize here is that all this extra anchoring and activation work we are doing beyond the seven levels of initiation will make the passing through future initiations much easier. Even though we are not taking the initiations, it is like we are completing a lot of the homework in advance. It is like being in high school but taking college courses that will apply to your college credits—extra credit, you might say.

The extra voltage of energy that is gained immensely adds to the power, radiation and magnetism of the world-service work one does. Of all the factors I have mentioned in this chapter, passing the initiations is the most important. If you don't know your level of initiation and light quotient, or chakra-anchoring level, and you would like to find out, contact me and I will help you find it out. If you also have not had your implants removed, I will help you get directed to the right people.

Planetary Bodies and the Ascension Process

To complete planetary ascension one must anchor and activate the first nine bodies of the twelve-body system. These nine bodies are described by the ascended master Djwhal Khul through Alice Bailey in *The Rays and the Initiations* as follows:

Plane	Bodies	Initiations	Quality
Material plane	Physical body	1st initiation	Instinct
Astral plane	Astral body	2nd initiation	Desire, feeling
Mental plane	Mental body	3rd initiation	Concrete mind
Buddhic plane	Buddhic body	4th initiation	Intuition
Atmic plane	Atma body	5th initiation	Spiritual will
Monadic plane	Monadic body	6th initiation	Divine intelligence
Logoic plane	Logoic body	7th initiation	Purity, divine grace

As you move upward in the initiation process, you keep moving into a higher dimension at each initiation and operate out of a higher body. Upon taking the seventh initiation you are operating out of the logoic body and have just entered the logoic plane as your stabilization point, so to speak. This is the continuing process of spiritual evolution.

One keeps moving into initiations, bodies, planes and/or dimensions and chakras. There are again seven sublevels between each initiation. These sublevels could also be correlated with the seven individual chakras in each chakra grid. For example, the first chakra in each grid could be correlated with the first sublevel of the particular initiation you are working on. As each individual chakra of that grid moves downward into your crown, you are in a sense going up another sublevel in your initiation process. In terms of light quotient one could say that at each sublevel, or chakra, is processed one-seventh of the light needed to complete that initiation.

I will also add here that there are two other bodies that need to be considered in the processing of the first seven levels of initiation before we actually get to the eighth and ninth body. The first is the etheric body, which is connected to the physical body and is of course the divine blueprint for the physical body. It is connected to the first initiation and the material plane, and the quality it embodies is vital force.

The one other body to be considered in this discussion is a second body connected to what might be called the higher mental plane. The lower mental plane is the concrete mind. This is your basic intellectual-type person. On the higher aspect of the mental plane, however, is the soul body, which Djwhal Khul has also called the causal body. It is where all one's good karma is stored from all his/her past lives and this life. It is the body that is burned up at the fourth initiation as the initiate begins to work directly with the monad and mighty I Am Presence, rather than just the soul or higher self. The quality of energy of the soul body is abstract mind. This is the quality used by your psychologist and metaphysician.

As you can see, each body is also connected to a quality or a particular characteristic. As you move up the initiation process you inhabit higher high-level bodies and hence more evolved characteristics and qualities.

You can see this progression in a child growing up. As an infant the child is just operating out of instinct and the flow of vital force, with no conscious directorship by the infant. As the child grows it begins to focus more out of the desire, or emotional body. In high school or thereabouts the mental body comes into play. Hopefully then the abstract mind grows and then intuition and spiritual will. One can also see how some people stay stuck or overidentify with certain bodies and their corresponding characteristics and qualities. The ideal is being balanced, of course.

Once you have completed the seven levels of initiations, you are operating now out of the logoic body on Earth. Then there are two more transitionary bodies that are still considered planetary bodies but become more transpersonal in nature. They are planetary collective bodies. These eighth and ninth bodies are: the group-soul body and the group-monadic body.

These two bodies are still connected to the seventh initiation as well as the eighth and ninth dimensions. They have a connection with the eighth- and ninth-dimensional chakra grids, or chakras 37 through 50. They embody a quality of group consciousness. These bodies are no longer dealing with your individual soul, or individual monad, but rather with the same principles on a planetary-group level.

The eighth-body integration has to do with merging in consciousness with all higher selves, oversouls, or souls (whatever you prefer), on the entire planetary level. The group-monadic level is the exact same thing, but one level up. This is the merging in consciousness with all monads or planetary mighty I Am Presences. We have moved here from individual focus of our own bodies to humanity's collective bodies that are connected to this planet.

As in the case with the chakras, these bodies need to be installed, activated and actualized. At the time of writing this section our core group has installed and activated up through this level and in the past couple months has begun working on the tenth, eleventh and twelfth bodies, which begins our discussion now of the cosmic bodies and cosmic ascension.

The Cosmic Bodies and Cosmic Ascension

The first three bodies I would like to consider in this discussion are the tenth, eleventh and twelfth bodies, which are the solar, galactic and universal bodies. These bodies, as can be seen from their names, are the first time we are now officially leaving the planetary ascension process and beginning the solar, galactic and universal ascension process, or collectively called the cosmic ascension process.

This is, of course, quite an exciting step. These bodies, as do all of the bodies on a planetary and cosmic level, need to be installed, activated and actualized. At the Wesak Festival in May 1995, our core group received a great blessing from his holiness, Lord Sai Baba, who installed all three bodies at that time. This is what we had asked for, and this special dispensation was granted to us.

Since that time I have had my Sherlock Holmes hat on and have been doing my research trying to figure out how this process works, since there is no written material on Earth really guiding the cosmic ascension process. The masters tell me that is my job, and that is why I am writing this book.

As I mentioned earlier, the masters can be kind of funny at times about giving out this kind of cosmic knowledge and sometimes you have to catch them at the right moment. You have probably heard the statement "when the student is ready, the teacher appears." I will add to this proverb "when the student is ready, the information appears." If they don't think we are ready, they often don't give the information. You, my beloved readers, will be happy to know I am very persevering and like Jacob in the Bible, I will not let go until they bless us.

In taking this stance and not being shy, I have learned a great many things. The first of these is that the process of installing and activating these three bodies is no small thing. My first clue about this was when they told me it would take five years to do it. Given that our core group had been processing our past three initiations in six months each, I knew this must be a big thing. The second major clue came when our core group received upon persistent questioning the understanding of the 330 cosmic chakras.

To put this in perspective, what we were basically asking for in installing and activating these bodies is the installation and activation of our first 200 chakras. In the next five years we are looking at having to install and activate another 150 chakras that correlate with these solar, galactic and universal bodies.

Now I think you will agree with me that this is awesome. I never even dreamed it would be possible to do such a thing—let alone in five years. Now I am not one to count my chickens before they hatch and a lot can happen in five years, but just the potentiality is staggering to me.

So as you, my reader, can see, it is truly possible to begin working on one's cosmic ascension on Earth. Melchizedek told us that it is in anchoring, activating and actualizing the universal, or twelfth, body that teleportation is possible. Another requirement to be able to do this Melchizedek told us is that one must clearly demonstrate an ability to get out of his/her negative ego or he will not be allowed to go beyond planetary ascension.

He also told us that one must also demonstrate to the masters a total commitment to service as his/her main purpose and goal. The basic attitude of our core group has been to pray for this and now completely surrender this process into Melchizedek's hands. He has stated to us what the timetable is and he has literally forbidden me to even ask about it for at least another year.

You have to realize that it has taken me this whole lifetime to anchor and activate my fifty chakras, and in truth it has taken me 250 lifetimes. We will be doing the next fifty chakras in the solar grid in a little more than a year and a half. This is equivalent to processing seven full initiations, even though we are not allowed to take these initiations on Earth.

We are then also talking about doing another fifty chakras for the galactic system and then another fifty for the universal system. The actual taking of the initiations that correspond to these levels will of course be much more time consuming. I was told that I would probably spend 150 years working in a leadership position in Djwhal Khul's ashram and then another 1000 years in the Great White Lodge on Sirius.

I honestly believe that the cosmic ascension work we are now doing is going to greatly speed up our cosmic evolution. I really do feel that we are starting to get an intuitive sense of how the process works in the very simplest cosmic sketch of the process. It is also important to enjoy the process and not try to rush it. I am very much looking forward to working in Djwhal Khul's ashram and to my future work in the Great White Lodge. It is like going to college and taking classes you love and helping millions of people whom you love.

What I am beginning to see now is that once you tap into the ascended masters and are working with them, at this level you are in a sense riding a wave, and all the invoking and activation work that was needed in the earlier stages is not needed as much now. At this level, the total focus is service. By becoming completely immersed in the process of service, one's personal evolutionary goals kind of take care of themselves.

For example, I am writing this book as a service project for you, my beloved readers. I don't need to write this book. I already understand the material myself. I write this for you. I don't need to focus on my personal evolutionary process, for my service work is pretty much my personal evolutionary process. Writing this book is the ultimate meditation for me, and I am having to run all the energies through my twelve-body system to write it.

The way I see the process is like staying in the Tao. Melchizedek has told us that it will take five years to do this. As long as the three of us stay in the Tao that has already been established through our hard work in the past, everything will just naturally progress without a lot of extra work on our part. It is like the understanding of developing good habits. From all our hard work our core group has developed good habits. Our spiritual lifestyle doesn't take a lot of extra energy because we already have the positive habit of doing all we are supposed to do. As long as the three of us stay in the flow we are in, focusing completely on service, our personal evolutionary goals will just take care of themselves.

It was important to pray and ask for these goals, but now that we have done this, it is time to let go and just be about the Father's business. To be perfectly honest, I really like this. For I have never liked having to be concerned about my own personal evolution. I finally feel I have gotten to the place where I don't have to concern myself with it anymore. Helping people as much as I can is my *sadhana* (spiritual practice), as Sai Baba would say. Sai Baba has also said that "hands that help are holier than lips that pray."

I also want to state here that one of the reasons that we are being allowed to move to this next level is because of the ascension buddy system, bonding and group consciousness that our core group has. I am absolutely positive, and we have been told this directly, that much of what we have experienced is because we have worked together in this cooperative venture in service of the Spiritual Hierarchy.

I am absolutely convinced that each of us would not have been given even one-third of what we have received if we hadn't formed a group body as we have. The three of us together form a much greater battery and group mind than any one of ourselves on our own. Our abilities also complement one another, which creates a more whole person and service vehicle.

Another reason we have been granted this dispensation is that the three of us have been given certain leadership positions in the Spiritual Government because of our unwavering focus and commitment to service. Because of this we are being allowed to do certain things and receive certain things that have not been available to the Earth before. In some areas we are functioning as prototypes, as others in the past have done for us. Most of the other masters have already done the things we are doing, but what is unique is that they did this work on the inner plane.

What is now being done on Earth in a physical body is totally unique. In some of the work we are doing, it is paving the way for others to follow. You are receiving the benefit of an enormous amount of hours of meditation and research to achieve this more refined and clarified understanding. You, I hope, will build and expand on many of the things I am writing about here, and will pave the way for others, just as the masters above are doing for us. This is the eternal chain and link of the spiritual and cosmic hierarchies. Brother and sister helping brother and sister.

On a slightly different subject, Melchizedek told us an interesting piece of information dealing with the issue of gender on the higher planes. Masters retain a feminine or masculine appearance up through all the cosmic dimensions back to their cosmic ascension. The body that is retained is usually the one in which you take your ascension.

Now, given the spiritual leadership positions our core group has been given, the group body we work out of and each of our unique abilities, I do want to make it clear here that not every person who reads this book will be operating from the same timetables we are. Some will complete their initiations in one year, some two years, some three years. We are not competing and it is not a race. Any one of these timetables is incredibly fast.

Djwhal Khul just fifty years ago took fourteen years to do one. Jesus took a whole lifetime to do just one. The same is true of cosmic ascension. Some might be able to do it in five years, some ten years, some fifteen years, some twenty years. Whatever it is, it is incredibly fast and in truth has almost never been done before in the 3.1 billion-year history of the Earth.

As prototypes in this area, I am giving you some timetables and potentialities of a general nature with which to work. When you reach these levels, do Huna prayers as I have outlined in *Beyond Ascension* and pray for these things. Use your intuition to request certain timetables for achieving these goals. Be realistic, and know that having these short-term goals for yourself can be extremely helpful. Also telling your own mighty I Am Presence and ascended masters your personal goals is extremely important.

What happens is that you are then placed in a group wave, so to speak. All those working at your level of evolution on the planet who have similar goals, be they conscious or unconscious, will be moved forward at the same speed. Your job is to remain in the Tao of the wave you are on. Some lose their focus, self-mastery, self-discipline and commitment and therefore lose the opportunity to be part of a more advanced wave.

There are infinite numbers of waves and everyone will eventually be on one of them. God's plan won't be complete until all souls return back to Source. The idea, as stated in *A Course in Miracles*, is to shorten the need for time. Time is a temporary concept that is being used for a temporary period of time to complete a certain phase of God's divine plan. When it has served its purpose, it will exist no more. Let us all work together as one massive group body and shorten the need for time and return home together. We will not return home without giving our hand in service and love to our brothers and sisters.

One last very important point I need to mention again is that in installing and activating the solar, galactic and universal bodies, we on this planet are actually only tapping into a small portion of their true power and realization. We might be tapping into only as much as five percent of their true power and magnitude. This is because we are doing this work from the consciousness of being seventh-level initiates.

As I told you before, we are not allowed to go beyond this level of initiation while still in a physical body. When we take our twentieth or thirtieth initiation, we will begin tapping into our solar, galactic and universal bodies' full power. Even tapping into just five percent of the full power of these bodies will be an enormous amount from the perspective of an Earthling and from the concept of planetary mastery.

For example, it will be enough to physically teleport and will greatly add to one's light quotient, overall spiritual radar system and spiritual battery and voltage. As Sai Baba has said, we are all like light bulbs. Some are 50 watts, some 75, some 100, some 150, some 200. Sai Baba is a 1000 watt-light bulb. We are all in the process of raising our spiritual wattage.

I think you can see why the masters are very discerning about who is allowed to move into these more cosmic levels and wattages. What if a person moves into these cosmic levels and is not clear of anger? He/she might be able to literally kill someone with the anger, with this level of wattage in his four-body system. Do you see that Earth is a school to practice with lesser wattage? As we master our lessons here and prove ourselves worthy at each stage, we are given more wattage with which to work.

There are some people going around the planet thinking that they are operating at the 352d level of the godhead. That is nothing but illusion and a massive ego trip. They are probably not even planetary masters. No one from the 352d level of the godhead would be living on Earth—this is a fact. Sai Baba is the highest being on the planet and he is only 30% there. There has never been a being of his magnitude incarnated on the planet before.

So again I say that these cosmic levels are available, but only if you are deserving of receiving them. The completion of planetary ascension is not as strict. All can achieve these levels. Cosmic ascension activations will only be granted if the spiritual voltages will not be misused and if you have proven yourself worthy over time to use your energies properly under all tests and in the face of great obstacles. You don't have to be perfect, but you do have to have a fundamental mastery over all aspects of your being in total service of love, God and humanity.

More Advanced Cosmic Bodies in the Ascension Process

There are also cosmic bodies that go beyond the solar, galactic and universal bodies that can be anchored and activated in your meditations. Some of the ones I mention here will be overlapping somewhat. The first, most easy way to understand the cosmic bodies that extend all the way back to the godhead are to consider the seven cosmic planes.

Cosmic Planes	Cosmic Bodies
Cosmic physical plane	Cosmic physical body
Cosmic astral plane	Cosmic astral body
Cosmic mental plane	Cosmic mental body
Cosmic buddhic plane	Cosmic buddhic body
Cosmic atmic plane	Cosmic atmic body
Cosmic monadic plane	Cosmic monadic body
Cosmic logoic plane	Cosmic logoic body

Just as we had seven planetary bodies that correlated with the seven subplanes of the cosmic physical plane, we also have seven cosmic bodies that correlate with the seven cosmic planes. These bodies can be called into your meditations upon completion of your seven levels of initiation, which will be triggers for the release of certain cosmic energies. I see many of these cosmic bodies and chakras functioning as keys that unlock certain cosmic energies. Some of the higher bodies in this list I am sure are probably not realistically available to us on Earth in any major way. Even if installation and activation doesn't occur, a certain type of overlighting and energy release might occur.

Cosmic Bodies and the Keys of Enoch

One other way of tapping into the cosmic and planetary bodies is to use the system of understanding brought forth by J. J. Hurtak in *The Book of Knowledge: The Keys of Enoch*. This is a most amazing book and has a certain Jewish, or more succinctly, Kabbalistic theme to it. In *The Keys of Enoch* Hurtak describes a series of twelve bodies as follows:

1. Lord's mystical body
2. Elohistic Lord's body
3. Paradise Sons' body
4. Order of the Sonship body
5. Anointed Christ overself body
6. Zohar body
7. Overself body
8. Electromagnetic body
9. EKA body
10. Epi-kinetic body
11. Gematrian body
12. Higher Adam Kadmon body

Some of the bodies I have listed here are dealing with the planetary body system and the ones on top, on a more cosmic level. Melchizedek has told us that the Lord's mystical body is the highest and most advanced body. It is literally the body of the 352d level of the godhead. The elohistic Lord's body is the body of our elohim-self, or Creator/God-self. The Paradise Sons' body is the body of our Paradise Sons-self.

We are recognizing here that we are multidimensional selves that have other aspects of our being already functioning on these higher levels. This is not hard to understand. We are already dealing with this in the planetary understanding that we have a higher self and monad, or mighty I Am Presence, functioning at a higher level. The same is true on the cosmic level. It is possible to call forth in meditation to anchor and activate these bodies in dealing with the cosmic ascension process.

Moving down the list we come to the Order of the Sonship body. This is another level within the cosmic dimensions that can be invoked. According to Melchizedek, the highest body within the planetary bodies is the anointed Christ overself body. This body functions as a trinity with the zohar body and the overself body. I have described these bodies in *Beyond Ascension*, so I will not repeat that information here.

The electromagnetic body deals with our whole electromagnetic field that is activated in the process of planetary ascension. The eka body and epi-kinetic body deal with time travel and teleportation. The gematrian body stores all the geometric bodies that program our whole program. I often call in these geometric codes for whatever it is I am trying to manifest. For example, if I want more energy I might call in the geometric codes to energize the etheric body and meridian system. I have called in the geometric codes from Melchizedek to live on light and for physical immortality. These codes facilitate the movement toward realizing these goals.

The last body is the higher Adam Kadmon, which is like the divine blueprint body. It replaces the old etheric blueprint that has been used from all your past lives. Not everybody realizes that the etheric body can be damaged from your past lives or from your experience in this lifetime. It is a good idea to request that it be repaired and replaced with the higher Adam Kadmon body, or divine blueprint body. This works very closely with the mayavarupa body, which is another divine blueprint body that can be used in the ascension process.

These Keys of Enoch bodies are another system to work with, which I happen to like very much. A multiuniversal body could also be added to the system of the solar, galactic and universal, which is the body used for exploring the forty-three christed universes for this Cosmic Day. Finally, call in the cosmic body.

In essence what I have given you here is three different systems to work with that are all overlapping. I personally use them all to make sure everything is covered. I want to make sure I haven't missed anything. These bodies I have mentioned are listed on the Cosmic Map at the beginning of the book, as is all the information I have discussed in this chapter. The Cosmic Map is a good tool for synthesizing this information.

The Twelve Strands of DNA and the Ascension Process

The twelve strands of DNA can be installed and activated within the etheric body early on in the planetary ascension process. It is just a matter of invoking them and asking your own mighty I Am Presence, soul and the ascended masters to help you do this. They will be happy to oblige for the asking. The key point here with all these things is that you must *ask*. Part of the reason I have gotten to where I am is that I am not afraid to ask questions and I am not afraid to invoke and pray for what I want. I am also not afraid to make mistakes and sometimes ask some rather "dumb" questions in the process of trying to find truth.

The masters have been very patient with me and over time have begun to greatly respect my investigative abilities. My goal is always to make all this abstract material easy to understand for people, and by the grace of God I feel that I have achieved this goal.

Anyway, let's get back to the twelve strands of DNA, which is quite a popular focus among lightworkers right now. The process begins, contrary to popular belief, in the etheric body. The first step is to get the twelve strands manifested there. The next phase is to work toward transferring them from the etheric body into the physical body.

Djwhal Khul and Melchizedek told us this won't be complete until one fully anchors and activates all twelve levels, or twelve bodies, or up through the twelfth dimension. Our core group is currently working on this process and is a natural byproduct and result of all the other things I have been speaking of in this chapter.

This is something that can occasionally be invoked and prayed for in your meditations. After a while, as you can see, all these facets of initiations, chakras, bodies, twelve strands of DNA, light quotient, monadic and soul anchorings, weave and come together. The achievement of one catalyzes and facilitates the achievements of the others. Each one of these things is like a window for looking at the planetary and cosmic ascension process. Taken all together you get a more full picture and multifaceted approach to how the planetary and cosmic ascension process is achieved.

Cosmic Light-Quotient Building Scale

As I have already stated, 99% on the planetary light-quotient building scale equals 10% on the cosmic light-quotient scale. To install, activate and actualize the solar level one must build his/her light quotient to the 20% level. To install, activate and actualize the galactic level one must build her light quotient to the 30% level. At the universal level one must build up her light quotient to 40% and at the multiuniversal level one must build her light quotient to the 60% level.

This information that Melchizedek has provided must be put in the context of those who are still in physical incarnation. This is because Melchizedek told us just today that we are accessing only 10% of the full voltage of the solar, galactic and universal levels even though we are fully completed seventh-degree initiates.

Sai Baba is still doing the same process at a much higher level of initiation, as are many, many masters on the inner plane. The numbers I have given are valid for just about every one of the six billion people on Earth except for Sai Baba and Lord Maitreya. This also might apply to a few others who have incarnated as a part of the externalization of the hierarchy and are senior members of Lord Maitreya's ashram. Other than these few exceptions, these are very accurate numbers, which in summation are:

10% light quotient for planetary activation
20% light quotient for solar activation
30% light quotient for galactic activation
40% light quotient for universal activation
60% for multiuniversal activation
100% Source activation while still in earthly incarnation.

We will move to a new scale again when we are out of incarnation and can take the initiations that go along with those activations. So looking at this logically, we have the potential on Earth to activate 10% of full Source energy while still a seventh-degree initiate. Said in another way, we have the potential here to activate 10% on Earth of our full cosmic ascension.

The work we are doing here is laying the foundation for moving through our cosmic initiations more quickly. For the time being we are stuck at the completion of the seventh no matter what, as long as we are still in physical incarnation. Upon passing over to the inner plane we will most probably immediately take our eighth initiation.

How to Make Progress on Your Cosmic Ascension

The first thing one must do, of course, is complete one's planetary ascension and seven levels of initiation. The keys to completing both processes are unconditional love, service and meditation. Meditation includes around-the-clock light-quotient building and spending a lot of time in the various ascension seats as will be described in the next chapter. The idea here is to make your life a continual meditation, besides the actual precise meditations you do.

I would intensively study my eight books and especially focus on the meditations in *The Complete Ascension Manual* and *Beyond Ascension.* I also have five ascension-activation tapes that can be acquired through contacting me directly. They can be bought as a set or individually, which literally covers the gamut. I would also recommend that you come to the major planetary event that I have committed to putting on each year at Wesak, on the full moon in May. This is something I have contracted to do with Lord Maitreya, Melchizedek and Djwhal Khul.

The event each year is for the purpose of celebrating the Wesak Festival (Buddha's birthday). The numbers of people coming range anywhere from 1200 to 5000. Can you imagine doing high-level world-service work with 1200 high-level initiates and ascended beings? Can you imagine doing the meditations I have recommended in my books and tapes with this type of group?

I coordinate and participate in this event each year. The spiritual benefits one gains from participating in this weekend celebration and activation is literally 1000 times more powerful than any meditation one could do by him/herself.

There is a miraculous exponential factor that occurs when this many masters gather in oneness, love and group consciousness. We all need each other and no one is an island unto him/herself. These gatherings and celebrations are truly a coming together of spiritual family.

The fact that we hold the festivals at Wesak (the holiest day of the year from the ascended masters' perspectives) during the full moon, which coincides with many people's initiations, makes the event 1000 times more powerful. The festivals are held every year—pretty much indefinitely until I am guided to leave this plane.

Later in this book I will give more information about Wesak and the Twelve Planetary Festivals. The fact that we hold the event in Mount Shasta, California, also has an extraordinary impact, as well as the fact that we are moving through the planetary window for mass ascension from 1995 through 2012.

These events are designed to be the major planetary events to activate the next set of mass-ascension waves and to help those who have taken them already to actualize their ascension. Consider yourself now officially invited. I guarantee that it will be one of the most powerful experiences of your entire life.

You will have the experience of working in a "group body," not just your own individual focus. During the entire weekend the whole group functions like a gigantic tuning fork for cosmic transmissions of energy. Nothing you will ever do will catapult your spiritual progression forward as fast as attending a celebration such as this.

What you experience will reverberate through your being for months afterward, if not for the whole year. The Wesak was designed by the ascended masters to be a time of renewal and a time for the spiritual family to take a break from its normal service work to come together to rejuvenate, regenerate and commune with fellow initiates and ascended beings, on both the inner and outer plane.

I have taken on the mantle of responsibility to help lightworkers around the globe remember this sacred festival and to celebrate it as the ascended masters do every year on the inner plane. It is time for the complete externalization of the Spiritual Hierarchy on all levels and this is one extremely important aspect of this process that is now taking place.

Could you imagine doing high-level world-service work like this with 5000 dedicated initiates and ascended beings? Melchizedek has told us that this is in the cards and not too far away, so let all your friends know about it, as well as the books. Melchizedek has told me that the books are the key to the whole process. The books will lay the foundation and do all the advertising, and these events will be the group experience of what is possible that will further the work of the planetary and cosmic hierarchy, which we are all representatives of on Earth.

The last essential process that comes to mind is the importance of prayer. In my book *Beyond Ascension* I have provided a very useful tool called the Huna Prayer Method, which I would highly recommend that you utilize. However, any kind of prayer will work. The ascended masters are not allowed to intervene in your life unless they receive a request. Let them know what your spiritual short-term and long-term goals are. Give them your timetable preferences or request your highest potentialities in this regard.

Probably the biggest reason I have made the progress that I have in my own spiritual evolution is that I have prayed and questioned and called for help constantly. As long as you are responsible in your life and practice that which you preach, the ascended masters are happy to oblige your every request if it is within your potentiality and the range of your personal Tao.

Pray, meditate constantly (even while watching TV, walking or doing errands), express unconditional love at all times, use moderation and balance in all things and practice holy encounter at all times. "Holy encounter" means God meeting God with every person, animal, plant or rock you meet, building the light quotient as a main focus, studying books, utilizing ascension seats and most of all dedicating your life to service of humanity and the Earth. This is the planetary and cosmic ascension ticket.

2

Instructions for Utilizing the Planetary and Cosmic Ascension Seats

O ne of the most important tools a person can utilize in the process of achieving and completing his/her ascension and eventually moving on to his cosmic ascension is the use of the ascension seats. I first introduced this tool in my book, *The Complete Ascension Manual* and then greatly added to the list in *Beyond Ascension*. In this book I have added to the list again. The following is my newest and most up-to-date list, which I have called the Cosmic Ladder of Ascension Seats. I have broken down the ascension seats into those on the cosmic level, those on the multiuniversal level, those on the universal, then galactic, solar and planetary levels.

Cosmic Ladder of Ascension Seats

1. Cosmic level
   - Godhead ascension seat under guidance of Melchizedek (only permissible after completing the seven levels of initiation and working with the multiuniversal ascension seat for two years' time)
   - Divine Mother and divine Father ascension seat
2. Multiuniversal level (forty-three universes from the Source of our Cosmic Day)
   - Many universes' ascension seats in the Great, Great Central Sun under guidance of Melchizedek (only permissible after completing seven levels of initiation)
3. Universal level
   - Golden Chamber of Melchizedek under auspices of Melchizedek

4. Galactic level
   - Great White Lodge ascension seat under guidance of the Lord of Sirius
   - Arcturian ascension seat under guidance of the Lord of Arcturus
   - Lenduce's ascension seat under guidance of Lenduce
   - Melchior's ascension seat in galactic core under guidance of Melchior
   - Lord of Pleiades ascension seat on the Pleiades
5. Solar ascension seats
   - Golden Chamber of Helios in Solar Core ascension seat
   - Shamballa ascension seat under guidance of Sanat Kumara and Lord Buddha
6. Planetary ascension seats
   - Serapis Bey's ascension seat in Luxor on the inner plane
   - Commander Ashtar and the Ashtar Command's ascension seat on their mothercraft
   - Inner plane atomic accelerator ascension seat in Table Mountain
   - Ascension seat in Telos, one mile below Mount Shasta on inner plane
   - Mount Shasta ascension seat inside mountain on surface of the planet
   - Shamballa ascension seat in center of the Earth
   - Great Pyramid of Giza, King's Chamber ascension seat
   - Sananda's ascension seat on his own spacecraft
   - Ascension seat on Venus under guidance of Planetary Logos of Venus.

Melchizedek gave us the following instructions as to the ascension seats' proper use. One should begin by focusing on planetary ascension. This applies to all initiates up through the beginning of the fifth initiation. One must understand that these ascension seats are very powerful. Your initiation really has to do with the level of spiritual voltage you are holding and stabilizing. One needs to pattern into the ascension seats when first using them anyway, and then one needs to deeply consider that more voltage is not necessarily better.

There are many souls in the history of the Earth who have died prematurely or damaged their physical, astral, mental or spiritual webbing from calling in too much energy before their nervous system and metaphysical bodies were able to handle it. There is no danger as long as you follow the instructions I am giving you. I am not making up these rules arbitrarily but was told this directly by Melchizedek, the Universal Logos. So please listen very clearly, especially to what I say about the cosmic ascension seats.

Begin with the planetary ascension seats—they are wonderful. It is important for your training that you work with them all. You will find certain ones to be your favorites—follow your intuition. The most important planetary ascension seat to achieve your ascension is the one in Luxor. Every disciple and initiate on planet Earth who is going to achieve his/her ascension must spend time in Luxor on the inner plane with Serapis Bey. He holds the planetary ascension "flame," so to speak.

The second most important ascension seat is in Mount Shasta, which is on the surface of the Earth and inside the mountain. This is what Melchizedek said and interestingly enough this was my personal experience. I worked a lot in the other ones however and enjoyed them all. If you want a little more energy, it is permissible to call on the master in charge to increase the voltage a little bit.

Spend as much time as you can in these ascension seats. As I mentioned in *Beyond Ascension* this can be done not only in meditation but also while watching television, walking, doing errands. Your spiritual self will bilocate there and you can in a sense be doing two things at once. The idea here is to make your life a meditation, because who has the time or desire to meditate all day!

I literally spend twenty-four hours a day, seven days a week meditating as I am living my life. If I am not in one of the ascension seats, I am doing light-quotient building—and this is the single most important reason why I have processed my initiations so quickly. Try it, for it is fun. The wide variety of ascension seats makes it less boring and monotonous.

Again, your first experience in the ascension seats should be at the planetary level. Once your nervous system and bodies get adjusted, those of you in the third initiation and above can also begin using the solar level ascension seats. Most people reading this book are at this level (you wouldn't be attracted to it if you weren't). Just prior to taking the fourth initiation you can also begin using the galactic ascension seats, except for the Great White Lodge ascension seat under guidance of the Lord of Sirius.

This gives almost everybody reading this book an extremely wide choice of ascension seats, which took me many years to research and uncover. The ascension seat on the Great White Lodge can be used as soon as you take your fifth initiation. If you don't know your initiation level, use your intuition at first. Some people can use a pendulum to find out. If you need further assistance, give me a call and I will help you get this information. This also applies to the issue of removing your alien implants and elementals if you haven't had them cleared.

I personally love these ascension seats. You can use them even when you are talking to friends on the phone. You can socialize and sit in the ascension seats simultaneously. If you ever sense the flow of spiritual current stopping, just call yourself back there again. The key here is the efficient use of your time and energy.

The universal-level ascension seat, called the Golden Chamber of Melchizedek, can also be used after you take your fifth initiation. Most of the people reading this book are much further along in your initiation process than you realize. I am privy to the initiation level of a great many people, and I am here to tell you that just about every person I meet is in the fourth, fifth or sixth initiation.

Completing these initiations is actually becoming commonplace these days for lightworkers. For those very dedicated lightworkers, you can figure two years for an initiation if you apply the information and meditations in my books. That is mind-bogglingly fast. Those who really focus and apply themselves might be able to do them even faster. It is all up to your commitment.

In actuality for most people reading this book, you have almost free access to all the ascension seats. The only exceptions to this rule are the two ascension seats on the multiuniversal level and cosmic level.

The multiuniversal level is the level of the forty-three christed universes of the Source of our Cosmic Day. This is an ascension seat you are only allowed to enter after you have fully completed your seven levels of initiation. These are direct orders from Melchizedek. He told us that there is an ascension seat above this that exists literally at the 352d level of the godhead, however at this point even the core group and I are not allowed to go there, even though we have completed all seven levels of initiation and fifty chakras, are working on our tenth body, or solar-body activation, and have stabilized our 99% light quotient.

Melchizedek told us that this ascension seat could burn our etheric webbing and nervous system in a flash. He said if we were ever to be allowed to use it in the future, it would have to be as a group body, which holds more spiritual voltage potential than our individual twelve-body systems do.

It is very important to follow these instructions. The masters don't take kindly to immature disciples trying to enter states of consciousness they don't belong in. There is a natural orderly process to spiritual growth and to try and skip levels is just a manifestation of negative ego that will karmically backfire on you if you try.

Being able to work as a fifth-degree initiate at galactic and universal levels is an enormous leap in and of itself. The galactic core just opened up in 1987 during the Harmonic Convergence. In the use of the Golden Chamber of Melchizedek you are being given direct access to the universal core. I feel the responsibility to share the entire picture, which will serve as a cosmic carrot of sorts for something to which you can look forward.

After taking your ascension you can begin to call in the energies of the five christed universes, then the twelve christed universes, then the forty-three christed universes. You will not be going to the ascension seat there, for that is not permissible until completion of the seventh initiation. However you can begin to call the energies in during your actual meditations. So as you can see, I am on your side. All the information that I am giving you here, in the next chapter on the cosmic rays and in *Beyond Ascension* will take you many years to integrate.

The Source or godhead ascension seat is only available after you have worked with the multiuniversal-level ascension seat for two full years to prepare your nervous system. This is two full years *after* you have completed your seven levels of initiation and 99% light quotient and anchored and activated nine bodies and all fifty chakras.

There are two more very profound ascension seats that the divine Mother and divine Father, who stand in essence on the right and left hand of God, have allowed me to bring forth in this book. These are the divine Mother ascension seat and the divine Father ascension seat. To be allowed to use these ascension seats you must at least be at the beginning of your sixth initiation. If you don't know your level of initiation, call me and I will set you up with a telephone reading to give you this information. Even if you are a sixth-degree initiate or higher you also must make the following request since this is such a high voltage: "I call forth only those energies that I can assimilate easily and comfortably at the level I am currently at while sitting in this (divine Mother/Father) ascension seat."

The Synthesis Ashram of Djwhal Khul

There is one more type of seat that is not an ascension seat but more aptly called a healing seat. Djwhal Khul has taken over Kuthumi's inner-plane ashram because Kuthumi is preparing to take over Lord Maitreya's position in the Spiritual Government as Planetary Christ in the not-too-distant future.

The second ray has to do with the spiritual education of the planet, and because of this focus it is the central pillar of the seven rays. So all souls regardless of ray type will spend some time working with Djwhal Khul on the inner plane. It must be realized that there is a great movement of disciples and initiates from ashram to ashram on the inner plane depending on their individual needs. All seven of the main ashrams under the guidance of the seven chohans are really in truth one ashram of Lord Maitreya, the Planetary Christ.

Anyway, Djwhal Khul has a healing seat in the synthesis ashram in which I highly recommend spending time. Call on Djwhal Khul and he will work with you there. This seat will give you access to everything I have written about in all my books, whether it is light-quotient building, implant removal, Arcturian technologies and so on. It is kind of a "jack-of-all-trades" healing seat.

The Love Seat of Sai Baba

I mentioned this seat in *Beyond Ascension* and it is another seat that can be called on at any level of initiation. This seat is again not an ascension seat but rather a seat for communing with Sai Baba and just receiving his love, sweetness and succor. There is nothing quite like the glory of Sai Baba, so I highly recommend calling on this seat.

How to Use the Ascension Seats

To utilize these ascension seats call forth the ascended master who is in charge of the particular ascension seat you are using and your own spiritual teacher, if you like. Then just make a prayer request to be taken to the location in your spiritual body to sit in the ascension seat. You will immediately begin to feel the flow of the spiritual current in the top of your head and throughout your entire body. Sometimes it takes a minute or two to get established, sometimes not.

I find that the higher you go in the ascension seats, the more warm-up time is needed so they don't blow your circuits. If you can't feel anything, ask a second time and also request an increase in the ascension-seat voltage. Always remember it is the energy that creates the acceleration. You don't have to be psychic, clairvoyant or hear voices. If you do, all the better; however, it is totally unnecessary. It is the flow of the spiritual current through your twelve-body system over time that builds the light quotient and creates the transformation. Be patient and persevering in your efforts and the results will be remarkable—I guarantee it.

One interesting insight is the fact that I also uncovered ascension seats on the Moon, Mercury, Mars, Neptune, Pluto, Uranus, Saturn and Jupiter. Melchizedek specifically guided me not to mention these with my basic list except for the one on Venus. He told me that these other ones were more extraterrestrial and fourth-dimensional in nature and he wanted me to keep my list to fifth-dimensional ascension seats and higher.

One of the real keys to the spiritual path is not to waste time and not to waste energy, but still to have fun. The use of the ascension seats might be one of the single most important spiritual tools for accelerating spiritual evolution this world has ever known. Take advantage of them and enjoy the process of being a cosmic traveler. God has given you everything you need to achieve ascension and liberation. You must use your free choice to take advantage of all that He has provided.

The Atomic Accelerator

The atomic accelerator in Table Mountain is the only one of the ascension seats I have listed that has been anchored in a third-dimensional sense. This ascension seat was brought in from the fifth dimension into the third dimension by a spaceship. The machinery that is developed in the fifth dimension does not have to be maintained in the same way as our third-dimensional machinery. It vibrates at a higher frequency.

The atomic accelerator is like the ultimate radionics machine. It was brought down to Earth through the efforts of Saint Germain and Sananda. It is also operated by the Arcturians, Ashtar Command and Pleiadians. It is nothing you will ever be able to find physically. We have been told that one must be beyond the seventh initiation to be able to use it. The atomic accelerator has the ability to give readouts in a similar way to Djwhal Khul's computer that creates light profiles of his disciples and initiates.

This ascension seat can be visited spiritually by anyone for the asking. In some of the channelings we were told that the atomic accelerator was somehow also connected with the elohim computers, which I found very interesting. If we ever receive permission to go to the physical atomic accelerator, you, my beloved readers, will be the first to know.

Anchoring of Ascension Seats

One more tool I would highly recommend that you utilize at whatever level you are working is to call forth on a permanent basis the anchoring of the ascension seat at your level of initiation into your four-body system, your home and your ascension column. Let's say you call forth the anchoring of the ascension seat in Luxor to be anchored in this manner. This way you will be living in the ascension seat on a full-time basis without even asking, and all who enter your home will walk into it.

As you progress you can ask for higher and higher levels of this type of anchoring. This past week we requested the anchoring of the multiuniversal ascension seat and Source ascension seat. In this process you will not be allowed to skip levels. Melchizedek was very stern with us about this. He gave examples of initiates who tried to skip levels and got greedy for cosmic energy, who then had a heart attack and died, damaging their etheric body.

Before anchoring this level you must anchor the planetary, solar, galactic and universal ascension seats in a gradual, systematic procedure, according to your level of initiation, light quotient, chakra anchoring and activation and body anchoring and activation. Your nervous system and etheric nadis must be prepared over a long period of time at each level. Be patient and over time all will be given to you—I wouldn't be writing about this in this book if it weren't so.

3

The Cosmic Rays

One of the most profound areas of research that has come through in recent times is in the area that I am calling the cosmic rays. This information along with the cosmology of the ascension seats is so exciting that it is hard to contain myself. Let me begin by laying the foundation for this discussion. Prior to 1960 this planet for the last 3.1 billion years basically dealt with seven major rays. These seven rays are:

1. First ray: power, will and purpose (red)
2. Second ray: love/wisdom (blue)
3. Third ray: active, or creative intelligence (yellow)
4. Fourth ray: harmony (emerald green)
5. Fifth ray: concrete science (orange)
6. Sixth ray: abstract idealism and devotion (indigo)
7. Seventh ray: ceremonial order and magic (violet)

Then in approximately 1960 a most extraordinary event occurred on this planet. There was a special dispensation to this planet of five new rays. These five new rays are:

8. Eighth ray: higher cleansing ray (seafoam green)
9. Ninth ray: joy, attracting the body of light (blue-green)
10. Tenth ray: anchoring of the body of light, inviting soul merge (pearlescent)
11. Eleventh ray: bridge to the new age (pink-orange)
12. Twelfth ray: anchoring of the new age and the Christ consciousness (gold).

The anchoring of these five higher rays was an extraordinary occurrence. The whole science of esoteric psychology and the twelve rays have been extensively written about in my first book, *The Complete Ascension Manual*. It is probably one of the most important spiritual sciences known to man. It predates and is the causative factor of even the science of astrology. It is absolutely mind-boggling to me to see how totally unknown this science is and how much inaccurate information is floating around in regard to it.

If you have not spent time calling in these twelve rays and experimenting with them, I recommend that you do so. It is essential that you do so for your spiritual training. The instructions for how to do this are in *The Compete Ascension Manual* [page 128], so I am not going to repeat myself here. These planetary rays function a lot like the ascension seats. It is just a matter of calling them forth and then bathing in their energy. They are there for the asking.

This is another one of these cases where God has given us everything, however most people, even lightworkers, don't know these rays are available or how to use them. It is really so simple. If you want personal power, call on the red ray. If you want cleansing, call on the eighth ray. If you are doing scientific work, call on the fifth ray. If you want devotion, call on the sixth ray. If you want transmutation, call on the seventh ray. If you want the pure Christ consciousness, call on the twelfth ray. If you want to attract your body of light, call on the ninth ray.

You can call the ray by number, color or quality. Each of these methods work equally well. The five higher rays, which are combinations of the first seven rays with the added ingredient of white light, are especially powerful.

Since completing my own planetary ascension and having worked with these twelve rays for a very long time, I was ready for the next step. One day I had the idea that maybe it would be possible to map out the cosmic rays beyond these most extraordinary planetary rays. I don't know why, I just hadn't thought of this before (probably because the timing wasn't right).

Our core group and I sat down over a couple of months and were able to actually come up with this information. This, along with the ascension seats and the process of cosmic ascension, is some of the most profound information I have ever come across. I have been more excited about writing this book than any of my other seven books to date, and that is amazing because I was absolutely on fire writing the other books.

What is exciting to me is the process of bringing forth new information on the cosmic levels of creation that has never been brought forth before to humanity. What is also exciting is that these cosmic rays can be called forth in the exact same way that the ascension seats can for accelerating planetary and cosmic ascension. It is another method for tapping in. The following chart, which I have called the Cosmic Rays Cosmology, is my first unveiling of this new information.

Cosmic Rays Cosmology
Godhead Level Clear light; translucent and invisible
The Twelve Cosmic Rays All twelve clear light; translucent and invisible
Multiuniversal Level Platinum ray
The Ten Lost Cosmic Rays of the Yod Spectrum All hues of platinum
Universal Level Golden Chamber of Melchizedek Purest and most refined gold
Great White Lodge on Sirius Gold; second-level purity
Melchior/Galactic Core Silver-gold
Helios/Solar Core Copper-gold
Shamballa/Sanat Kumara White light

Twelve Planetary Rays		
1: Red *P. power*	5: Orange	9: Blue-green *Joy*
2: Blue *Love/Wisdom*	6: Indigo *Devotion*	10: Pearlescent
3: Yellow *C. Intelligence*	7: Violet *Transmutation*	11: Pink-orange
4: Emerald Green *harmony*	8: Seafoam Green *Cleansing*	12: Gold (third-level purity)

At the very top of the chart we have the Source or godhead level. This is the level of God from which all creation fans out. This might be called the place from where the first-ray emanation stems. Melchizedek told us that the color of the first emanation is clear light. It is so pure and refined that it has no color. It is translucent and invisible.

The second level of the diagram leads one to the second step of creation, which is the creation of the twelve cosmic rays. Just so there is no misunderstanding, I am talking about the twelve cosmic rays here, not the twelve planetary rays that I spoke of earlier. These twelve rays are connected with the Cosmic Council of Twelve at the 352d level of the godhead.

The twelve cosmic beings literally run God's infinite universe. This is God's leadership group and core ashram members. These twelve beings are so infinite and vast "they are almost unfathomable." Each of these Cosmic Council of Twelve members is connected to a cosmic monad (not planetary monad), which all of us come from. All the beings in God's infinite universe emanate from one of these twelve cosmic monads.

Cosmic ascension is the merger with this cosmic monad. Each member of the Cosmic Council of Twelve is in charge of one of the cosmic rays. The planetary rays that we deal with at our level are stepped down hundreds of times so the voltage doesn't burn us up.

I asked Melchizedek what color these twelve cosmic rays are and he said they are so refined and rarefied that they also have no color. At this stage they are translucent and invisible. This reminds me of the Tree of Life and the very top sephirah called Kether, which is the crown of the cosmic tree. At this stage we have not moved down the Tree to the next two sephiroth, Binah and Chokmah, where creation as we know it begins to exist. In other words, we are still in the unmanifest rather than the manifest state. The prism of God has not begun to refract color yet.

This then brings us down the Tree of Life to the multiuniversal level, which is the source of the forty-three christed universes for our Cosmic Day. Manifested reality begins here. The first refracted color in the prism of divinity at the multiuniversal level is platinum. The platinum ray would correspond to the multiuniversal ascension seat that I spoke of in the previous chapter.

Here begins another way to access this level rather than going to the actual ascension seat there. It is to call on the platinum ray from Melchizedek or Metatron. This is also a little less dangerous in the sense that in working with the ascension seat you are actually going to the source of that ray rather than just calling forth the ray and experiencing it. It is kind of like calling on the energies of the forty-three christed universes. Here however we are specifically dealing with the cosmic rays.

That brings us now to the next level—a most extraordinary insight. This is what Melchizedek referred to as the ten lost cosmic rays of the yod spectrum. These ten rays have been lost by humanity until now. The ten lost cosmic rays are emanating from the multiuniversal level and can be brought forth by calling Melchizedek, Metatron or Lord Michael, the down-flow of the yod spectrum and the ten lost cosmic rays.

Melchizedek has said that this work should not be done until you complete your seventh initiation. You can begin if you like as soon as you take your seventh. The yod spectrum is a term I first became acquainted with through *The Keys of Enoch*, and refers to the cosmic yod spectrum not the planetary yod spectrum. The yod spectrum is the light spectrum and the planetary yod spectrum is the full scope of the twelve planetary rays.

This brings us down to the next level, which is the Golden Chamber of Melchizedek. It is so funny to use the phrase "come down to the Golden Chamber of Melchizedek," because this chamber is such an extraordinarily high level of consciousness. Melchizedek told us that this universal core emanates a most refined and purified God energy.

Each color that one can work with has three graduations of purity, refinement and clarity. This gold color from the universal core and Melchizedek is the most refined gold color and ray in existence. It is the cosmic ray at the core essence of our universe. You experience this energy when you sit in the Golden Chamber of Melchizedek. Melchizedek said you can begin calling in this cosmic ray at the beginning of the sixth initiation. The cosmic gold ray is different from the twelfth-ray gold of the planetary rays. That is the highest gold of our planetary system but not of the solar, galactic and universal system.

The next level on the chart is the Great White Lodge on Sirius, which is governed by the Lord of Sirius on the inner plane. This is not the extraterrestrial Sirius but the inner-plane Sirius. It is the true home of the Spiritual Hierarchy of which Shamballa is an outpost. It is where most of humanity will go in terms of the seven paths to higher evolution, which I speak of in *Beyond Ascension.*

The cosmic ray emanating from the Great White Lodge is again the color gold, but it is a second-level purity just beneath that of the Golden Chamber of Melchizedek, still extremely high in vibration.

This brings us to the galactic core, which is the home and charge of Melchior, the Galactic Logos. Melchizedek told us that the cosmic ray emanating from here is silver-gold. This is the energy that emanates when you sit in Melchior's ascension seat. It can be called forth once you attain the fourth or fifth initiation.

Continuing to move down the chart we come to Helios, the Solar Logos of the solar core. This is the cosmic ray of copper-gold. This is the energy that you experience when sitting in Helios' Central Sun ascension seat.

Moving down the chart we come to Shamballa, currently the home of Sanat Kumara and Lord Buddha. The cosmic ray emanating from here is the pure white light. This is the energy you experience when you sit in the Shamballa ascension seat of Sanat Kumara and Lord Buddha, which is another very important and most excellent ascension seat, also one of my favorites for a very long time.

We then have the twelve planetary rays. In going down this list it makes it sound like these twelve planetary rays are lowly unimportant rays that are not very powerful—nothing could be further from the truth. These twelve rays are awesome, even the first seven, let alone the last five.

You must realize and put into perspective that I am mapping out God's infinite universe and we are all planetary masters. We are all just little infants and babies in terms of cosmic evolution. I spoke in a previous chapter of our potential to activate ten percent of our cosmic evolution while still on Earth. This a great potentiality, however no one has ever done it, and I am not sure anyone ever will. In actuality, if we could achieve one or two percent of our cosmic evolution while still on Earth, that would be enormous.

Please remember we are talking about God's infinite universe now, not just one planet. There are ten billion planets just in our universe, and there are infinite numbers of universes. The Source of our Cosmic Day, or the source of our forty-three christed universes, is just one source of infinite numbers of sources that make up God's infinite universe. Do you have this in perspective? Even just one percent of God's full cosmic energy would be enormous. We are talking about the difference of being a fifty-watt light bulb versus being a million-watt light bulb. So please keep this in perspective as I give you these minimal restrictions I have outlined from Melchizedek.

The full installment, activation and actualization of your solar, galactic and universal bodies and/or 30% light-quotient scale would be only an increase of 3% on the scale Sai Baba is working in. There are three light-quotient scales: one for the planetary level, one for the cosmic level for seventh-level completed initiates and a third light-quotient scale for masters who have gone beyond the seven levels of initiations who are avatars on Earth. The true meaning of an avatar is one who is totally God-realized at birth. This would also be the light quotient of those ascended masters who are out of incarnation.

So my personal goal at this time is to get to this 30% level and not only to install and activate this level but also to actualize it. It is in the actualization, or third stage, that all the advanced ascended-master abilities that we have associated with the ascension process come. We are actually going much further than ascended masters in the past went in terms of installation and activation of cosmic energies. However, we are going slower in terms of the development of the advanced ascended-master abilities. This has a lot to do with the speed at which we are all going through this process and the fact that we are living in a period of mass ascension, which is a different dispensation and program than that which masters went through in the past.

Summation and a Few Shortcuts

Call on the rays that are appropriate to the level of initiation you are working with. The use of these planetary and cosmic rays is another awesome tool in conjunction with the ascension seats, light-quotient building, chakra anchoring and all the other ascension techniques and tools I have mentioned in my books. It also provides a variety, which is nice since I am recommending that you work with this twenty-four hours a day, seven days a week.

Even request before going to bed what process you want to work with. Now, I should mention here that you can overdo it, not so much with light-quotient building as with the more intensive meditations in some of my other books. Use your intuition and cut back if you start not feeling well. In the beginning you will be releasing a lot of toxins. Drink plenty of water and eat as pure a diet as you possibly can. Once you clean out your physical, astral, mental, etheric and spiritual bodies you will be able to bring in more and more light.

If you ever have any physical health problems, call on the ascended masters, the angels of healing and the Arcturians. I myself have had some chronic health lessons and call on the Lord of Arcturus and Arcturians for light-quotient building and for healing whatever is ailing me. They work on both simultaneously.

I find that when I go for my "ascension walks" I prefer using the galactic-level ascension seats and energies more because they are a little less refined than the universal level. That is just my preference. I like to call on the Arcturians early in the morning to get my energies flowing and to build my light quotient, which has a strengthening effect on my overall physical body and digestive system. I seem to be able to type and write for much longer periods of time by asking for their help in this manner. I like to call on the cosmic rays while meditating, if I need a particular quality of energy or if I am watching television.

I actually have some of my best meditations while watching television—sounds crazy, but it's true. I can soak in the energies for three hours and not get ants in my pants, as I do sometimes when I meditate. Once the spiritual current is activated you can do other things and it continues to flow quite nicely. If the current is too strong or too weak, you can always ask the masters to make the appropriate adjustment. Day by day, by doing this, your light quotient will slowly but surely build. Just make it part of your daily routine and soon it will become a positive habit. It will also help you to feel like you are making progress and accomplishing something. More and more as time has gone on I do less actual meditating and more and more making my life my meditation. It is amazing how much spiritual work you can get done standing in line at the bank or market. You can do it inwardly in your mind and it takes all of five seconds to invoke. I have worked out systems with the masters where all I have to say is five words and the whole process is activated. I will share a few of these with you:

- "Melchizedek, Golden Chamber, ascension seat." (This is all I say and it is immediately activated. The first time you might need to use more words to make sure you are connected; however, after a while it just takes a few words.)
- "Metatron, call forth twelfth ray."
- "Mighty I Am Presence, I call forth transmuting flame."
- "Helios, copper-gold ray."
- "Lord of Sirius, Great White Lodge ascension seat."
- "Sanat Kumara, Shamballa, ascension seat."
- "Call forth Serapis Bey, Luxor, ascension seat."
- "Metatron, 100% light-quotient increase."
- "Lord of Arcturus, Arcturians, 100% light-quotient increase, heal and strengthen digestive system."
- "Metatron, 100% light-quotient increase, revitalize."

I think you can get an idea of how the process works from these examples. By having these short invocations I can do them in my mind. If I want to do them out loud, I can just whisper them and put my hand to my face while standing in line at the post office and do light-quotient building while waiting.

4

Cosmic Evolution and the
Organization of the Higher Mind

In one of Melchizedek's channelings during a meditation, he gave us some fascinating information on the properties of the mind. The most important characteristic of the mind, Melchizedek said, is the will. The will interrelates the intuition and the intellect. He said the intuition could visually be seen on the inner plane as a spiral with the intellect being like a checkerboard.

In the third dimension perception is separate, like a string of beads. In the fourth dimension you have inner and outer, psychic and metaphysical. There is the understanding that there is a metaphor for everything, that there are multidimensions and that everything relates. There are things that are simultaneous, synchronistic and paradoxical.

This is a big step; however, it isn't until the fifth dimension that the infinite is really opened up. Only in the fifth dimension do you understand that everything is related to everything and that you cannot take in one thing without taking in all things. The problem is that we select our focus ordinarily on three-dimensional thinking, and that is why we cannot stay in Melchizedek's vibration as we would like.

When we adapt ourselves to taking in everything without feeling lost, or feeling that we don't understand or that we don't have a word for, then we will begin to function on a fully realized fifth-dimensional possibility of communication and energy without disruption. We will then be able to allow this to continue while we also communicate in a third-dimensional world. It is the will raised up to its highest potential that allows us to take this leap. It is no longer a will that forms its attention in opinions but that works as a circuitry to lace together all elements of reality—the greater reality that has everything contained within it. It is a nonselective reality.

Is it possible, Melchizedek questioned, for us to live in a nonselective reality, where we experienced all possibilities and were not lost in the profusion, were able to see the rhythm and relationship like a great hologram and still carried on daily functions? Again he asked us if we could imagine ourselves in a field of this nature. This is a much greater sensitivity of reception.

Melchizedek then said that even the most advanced lightworkers are not practicing this at this time. Unlimited and unbiased, it is without a personal perspective. It transcends all boundaries of culture conditioning. It sees only from a cosmic vantage point. It is without a personal perspective. Where third and fourth dimensions is seeing from the four or five vantage points, as mentioned earlier, this fifth-dimensional consciousness adds genetic programming, our physical makeup, our religious and moral upbringing and cultural orientation.

Each of these aspects are like lenses that color our opinions of which we as lightworkers are not always conscious. These lenses cause an intellectual opinion, a sensual experience, an intuitive assumption. Mass consciousness then decides that this is the reality. It is in a sense mass hypnosis. Melchizedek is trying to help us leave all these innumerable lenses and see from his perspective, free from the personal and planetary pull.

In this process the core group and I, forming a group body, have begun an experiment to see as many instead of as just one. I spoke of this process in my book, *Revelations of a Melchizedek Initiate*. To live and see from a body of many instead of one goes against all personal mass-consciousness training. Melchizedek spoke of this as quite a challenge and growth process of perceptual training. The idea here is to allow everything to flow in with no restrictions and no lenses. This group-body experiment removes all boundaries of polarity. Everything is experienced as compatible.

Melchizedek gave us the example of physical health lessons we all were working with. He said that these have to do with the body being reworked and recircuited. We were told that all health problems, whatever the cause, should not be seen as different, disharmonious or limiting, even in the case of chronic health lessons. Nothing can be seen through the lens of limitation, pain or disharmony. Everything has a purpose and there is nothing to get rid of—it all functions together for the perfection. Value judgments are removed.

Melchizedek even said that deciding that something hurts is a value judgment. From a third-dimensional understanding this would seem to be an insane or absurd way of looking at things. People would say that we are not in touch with reality if we don't acknowledge something that hurts. In fifth-dimensional consciousness, all is working together. There is no separation. One cannot say this is good and this is bad, this is dark and this is light, this hurts and this doesn't hurt, this feels good and this doesn't feel good, or say this is good for me and this is not good for me.

All synapses must work together. All brain secretions, fluids and chakra impulses must work together. We can no longer just partially activate the chakras. Each chakra has forty-eight sections and it is no longer appropriate to just light up a few of the sections in each chakra. It is the same as thinking about lighting up only certain cells in the body rather than all the cells.

Melchizedek said that the one Eastern discipline that does work on this is tai chi. He said it is not that one needs to take tai chi but rather to function as that, metaphorically. Those who take tai chi often focus on this at the physical level, but he said he is talking about all levels.

Melchizedek said that the beginning way to work with this whole understanding is through the "blessing system"—looking at everything as a gift. As Sai Baba says, welcome adversity. Paul Solomon once said to say to everything that happens in life, "Not my will but Thine." This is is the beginning step to what Melchizedek is saying here. He told us that it is essential for us to come to terms with this lesson and understanding if we were to eventually take over Djwhal Khul's synthesis ashram when Djwhal moves on to his cosmic evolution. Help will be given to us on this.

Melchizedek also said that this concept is something that very much gets in the way of the channeling process. He spoke of how this third- and fourth-dimensional view would color the teachings of even such great channels as Alice Bailey and Madam Blavatsky. The third- and fourth-dimensional mind in almost all channelings on Earth reinterprets it into this worldly mass-consciousness presentation. This might manifest as rules or regulations, which is really third-dimensional reinterpretation of the ultimate message.

This is not a judgment, just a cultural phenomenon on our planet. Melchizedek said that Djwhal Khul mastered the art of dematerialization through the harmonizing of every aspect of his being through his mind. This is part of what it truly means to complete the seven levels of initiation and work from the eighth and ninth dimensions.

I asked Melchizedek how the concept of spiritual discernment fit in with what he was talking about. His response made me glad to hear that this was something that fit in very well. We are not to let go of our spiritual discernment, just the untold number of value judgments we unconsciously make from all the lenses that metaphorically cover our brain, face and head. Spiritual discernment guides our actions without judging.

The idea is to move through life as if we are doing tai chi or practicing aikido. Do not stop and ask, "What should I do here? Is this right, or that right?" but rather simply move, and the moving or going is the discernment. The going is not a limited movement but bringing everything. Then we are able to move in the marketplace, and all those in the marketplace are brought into this movement instantly. The word I can come up with in my own mind is "flow," a kind of ability to flow with things in a much more refined and fluid fashion.

To be completely honest, I don't claim to understand everything Melchizedek is saying in this channeling. I feel like he is stretching all who read this to a higher level and I do sense the truth of what he is saying. The idea of letting go of value judgments and all these different planetary lenses sounds really good to me. Also I have always loved the blessings system, which sometimes is easy to forget to use consciously. I also love the idea of being more flowing and infinite in perspective, like a satellite dish.

The spiral relates everything to Source. The intellect fills in the universe piece by piece and is organized in sections. Wholes relate to Source and the pieces relate to structure. The will brings the structure and intuition together. It forces one to place the unruly and nonlinear musings of the universe into an organized field within an individual. Each individual within his/her grasp has the entire thought form of creation.

It is laid out in a spiral directly from Source—this is the true shape of the mind. The Source sends forth an impulse that spirals through the chakras and stimulates the brain. In an instant an insight is stimulated through that electrical current of experience coming from the Source.

Without the intellectual component one would experience existence instant by instant as insight. This is where one eventually comes to: It is both the beginning and the end. In between, one experiences a structure. In this structure the intellect is a stepping-down of the divine plan into its components, which translates as a stream of intellectually related facts or thoughts about the experience, explaining the impulse or current that is given. We operate simultaneously.

The will brings this together and issues forth a communication that focuses the insight about an experience in a structure. The structure is the brain, not in the physical sense but in the computer sense, and it has a network of corresponding components. Only through conditioning is this reduced to object-oriented rationale. It is up to us to determine for ourselves if we want to divorce ourselves from this conditioning, which traps the impulses into this known structure. This prevents one from completely functioning as a master who can, for example, materialize and dematerialize things.

We have been bound and tied to a grid or structure of information that places everything in a context. So long as we are tied to this structure of past conditioning and format, with all our impulses and intuitive insights into this structure, then we are in a form that prevents full transfiguration or transformation. On the other hand, the intuition places nothing in a context and only experiences pure energy. The work the masters have been doing with us is to help reconnect us with this pure energy and develop a style of communication in which we are not entrapped in the logic of past conditioning. Instead we are able to create new pathways throughout the chakras, which circuit the self to an infinite range of experience.

In essence, what this means is to see everything through the eyes of the anointed Christ overself body. This means the transcendence of all negative-ego perception and only thinking thoughts from the Christ-mind, completely untainted by limitations. The idea, Melchizedek said, is not to put anything you are reading now in a past-reference context but to break away from the encrustation of formulated ideas.

This is something we lightworkers have been doing for a long time; however, there seems to be another leap we all need to make to transcend all physical laws. "Contextlessness living" is what Melchizedek called this: the removal of all familiar boundaries of concept. He defined this process as both a cognitive exercise and energetic experience.

The Keys of Enoch has referred to there being seventy-two areas of the mind. Third- and fourth-dimensional consciousness only deals with three or four of these areas. In the third dimension these four areas are: the intellectual, the intuitive, the will and the sensing function. In the fourth-dimensional consciousness one more function is added to this list: the psychic. The fifth-dimensional view begins to understand the infinite possibility of looking at the whole rather than the parts. In the fourth dimension everything is broken into duality. In the third dimension you have duality plus the physical versus the nonphysical, which adds the emotional and sensual. It is only at the fifth level that you see that you can tune into more and more channels, like a satellite dish.

Solar Activation

For solar activation I recommend working with Helios and Vesta. Solar activation is not something you are ready for until you complete the seven levels of initiation, then anchor and activate your fifty chakras and install and activate your first nine bodies, which I have already talked about in previous chapters.

The process of solar activation involves six main principles: (1) solar body; (2) solar chakras; (3) solar sun; (4) solar braiding; (5) solar overlay; and (6) solar bridging.

To ask for this before planetary ascension is achieved would be a waste of energy and time. You have enough to deal with in the process of anchoring your fifty chakras, 99% light quotient, seven levels of initiation and nine bodies. All of you reading this book can and will achieve this if you utilize the information and ascension meditations in my books. It is actually much easier than you think, and I really mean this. If you have the right information and tools, the process will go very quickly. When you do achieve it, and you will soon if you are committed and focused, solar activation is the next step.

Ask to be taken to the solar core to have an interview with Helios and Vesta. The process begins with asking them to start building the electrical bridge of circuitry to your solar body and solar chakras. If you want you can also ask for help from Vywamus, the Lord of Arcturus and the Arcturians in this work.

The process of anchoring and activating these six principles might take from two to five years. You must realize it took you an entire lifetime to anchor and activate your fifty chakras. Now you are basically asking to anchor fifty more. This is no small endeavor.

The next step is to ask for the soul-braiding process. This will interweave the characteristics of the solar-life pattern into your four-body system. Then request the permanent installation and activation of your solar overlay, which is the solar divine blueprint. Every level of creation has one—this is very important.

Then request the permanent installation and activation of the solar sun into your being by Helios and Vesta. The solar sun will not be able to remain permanently until your electrical system, solar body and chakras are more in place. The idea is to keep asking for this anchoring in every meditation until it finally remains permanent. This is the process with all levels of creation.

The final step is to ask for the installation and activation of the solar chakras 50 through 100. If you want to be more specific, which might be a good idea, begin with solar chakras 50 through 57.

The process, as with all this work, has three stages: installation, activation and actualization. The first stage is to work on installation, which could take a year or more. Simultaneously keep praying for activation. Actualization is the hardest. As I have stated, I have previously installed and activated my fifty chakras, however, I have not fully actualized them yet.

Full actualization is the development of the advanced ascended-master abilities everyone is so interested in. Due to this extraordinary time in Earth's history, a new dispensation has been given that allows us to install and activate levels of energy that are light-years beyond anything that was ever permissible before. All this work that we are doing will make our future initiation processes on cosmic planes much easier. This might be called "extra credit," which we all remember so well having gone through earthly school.

It is at the fifth initiation that the mayavarupa overlay, or divine blueprint, comes in. The soul braid also comes in at the fifth initiation. I am speaking here of the soul braid, not the solar soul braid. The overlay is the blueprint that is the potential for whatever level overlay you are installing. There is an overlay, or divine blueprint, for every level all the way back to the godhead.

The seventh and final thing that needs to be anchored is the solar light-quotient level on an ongoing basis, which is approximately ten to twenty percent of the cosmic light-quotient scale.

Galactic Activation

Galactic activation will use the exact same procedure, however, instead you will go to the Great White Lodge on Sirius and work with the Lord of Sirius and the Lady Master from Sirius. You also may go in meditations to the galactic core and work with Melchior, Vywamus and Lenduce.

In talking about this I am of course getting way ahead of myself—the core group and I are just working on the beginning stage of the solar level. Because this is a book on cosmic ascension, I am laying out the map and procedures for the upcoming levels. The six aspects to work on for cosmic ascension are: (1) galactic body; (2) galactic chakras; (3) galactic sun; (4) galactic soul braiding; (5) galactic overlay; and (6) galactic bridging.

The procedures are exactly the same as on the solar level except you have moved up another major octave. These masters will help you build in the electrical bridging that will allow you to begin the process of installing the galactic body and chakras 100 through 150. Again, you see how ridiculous it would be to invoke these things if you haven't even completed the installation and activation of the first fifty chakras.

Next, you would call in the galactic sun, galactic soul braiding, galactic overlay and galactic bridging. This whole process will probably take another two to five years, for we are talking about another fifty chakras. Most of the lightworkers on the planet are working on anchoring chakras 10 through 22 at most. Once you understand these principles the process, no matter what level you are, can be speeded up literally ten thousandfold.

The problem is that no one has ever understood these things. I am a well-read and studious person, yet I have never read in any other book this understanding of installing, activating and actualizing chakras in the manner spoken of here and in my other books. This understanding is a golden key to accelerating evolution. This is why the things I speak of in this book are in the realm of possibility for *all* lightworkers.

The last and seventh thing that needs to be anchored here is the galactic light quotient, which is twenty to thirty percent of the cosmic light-quotient scale.

Universal Activation

The process for universal activation is again exactly the same. Instead, now you will be moving up to the next octave. For this I recommend calling upon Melchizedek, Metatron and possibly Sai Baba for help. Ask to be taken to the Golden Chamber of Melchizedek where you will also be worked on by his high-level universal initiates. The same six principles apply: (1) universal body; (2) universal chakras; (3) universal sun; (4) universal soul braiding; (5) universal overlay; and (6) universal bridging.

The process begins with requesting the electrical bridging or rewiring to prepare your twelve-body system for the next higher voltage of energies. At this level you will be bringing in the next fifty chakras, or chakras 150 to 200. In the beginning you can again focus on 150 through 157. Once the bridge work is done, then continual calling forth of the universal, or zohar, body begins, as well as the universal sun, universal chakras, universal soul braiding and universal overlay, or divine blueprint.

This might seem to you like useless information and something you will never be allowed to take advantage of. I assure you this is not the case. I have already told you that it is possible to move though your initiations every two years if you are really focused and committed and use the material and information in these books. Following this pace, all of you will complete your seven levels of initiation in a relatively short period of time. If you want to know your initiation level, call me and I will provide information for you to access this knowledge.

The eighth- and ninth-dimensional integration will be about the same; let's say two years apiece. Figure out the pace that you are moving in terms of your evolution by using this timetable. Even if it takes ten or fifteen years, that is nothing. Melchizedek told us that it was within our potentiality to move from the ninth to the twelfth level in five years. This potentiality is very vast and part of this is that we are acting as prototypes, given the leadership positions we have been assigned in Djwhal Khul's ashram and the fact that we are working in a group body.

A group-consciousness understanding has allowed us to speed up what normally would take much, much longer. Even if it took ten years to anchor the solar, galactic and universal levels or even twenty years, that is nothing. We are talking here about anchoring and activating two hundred chakras.

Do you realize how profound this is? Melchizedek said it was in the anchoring of the twelfth body, or the universal body, that the advanced ascended-master ability of teleportation comes in. Now, the installation can come very fast in terms of these three levels and the activation is what will take five to ten years. The actualization of all these chakras and bodies will probably take another twenty years if not the rest of the lifetime. Melchizedek told us in 1995 that by the year 2000 we could have our two hundred chakras and solar, galactic and universal bodies installed and activated. But I am not counting my chickens before they are hatched, that is for sure.

I have learned on the spiritual path that things are always changing. The slightest downturn on any one of our parts could delay this indefinitely. All I am saying is that it is a potentiality. Melchizedek said that for the most advanced lightworkers five to fifteen years is a good estimate of the potentiality factor here. Having the information that I have given you will greatly accelerate this process. What this whole process comes down to really is asking. "Ask, and it shall be given you; . . . knock, and it shall be opened unto you" [Matt. 7:7]. These understandings and tools have always been available to humanity. The problem is that no one *asked*.

There is no faster path of spiritual growth on the planet than working with the ascended masters. I am absolutely convinced of that, and I speak from firsthand experience, having checked out just about everything. I write these books with an open heart, wanting to share with you the insights and tools that I have discovered which have been helpful.

In the past these things have been kept secret and hidden. I have made the choice to share everything—and I mean *everything*—that I have learned. I am literally holding back nothing. Every single insight and tool that I have used to get where I am, I have shared with you in one of my books. I am not special and neither is the core group. God loves all His sons and daughters equally. What has worked for us will work exactly the same for you. All we are really doing here is applying universal laws—they work every time.

Take advantage of the literal "spiritual gold" you are being offered. You will never have a better opportunity than you have right now. Part of the reason the core group and I have been accelerated so quickly also has to do with the times we are living in. The time period between the years 1995 to 2000 is the window for mass ascension. We are timing the solar, galactic and universal activation exactly with this mass-ascension window. You can take advantage of this window also, whatever level you are on. The real window here really lasts until the year 2012, which is the end of the Mayan Calendar. There is an enormous spiritual wave riding through this planet, this solar system, this galaxy and this universe.

I am putting out the clarion call to that which is highest within you to take advantage of this planetary, solar, galactic and universal wave. There might not be one like it for eons to come. The core group and I are on this wave and taking it full tilt toward God and service of humanity. The many of us reach out our hands in total love and friendship and ask you to join us, for there is room for everybody on planet Earth. As said in *A Course in Miracles*, "All are chosen."

Melchizedek and Djwhal Khul told us that the goal of the Spiritual Hierarchy is to have all of humanity take its third initiation by the year 2012. The third initiation is the soul merge. The people reading this book, however, will obviously be much more advanced, for a person below the third initiation would probably not be interested in reading this book. One must be guided by the soul to be interested in such things.

Can you imagine every person on Earth taking his/her third initiation? That would be awesome. The goal for the advanced lightworkers is to have everyone complete the ascension and seven levels of initiation and to move into spiritual leadership, world service and cosmic ascension processing. Take advantage of this wave, for it is probably the number-one reason why we have been allowed to accelerate as quickly as we have. This applies equally to you as well.

My beloved brothers and sisters, the clarion call has sounded from the deepest recesses of the universal, galactic, solar and planetary core for God's sons and daughters to come home and bring as many of His children as we can with us. Let us join hands, minds, spirits and hearts together in total focus and commitment to take advantage of the most extraordinary time in Earth's history.

The last and final thing that needs to be anchored here on an ongoing basis is the universal light-quotient level, which is approximately 30 to 40% on the cosmic light-quotient scale.

A Mind Map of Consciousness

The core group and I received some fascinating information from Melchizedek that he called a Mind Map of Consciousness. It is a map not of the physical brain but rather of the energy fields of consciousness that surround the human brain, chakra system and physical human body [see diagram on next page]. This field also serves to link the mental field with the astral field. It was at this point that Lord Maitreya and Djwhal Khul also joined the discussion.

The spiral funnels in the spiritual energies to the brain. It funnels in vibration and knowledge to overlay and intermingle with the will aspect and the intellectual pieces. In an integrated person the spiral would be superimposed over the checkerboard. This has been referred to in the initiation process as the soul merge and monadic merge; however, now we are beginning to get a visual of what this process actually looks like from Melchizedek's universal perspective.

These two aspects are linked together by a healthy, functioning will. This might be looked at as the two halves of the brain merging and integrating. This could also be looked at as the yin and yang becoming integrated, or the feminine (spiral) and the masculine (intellect). In an unintegrated person these aspects remain either dormant and unawakened or just a very small portion of the spiral is let in and kept very separate. It is not fused with the concrete mind. Here we have the scientist who is totally cut off from the soul or spiritual aspect of life. This can also become a very disturbed state of affairs causing great confusion, spaciness, madness, delusion, possession and so on.

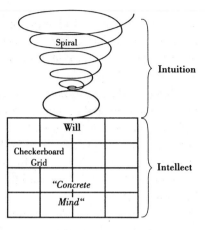

The goal here is to integrate the third- fourth- and fifth-dimensional states of consciousness. The fourth-dimensional functioning is a type of bridge in the ideal state of affairs. Ascension, of course, is the fifth-dimensional state of consciousness.

As the disciples and initiates move through their initiations and grow in light quotient, the clearer they become in their ability to channel the pure information and energy from this spiral without contamination. Melchizedek said that this can never be done one hundred percent, for there are always lenses of some kind. However, the higher one goes in his/her spiritual development, the clearer he becomes in the process.

Everyone has a lens because everyone has an ego, or personality, which the spiral must come through. I am not talking here about a negative ego, but just an ego that in the ideal state must be spiritualized, rather than become a negative ego and instrument of the lower self and Dark Brotherhood.

It is the clearing of the negative ego, the proper integration of the twelve archetypes, the twelve rays and the twelve signs of the zodiac in their highest expression and mastery and the study of psychology from the perspective of the soul that allow the ego to be a clear channel for spirit.

When a person is undeveloped spiritually and psychologically and/or run by the negative ego, the spiral begins to shrink and become very narrow. In the advanced initiate the reverse is true—the spiral is very wide and very large. The spiral is actually the map and increases in size like a spectrum. It increases in velocity, vibration and girth as it moves into higher dimensions. It resembles a tornado.

The antakarana, or bridge of light, that connects one's personality with his/her soul and monad is a part of this spiral. However the spiral is much larger and more massive than the antakarana. The need to build the antakarana and to make it as wide as possible, as well as to do so with the ascension column and chakra column, is essential to being able to receive all the energies in the spiral. It is also essential to keep one's antakarana,

ascension column and chakra column, which in the advanced stages become one, clear from any and all contamination. The ascension techniques
in *The Complete Ascension Manual* and *Beyond Ascension* when practiced
regularly will help to do this.

Keeping the antakarana, ascension column and chakra column as wide
open as possible and as uncontaminated as possible functions as a satellite
dish that allows for the greatest possible attunement to higher-frequency
energies and information. This is the ultimate cable TV station, where all
channels are open. The more the negative ego is in control, the more the
channels will be shut down and the narrower and more tunneled the band
frequency will be.

Through spiritual development and meditation, illumination of the
brain occurs and there is the anchoring of what Djwhal Khul called the Star
of David. This is really a tetrahedron that is able to funnel into it the ema-
nations from the higher mind and the spiral of spiritual energies. When this
happens the lower mind, or concrete mind, begins to expand and lose its
boundaries and fuses with the higher mind.

This Star of David is really an unlimited satellite dish. The concrete
mind is just dealing with the conscious and subconscious mind. It is only
when the concrete mind fuses with the superconscious mind (see "Integrating the Three Minds and the Four Bodies" in Soul Psychology), that full satellite attunement can be achieved. All light technology is for the purpose of
opening up this unlimited capacity. The lower-mind functions now are
transformed into higher-mind functions. The six-pointed Star of David
would be the symbol of awakening—as above, so below; as within, so without.

This initial anchoring of the Star of David into the brain/mind is the beginning of ascension consciousness. It is obviously connected here with the
merger of the soul and monad, or mighty I Am Presence. Ascension in truth
is descension. The spiral becomes wider as this initial step is achieved.

Now, it is essential to understand here that even though this has taken
place in some very high-level initiates, this process can be deflated or nar-
rowed down again if contamination occurs or if the negative ego is allowed
to get out of control.

I repeat again: Just because a person has achieved his/her ascension
and/or completed the seven levels of initiation doesn't mean that she is invulnerable to being taken over by the negative ego. The story of Lucifer in
the Bible is that of an extremely high being who chooses to reverse his
course to the Dark Brotherhood. This process can happen consciously or
unconsciously. It doesn't even have to be the Dark Brotherhood per se; it
can also just be taken over by self-inflation, criticalness, depression from a
physical illness or loss of some kind. Power trips, greed, glamour or fame

can all be contaminants that deflate this program.

There is not a single person on planet Earth, including myself, who doesn't have to be constantly vigilant of the sly tricks of the negative ego and its cohorts of glamour, maya and illusion. No one, and I mean no one, is invulnerable to this danger. One surefire sign to know that you are in danger is that you think you are not—as the Bible says, "After pride cometh the fall."

It is the antakarana, ascension column and chakra column that can be contracted and the greater spiral that too can become contracted. The spiral that ideally overlays each individual receives its energies from the Source. Melchizedek gave the example that this is like letting the air out of a balloon, and that is how quickly this collapse and contamination can take place. Contamination can be equated with a person's lack of ability to maintain unconditional love.

The ability to shift dimensions is the very thing that the yogic path has always maintained. In the Western path because of Judaic-Christian dogma, the soul has been seen as outside the body. Only through the path of ascension is the merger of the soul, monad and personality being emphasized on Earth. This again is why ascension, in truth, is really descension of the soul and monad into the personality and four body-system and why it has become so popular. This is also why the yogic practices have learned to develop a lot of the ascended-master abilities that the Western world has not been able to develop other than an occasional master such as Jesus.

The fourth dimension is the bridge that most do not cross over because of the psychic charge of polarity. This is the level where the Dark Brotherhood wages its entire battleground. Djwhal Khul said that most people who have taken their sixth and seventh initiations have, in truth, only achieved their partial ascension. They have completed their ascension initiations and broken the wheel of rebirth, however, do not always see the whole picture. Part of this is because they have not completed their work in the fourth dimension, which is astral and causal mentality.

They have not completed the cleanup work of the second to fourth initiations even though they have passed the initiations from the perspective of Sanat Kumara, Lord Buddha and Lord Maitreya. They have in other words claimed soul and monadic merger by taking these initiations but have not claimed in reality the soul and monadic fragments of self. This has to do with the proper clearing and integration of the archetypes, rays, astrological signs, houses and planets. They, in essence, have not merged with all the thoughts, feelings and attributes of the soul.

Just because you achieve soul merge at the third initiation or monadic merger at the fifth, sixth and seventh initiation doesn't mean you have realized Christ consciousness on the mental, emotional or physical level. On the physical level you might pass these initiations but still have physical health lessons. On the emotional level you might still be filled with negative emotions and on the mental level still filled with a lot of negative thoughts, lack of understanding and improper philosophies. The myth of ascension is that people think ascension means the automatic attainment of these things when they pass these initiations, but it doesn't. In truth, as I have said many times, initiations have more to do with light quotient than anything else. You can have high light quotient and be an egomaniac and an emotional victim at the psychological level. This might be hard for people to accept, but it is true. Even though people have taken these initiations they must learn to master their archetypes, subpersonalities, past-life aspects, four bodies, three minds, inner parent and inner child and all that goes along with developing a healthy spiritual psychology.

Lightworkers tend to be much enamored by the ephemeral and celestial realms and are not well grounded on this psychological level. In essence one must work the three levels simultaneously on the spiritual path. One must work on the physical level in terms of diet, exercise, herbs, homeopathics, sunshine and so on. Then one must work on the psychological level in regard to the in-depth study of spiritual and soul psychology. Thirdly, one needs to work on the spiritual level.

I meet an enormous number of lightworkers who are totally preoccupied with the spiritual level and channeling and all these wonderful beings and dimensions, but are not balanced and integrated themselves. They are not in control of their emotional body or of their desire body. They are not in control of their negative ego. They have not mastered their finances. They do not have inner peace. Their relationships aren't working. They have too many negative thoughts. They have physical health lessons. They are tired all the time. They are filled with too many negative emotions. The philosophies they hold on a conscious level are not always balanced and integrated. They do not remain in a state of oneness, unconditional love, inner peace and joy at all times. If you relate to any of these, this is not a judgment, just a sign that your physical-level reality and psychological-level reality need more focus and attention. The goal is balanced self-realization.

Djwhal Khul told me a very fascinating thing in regard to this whole process. He said that it was only since 1993 that permission was given for lightworkers to go beyond the fifth initiation before completing this psychological-clearing work. Djwhal said that this was in a sense an experiment on their part and might not have been such a good idea. They did this because we are living in such an extraordinary time in Earth's history and closing in on the beginning of the new millennium, and as many planetary lightworkers as possible need to take their place.

Djwhal also said that all must do their inner cleanup work before they will be able to complete their seven levels of initiation. They will move to the seventh sublevel of the seventh initiation but will not be allowed to cross over and be called fully completed ascended masters and seventh-degree initiates until the proper psychological, physical and soul-extension clearing and integration work is achieved. This full integration and mastery of all three levels takes great depth of maturity. This is why you will see many at this time taking their sixth and seventh initiations, but in many ways they are still like children, for the full maturation of what it really means to be an ascended master has not flowered yet.

So again, what we have here is that one's spiritual body might have merged into fifth-dimensional consciousness at sixth and seventh initiations, however, the mental, emotional and physical body might in truth not be spending too much time there. Do you see now?

Initiations are given when the spiritual body touches in through higher light quotient. Most have been graced to be allowed to take these initiations before all four bodies have matured into the ability to hold and maintain this state of consciousness all the time, no matter what is going on outside of self. The misconception is that people take these initiations and think that they are ascended masters and that their work is done. Nothing could be further from the truth. In reality their work is just beginning.

Now, the work is to see if you can keep your entire four-body system in that state of consciousness all the time without slipping out. This is true ascended-master maturity. This is also why the advanced ascended-master abilities are not being given out after taking one's ascension. Do you really think after everything I have explained here that lightworkers are really ready for this responsibility? Would you want someone who was extremely psychologically unclear, run by the negative ego, operating out of victim consciousness and not having achieved full unity consciousness in his/her four-body system, possessing these kinds of abilities?

In this more accelerated phase of evolution this is why advanced ascended-master abilities don't come until the full solar, galactic and universal levels are installed, activated and actualized. I think this section clears up a lot of the previous misconceptions about ascension that we have held in the past.

Dimensions of Consciousness

The true testing ground of the soul is the fourth dimension. This is the battleground that lightworkers must master to move into fifth-dimensional consciousness, which is the realm of immortality and the breaking of the wheel of reincarnation. Many lifetimes are fought on this fourth-dimensional level and it is the true testing ground of the soul. The fifth dimension is the

realm of ascension. Third dimension is the realm of pure materialistic consciousness. In the fourth dimension one begins the bridging process from
materialistic consciousness to full spiritual maturation.

The seventh initiation actually moves one into sixth-dimensional consciousness. This again, however, is usually just the spiritual body that
touches in. It is a rare lightworker who can keep his/her mental, emotional
and physical body there unceasingly. To move into seventh-dimensional
consciousness one must fully complete the seven levels of initiation, do all
the clearing work on the psychological and physical level and truly achieve
the full depth of maturity of what it really means to be an ascended master
on all levels.

To move into eighth-dimensional consciousness one must move completely into group consciousness, on a soul level. This is beyond the union
of just one's individual soul and monad but has now moved to groups of
souls that work together. The ninth dimension takes the same principle one
step higher, which is group-monadic level. This is the merger with your individual monad.

The tenth dimension is merger with monads on even a larger scale on a
solar level. The eleventh dimension is merger with monads on a galactic
scale. Twelfth dimension is merger with monads on a universal level.
These last three are a much slower process than the speed at which initiations five, six, seven, eight and nine can be worked through. The solar, galactic and universal levels are much vaster in scope and, as I mentioned in
a previous chapter, contain fifty chakras to be integrated at each step,
where the first nine levels were only fifty chakras.

Dimensional Spectrum of Consciousness

12th dimension	Realization of universal chakras 150 to 200 and realization of anointed Christ overself body, zohar body and/or universal body of light; twelve strands of DNA fully realized; 40% cosmic light quotient achieved; ultimate monadic ascension
11th dimension	Realization of galactic chakras 100 to 150 and realization of galactic body
10th dimension	Realization of solar chakras 50 to 100 and realization of solar body
9th dimension	Realization of chakras 44 to 50
8th dimension	Realization of chakras 37 to 43 and group-soul body activated and actualized
7th dimension	Completion of seven levels of initiation, full

realization of seventh, or logoic, body

6th dimension   Seventh initiation

5th dimension   Beginning stage of ascension, sixth initiation

4th dimension   Bridge to ascension, testing ground

3rd dimension   Materialistic consciousness

The Eighth- and Ninth-Dimensional Levels

After you complete your seven levels of initiation you then begin the process of not working on attaining initiations anymore but rather anchoring dimensional levels. This is done as I have previously mentioned by anchoring, activating and actualizing chakra grids, higher bodies and cosmic light quotient. It is also done by expanding one's understanding of light quotient. In one of our group meditations Djwhal Khul and Melchizedek began to explain to us how this process works at the eighth- and ninth-dimensional levels.

In the first seven dimensional levels one is working for monadic ascension, which is the ascension of all twelve oversouls into your monad and is a longer process. One has to achieve planetary ascension in all twelve oversouls, not just your own oversoul. Here you see your evolution is totally dependent upon eleven other high-level initiates who will be doing this process for their oversoul families of twelve. While this ultimate monadic-ascension process continues you will, as you move past your seven levels of initiation, also begin to form groups of souls and monads, which then merge together in unity consciousness. This must be done to realize the eighth- and ninth-dimensional levels, bodies and chakras.

The best way to explain this is to share what Djwhal Khul told us about our core group. He said that in giving us the job to take over his inner-plane ashram in the year 2012 when he moves on to the Great White Lodge on Sirius, he is in a group-monadic connection with us. He told us that there were six monads that we combined together in this group matrix. It is almost like six molecules coming together to form a larger molecule. To realize the eighth and ninth levels of group-soul and group-monadic consciousness one does this through this group of six.

Then each of us in our individual monads has our own smaller group of six that form a type of group-monadic family. This is different now than what I was speaking about in planetary ascension of one's soul and monadic family. It is different because we are now dealing with the combining of other monads, not just soul extensions and oversouls from the same monad. The following diagram [see p. 64] shows this geometric group matrix.

Djwhal Khul told me that from the frame of reference of this larger group module, I am one of his soul extensions and he mine. We are not

Group-Monadic Module

An example of how this structure works can be seen by using some of the people currently working out of the Los Angeles ashram.

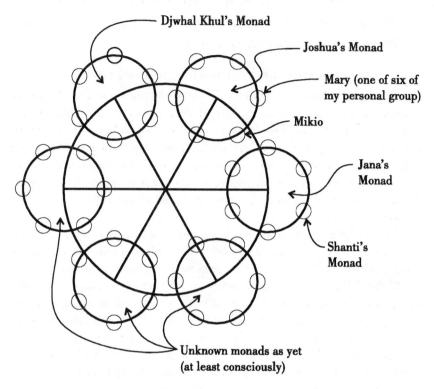

Djwhal Khul's Monad

Joshua's Monad

Mary (one of six of my personal group)

Mikio

Jana's Monad

Shanti's Monad

Unknown monads as yet (at least consciously)

from the same individual monad: We are each soul extensions from the larger group module. Each individual monad has 144 soul extensions. If you multiply this by six monads, you have 864 soul extensions that make up this larger group module. Do you see how this works now?

We each have an oversoul family of twelve. We each have a monadic soul family of 144. On the next level we have a group monadic family of 864. In planetary ascension you are dependent on 144 soul extensions from your oversoul to all work together to ascend.

In the process of ultimate monadic ascension you are dependent on 144 soul extensions, which are all your soul extensions from your twelve oversouls. In this group module you could say you are interdependent upon 864 soul extensions. The actual numbers are not really that important. What is important is to see how interdependent we are on soul family, monadic family, ultimate monadic family and group-module monadic family. For example, with the core group and I, our evolution is totally tied to one another. If one falters, the entire group will falter. This is why this concept of group consciousness is so important.

The negative ego will tell you that you are evolving on your own. This is illusion. If your eleven other soul extensions are not clear and properly integrated, your ascension will be held back. You are interdependent on them whether you like this or not. This is even easier to see in the concept of the ultimate monadic ascension, where the ascension of your entire monad is totally dependent on one of your soul extensions from each of your twelve oversouls achieving their ascension, before all twelve oversouls can completely rejoin with the monad and hence achieve ultimate monadic ascension.

You can help in this process, but your fate is totally tied up now with other beings in your monadic family who are working on their evolution just as you are. In an even larger context still, the evolutionary fate of our group module is not dependent on just your own personal monadic family but also with the monadic families of six other monads. No person is an island unto him/herself. If you hold onto such a concept, you will not progress.

Do you see now why it is so important to transcend negative-ego consciousness. We all must learn to cooperate, live in harmony and be our brother's and sister's keeper. Interdependence and group consciousness are the keynotes and touchstones for the new age and the next millennium.

The entire universe is comprised of these triadic, honeycombed modules that keep fitting together in larger and larger matrices the higher one goes in his/her cosmic evolution. All are connected in the ultimate honeycombed module that is God. "Honeycombed" is a good way to describe this, for isn't God sweet like the finest honey money can buy? These ultimate group modules that get larger as you move up the solar, galactic, universal and multiuniversal levels are also connected at the highest Source level with the twelve cosmic rays and the Cosmic Council of Twelve.

The group module that the core group and I are connected with is a second-ray module. Now, this gets complicated because our entire solar system is a second-ray solar system. So even though we each might have different rays that make up our soul monad, personality and so on, in the ultimate cosmic sense, we might all come from the second cosmic ray. I am not speaking here of the twelve planetary rays that I spoke of in my first book, *The Complete Ascension Manual*. These rays are in truth subrays of one single cosmic ray. I will have to ask Melchizedek what ray our galaxy and universe are—that will be an interesting discussion.

So getting back to the main point, the group modules are connected to a cosmic ray and Cosmic Council of Twelve members. On this cosmic level we have cosmic modules interfacing because Melchizedek said certain cosmic rays group together in triad formations, just as we do at our level. Each of these group modules could be looked at as atoms, electrons, cells, molecules and, ultimately, as glands and organs in God's infinite body.

Even if each of us is only an electron in God's infinite body, He will not be perfectly healthy if we do not do our job. So ultimately we don't work for our oversoul, monad, group module, group-solar module, group-galactic module, group-universal module or group-multiuniversal module. We are really working for God and His God module. Each of these are just steps along the way that must be taken and actualized to realize this ultimate goal—true God-realization.

This whole understanding completely breaks up the veil of the ego's identity. As Sai Baba has said so eloquently, "God is hidden by the mountain range of ego." The essence of the negative ego's philosophy is separation. As one embraces this process of self-realization and God-realization, these veils and imaginary fences of identity begin to fall away.

Djwhal Khul said that the eighth dimension, or group-soul level, is achieved when you merge with the oversoul of your six monads in your group module. You are really doing it for the entire planetary group-soul level. All possible combinations on the planetary level are in this pattern of six. Merging with the six is the way God has set it up for the entire group-soul planetary level. This is the sacred geometry of the universe.

5

A Cosmic Day and a Cosmic Night

Those who have read my books know that a Cosmic Day lasts for 4.3 billion years. Then there is the Cosmic Night, which lasts for a similar amount of time. This has been termed the inbreath and outbreath of Brahma. We on Earth have used up 3.1 billion years of our Cosmic Day and therefore have 1.2 billion years before our Cosmic Night begins. I have always been interested in what goes on during the Cosmic Night, so I put on my Sherlock Holmes hat and attempted to pin the masters down on this point.

During the Cosmic Night there is kind of an incubation period before Brahma, or God, takes His next outbreath. In a Cosmic Night the physical planets do not evolve but souls who are now out of incarnation do still evolve. Melchizedek said that incarnations in a sense continue not on the physical plane but rather on the astral plane, which was a total surprise and new concept to me, yet it made total sense.

The physical planets go into hibernation. There also seems to be a speeding up on the inner plane because of the lack of resistance that is brought about because of the fact that material existence does not have to be dealt with at this time. Souls continue to reincarnate on the astral plane until they break the wheel of reincarnation and transcend the physical laws. This again is the attaining of the seventh initiation.

Melchizedek said that whatever kind of role the given soul was playing in the physical, that soul plays the opposite in the astral plane, just like the contrast of day and night. This allows for balanced growth and the proper integration of all archetypes.

An example of this might be someone who has been very intent on making money as his/her main focus and was very wealthy and miserly. In the Cosmic Night the person would incarnate on an astral plane where he would be very poor in terms of monetary wealth and hence would be forced to learn how to grow spiritually without this attachment. The Cosmic Night also allows each soul an enormously long period of time to think, introspect and digest its hundreds of lifetimes in material existence and its many thousands of lifetimes of its oversoul, which is made of each person's eleven other soul extensions.

Each soul extension usually has from 200 to 250 incarnations. This is similar to the time each of us have had between our incarnations during a Cosmic Day. This is really the break time for an incarnation of an entire universe between incarnations. You must realize here that we are only talking about one Cosmic Day. Think of how long a year of Brahma is, or one hundred years of Brahma, which is the period of one solar system. I have enclosed a chart from *The Complete Ascension Manual* that deals with this time line and that is originally from the Alice Bailey material. God's infinite universes are made up of infinite numbers of these occult or cosmic centuries, which is a concept that cannot even be fathomed by the linear mind.

a. One hundred years of Brahma	An occult century; the period of a solar system
b. One year of Brahma	The period of seven chains, where the seven planetary schemes are concerned
c. One week of Brahma	The period of seven rounds in one scheme; it has a chain significance
d. One day of Brahma	The occult period of a round
e. One hour of Brahma	Concerns interchain affairs
f. One Brahmic minute	Concerns the planetary centers and therefore egoic groups
g. One Brahmic moment	Concerns an egoic group and its relation to the whole

As an evolving being we receive the whole balance of cosmic experience by moving in and out of these Cosmic Days and Cosmic Nights every 4.3 billion years. On a microcosmic level we do this every Earth day. Every twenty-four-hour Earth day we have a microcosmic day (waking hours) and a microcosmic night (sleep time). Did not Hermes/Thoth say,

"As within, so without. As above, so below"? Understand the atom and you can understand the infinite universe. Know thyself, and hence you can know God.

Earth – courage

Once one incarnates into a particular universe (and there are infinite numbers of universes, each with a different cosmic theme), one does not leave that universe until he/she graduates, which would mean becoming a full-fledged Melchizedek, not in the earthly sense of the term but in the highest universal sense of the term, as a Sai Baba, for example. He is the only being in incarnation even close to operating at that level.

So there might be what is called a planetary Melchizedek, a solar Melchizedek, a galactic Melchizedek (Lord Maitreya) and a universal Melchizedek (Sai Baba). There is one level after this, the multiuniversal level Melchizedek, which would be full and complete graduation from the Melchizedek school. The next step after this is Source, or God, merger. This is the step that Melchizedek, our Universal Logos, who runs the universe, is now moving toward. So even *he* is in a state of evolution, as is Sai Baba.

Part of the work of the Cosmic Night is to prepare oneself and to do all the work to prepare for one's next evolution in the Cosmic Day. This is the same principle between incarnations. Most souls do not incarnate immediately after passing on. A rest period is needed and a time for introspection and review.

The same principle is in operation on the universal level, a period of activity and nonactivity, in a material sense. On a psychic or spiritual sense, just like our inner-plane dreamtime, it is still very active. If you realized how much you do every night while you are asleep, you would be amazed. Most of us remember only one-tenth of one percent of all the spiritual work and service work we are involved in. On the psychic or spiritual level this never stops.

Melchizedek and Djwhal Khul told us that in the original design of the Cosmic Day it was thought that souls would only do physical evolving and not astral incarnations. It was found, however, that this was much too taxing on the mental body. Because of this the process of astral incarnations was instituted so the mental body could rest from the taxing process of creating physical form. The masters said that the Cosmic Night is speeded up in some mysterious way because of the nonmaterial existence, so in truth it isn't as long as a Cosmic Day.

This process of astral incarnations reminds me of what has taken place during the initiations in the Great Pyramid of Giza in the King's Chamber while lying in the sarcophagus. Souls were allowed to accelerate evolution by living out incarnations in the dream state in the Great Pyramid to achieve the process of becoming a planetary Melchizedek in a shorter period of time (*Hidden Mysteries* details this in chapters on the

Egyptian mysteries).

During a Cosmic Night the physical universe still exists, but is in a state of suspended animation waiting for the incarnation cycle to begin again. The masters then chimed in with another amazing piece of information that they said was a side note to this whole line of questioning. They said that the key to our learning dematerialization and materialization lay within this understanding of the Cosmic Day and Cosmic Night.

The next piece of information transported us into the Twilight Zone, and you will see what I mean when you hear this. To be honest it is hard for me to believe that this is true. I think I once saw an actual *Twilight Zone* TV episode using a similar theme (you probably saw this one, too). If this came through accurately, what they said is that when the Cosmic Night actually begins the six billion don't physically instantly die on our planet and on the ten billion planets with life in the universe.

I asked if they don't physically die, what happens to them? The masters said they are held in suspended animation with the rest of the universe and the essence, or souls, in incarnation live on. In the exact moment of the beginning of the Cosmic Day again 4.3 billion years later (no real time on the inner: it is a concept of material existence), everything begins exactly where things left off with everyone in the universe back in incarnation exactly the way they were before they left—except 4.3 billion years wiser.

Is that a trip, or is that a trip! Do you remember the *Twilight Zone* episode where the man somehow obtained a pocket watch that could stop time for everyone on Earth except for himself? Everyone else was frozen in time, but he could move around. I can't remember how it ended, but I think at first he liked it and then he began to hate it, and then at the end I think he dropped the watch and it cracked and broke and he was stuck in the Cosmic Night.

I remember reading something in a metaphysical book and never have asked the masters if this is true or not; however, for some reason it has always stuck in my mind. What was said is that if a person who was still involved in the reincarnation cycle died in the month of December as a Sagittarius, then he/she would be reborn her next life as a Sagittarius according to Cosmic Law.

This concept of suspended animation and picking up exactly where one left off 4.3 billion years earlier reminded me of this. I don't know if this theory is true; I will have to check this out the next time I meditate. It sure is an interesting thought, however, and does make sense. As Edgar Cayce said in regard to the law of karma, "Every jot and tittle of the law is fulfilled." What you sow, you reap. And what you put out comes back to you. No one gets something for nothing. The masters call this a stop-action frame.

If you think about this, it is exactly what goes on every night when we go to sleep. The physical body is held in a state of suspended animation and the etheric, astral, mental, buddhic, atmic, monadic, logoic and soul bodies are off to their different planes of existence. When we wake up in the morning we continue exactly where we left off, one planetary night wiser. In a cosmic sense, it is like going to sleep for a Cosmic Night, instead of just a planetary night. You have to admit, it makes a lot of sense: Whenever there is the correlation between the microcosm and the macrocosm, there is always a ring of truth. This would make a great story line for a Star Trek movie, wouldn't you agree?

The masters continued on with their discussion telling us that this could be equated to time travel. Look at when we dream, it feels like hours and days go by and in true chronological time it has been only seconds. This process is the exact reverse: Eons of time go by and from the perspective of the physical body it has not even been a second. This is possible because we are dealing with nontime and space realities. Time is a linear concept created by the third-dimensional mind. It is multidimensional and simultaneous in the spiritual world.

I then asked, when does a universe achieve its ascension? The universe achieves its ascension when all the souls incarnated in the entire universe achieve cosmic ascension in their given universal school. Our universal school is the Melchizedek school. Other universes have different cosmic themes (as I talked about in *Beyond Ascension*).

The theme for our Cosmic Day is *courage* in the Melchizedek school or university. Other universes, of which there are infinite numbers, each have a different Universal Logos, hence a different school and a different cosmic theme. A very interesting side note here is that Vywamus, in one of his channelings through Janet McClure, said that the extraterrestrials called the Grays, who are connected with Zeta Reticuli, are very sick physically and are affected this way because they traveled in spaceships from a different universe. He said they will never recover on their own without cosmic spiritual help, for they weren't created to evolve through this universe. I personally find this absolutely fascinating.

When all beings graduate from Melchizedek's cosmic school, Melchizedek said that the universe dissolves into light, and the next universe is created. Metatron refers to this in *The Book of Knowledge: The Keys of Enoch* when he speaks of the possibility of receiving the information from the next universe and the pyramid grid from the next universe. Just as Arcturus is the future self, or prototype, for planet Earth, being the most evolved civilization in our galaxy, so planets, solar systems, galaxies, universes and multiuniverses are all in a state of evolution and ascension as well as ourselves.

In the Alice Bailey books Djwhal Khul spoke of the Jewish race being the most evolved race from the previous, or third solar system. We are now in the fourth solar system. This ties into the understanding that was brought forth in the Alice Bailey books and in the theosophical books of Madam Blavatsky of an occult period of a round, involving seven rounds that make up one scheme and seven schemes that make up one occult century.

On our planet this is divided on a more microcosmic level into the seven root races, which I have reprinted here from *The Complete Ascension Manual*. Each root race is connected to the evolution of one planetary chakra. The universe is as ordered and mathematical in its evolution as a Swiss-made watch. Everything in God's universe is governed by laws, including God. To get even a glimpse of this process puts one into a state of absolute awesome amazement.

After a universe's completion, graduation and ascension, there is a new universe created with a new and more evolved cosmic theme, just as the lightworkers on this planet and others like it will eventually fill those posts. The galactic masters will ultimately evolve to fill the posts in the universal level of government. The universal masters such as Melchizedek will ultimately move on to the multiuniversal level and beyond back to Source to fill cosmic posts in the ultimate cosmic government.

This is the cosmic hierarchy of creation and a vision of our cosmic journey. Can you imagine being in charge of an entire universe? It is sometimes hard enough just being in charge of a physical, emotional and mental body. This is why we have to master each level of school—planetary, solar, galactic, universal, multiuniversal and cosmic—step by step. It is a long journey, but again what is the rush? There is no such thing as death, so in truth we have all the time in the world. It also gets much easier and much more fun the higher you go. The material universe and this schoolhouse called Earth is definitely one of the tougher schools. It will be a big plus on your cosmic résumé that you went to planetary college here.

When I say that you have a cosmic résumé, this is no joke and not just a metaphor. As you move up this ladder of consciousness you might be offered jobs in other solar systems, other galaxies, other universes and other multiuniverses. When a given ascended master is gifted at what he does, word gets around. The same is true on a microcosmic level on Earth. This is true in all professions, sports and/or the spiritual movement. The same is true in the solar system, galaxy, universe and multiuniverse.

Other solar, galactic or universal hierarchies might offer you job opportunities you can't refuse, not because of the money they offer you but because of the service and growth potential. There is no competition between galaxies, for example, because God is the guiding force for all. On that level what you choose will be God's will. There are, in truth, unlimited opportunities for your particular service skills.

There are vast cycles of evolution involving the inbreath and outbreath of Brahma. For example, I mentioned earlier an occult century is one hundred years of Brahma. In the Alice Bailey books Djwhal Khul said that this period of time constitutes the whole period of Brahma's age, which is esoterically referred to as a *mahakalpa*.

You think one Cosmic Day is long, being 4.3 billion years and then another 4.3 billion years for a Cosmic Night. A mahakalpa is 311 trillion, 40 billion years. To put this in perspective, humankind has only been on the Earth, according to Edgar Cayce, for 10.5 million years. Sanat Kumara has been the Planetary Logos for 18.5 million. We are talking about trillions and billions of years.

Since the focus of this book is cosmic ascension, it would not be complete without integrating the view of the cosmos from *The Urantia Book*. Because many people might be reading this book before reading some of my others, I am quoting two paragraphs from my book *Hidden Mysteries*.

The Urantia Book, for those of you who are not familiar with it, is another book that is truly a revelation of God. It was written by a commission of universal beings who reside in the capital of our superuniverse. In their writings they refer to Earth as "Urantia." The following paragraphs describe the physical organization of the universe as depicted in *The Urantia Book*:

> Your world, Urantia, is one of many similar inhabited planets which comprise the local universe of "Nebadon." This universe, together with similar creations, makes up the superuniverse of "Orvonton," from evolutionary superuniverses of time and space which circle the never-beginning, never-ending creation of divine perfection—the central universe of "Havona." At the heart of this eternal and central universe is the stationary "Isle of Paradise," the geographic center of infinity and the dwelling place of the Eternal God.

> The seven evolving superuniverses in association with the central and divine universe, we commonly refer to as the "grand universe." These are the now organized and inhabited creations. They are all a part of the master universe, which also embraces the uninhabited but mobilizing universes of outer space [excerpted from *Hidden Mysteries*, this information is sourced from *The Urantia Book*].

As I began to meditate on this description what I realized is that the entire infinite universe is like one gigantic atom. The stationary Isle of Paradise is the only stationary point in all of creation. Hence, it is like the nucleus of the atom. The superuniverses, universes, galaxies and solar systems are like the electrons, protons and neutrons.

Djwhal Khul once told me that the monad had a nucleus to it. This made sense to me, for the microcosm is like the macrocosm. To look at the smallest physical particle in the material universe is to get a glimpse of God at the macrocosmic level also.

The Urantia Book also states that the physical universe extends infinitely. The stationary Isle of Paradise is not a time creation but an eternal existence. It is the perfect and eternal nucleus of the master universe. The master universe includes all that I have told you about so far and also embraces the uninhabited but mobilizing universes of outer space. The Urantia Book then divides the outer space regions into four levels: first, second, third and fourth.

The fifth level is called open space. It states that the grand universe has an aggregate evolutionary potential of seven trillion inhabited planets. The grand universe includes everything in the universe except for the outer space levels just mentioned. There is potential for even more inhabited planets if the outer space levels are included. Our particular universe of Nebadon is one of the new universes in God's creation. It lies on the outer edge of the grand universe.

So our universe is on the outer edge from the geographic or physical standpoint of the center of the universe. This has no effect from a spiritual standpoint of being close to God because time and space is really only an illusion of linear time.

More on Universal Evolution

One by one every universe in God's creation will ascend just as every individual will. We can visit these other universes in the dream state. I remember one night I was taken to the Govinda Galaxy in dream state. I was told that I was given this experience to accelerate my ascension and permanently anchor the love vibration. Each universe and galaxy has a different vibration. Ask in meditation or in dream state to be taken by the masters to visit another universe to see how it feels. We can visit other universes all we want, but we are not allowed to permanently leave this universe until we graduate.

Whether or not the cosmology of The Urantia Book concerning the organization of the physical universe is true, I am not sure. I will say it is very interesting food for thought. I like this idea of there being a stationary Isle of Paradise. It sounds like Shamballa on a cosmic level. I think this would make another really good Star Trek movie.

I then asked Melchizedek why this process of incarnation into matter began. I asked whether this was our choice or if we had to do this as part of God's plan. Melchizedek smiled on the inner plane and then with his quick wit said, "It seemed like a good idea at the time." He said that God's plan was to extend God's kingdom into the dense vibration. In essence this was an experiment that was greatly determined by the use of our free choice or free will.

I then asked Melchizedek what will happen when all souls return not only to Melchizedek, but on a larger scale, all the way back to God. He said immediately that there is the inbreath and outbreath again. Once God has breathed all souls back into His heart there will emerge a new ultimate evolutionary cycle with a new theme at a much higher level—a new creative experiment begins. The difference being, however, that we have returned home conscious.

Previous to this in our creation we were not conscious in the same way we are now or will be after traversing planetary, solar, galactic, universal and multiuniversal levels to return home again. Eventually we will integrate and absorb universes in a way similar to how we now absorb our eleven other soul extensions or 144 monadic soul extensions, which enable us to ascend.

Do you see here again how the microcosm is like the macrocosm? Melchizedek is the archetypal being to which we are all heading for our universe. From what we were given in this session, he is in charge of the forty-three other universes from the Source of our Cosmic Day. The exact number forty-three might not be completely accurate (however, this is not important). When one goes to the multiuniversal-level ascension seat, one is tapping into the essence of these universes, which is why this is so profound.

I had previously thought that Melchizedek was in charge of all forty-three universes (or whatever number it is). Melchizedek is in charge of only our universe but does sit on the Multiuniversal Council since he is one of the Universal Logoi.

Well, Melchizedek is the ultimate fully integrated universal archetype, who is our ultimate leader and president, so to speak. So there is a being who we will refer to as the Source of this Cosmic Day, who is in charge of coordinating the many universes that make up the multiuniversal level. There are infinite numbers of sources who then report to God, the ultimate Source.

The evolution of a universe is, of course, dependent on the evolution of the astronomical number of galaxies, solar systems, planets and incarnated souls that make up a given planetary system. Each individual soul is like a cell in the universe: each country a molecule; each planet a grouping of cells; each solar system a part of an organ system; each galaxy like an organ or gland; the entire universe, the full body of Melchizedek. The multiuniverse has many individual bodies. At the highest cosmic level is the infinite number of bodies that make up the omnipresent, omnipotent and omniscient body of God, who contains and expresses through them all.

When a universe ascends, in a sense it merges with the Multiuniversal Source at the next level above itself before the Source of our Cosmic Day breathes out another universe. All the infinite number of universes in God's body are evolving at a different rate of speed.

Again, as I mentioned in *Beyond Ascension*, some universes are closed down early and brought into the cosmic laboratory and completed, for the theme of that particular universe was not working. The example that Vywamus once gave was the reading of a bad book. Why continue reading it? The Source closes it down and completes it in the cosmic laboratory and makes the ensuing knowledge and wisdom gained available to all. Vywamus said that ten universes were closed down from the Source of our Cosmic Day in 1988 [see "The Twenty-Four Dimensions of Reality" in *Beyond Ascension*].

Currently, we are in a cosmic inbreath cycle, which means we are all returning to Source. There obviously is no rush, but there is a big push by the "powers that be" in the cosmos to make as much progress as possible given that we have completed three-quarters of our current Cosmic Day and have only one-quarter left.

From our perspective the 1.2 billion years left seems like an eternity given that humanity has only lived on Earth for 10.5 million years. From the perspective of the Source of our Cosmic Day it is like thinking in terms of possibly millions of occult centuries, which again is one hundred years of Brahma to us. One twenty-four-hour day seems like a long time to us, but to the Source it is 8.6 billion years. A lifetime for us is one hundred years. A lifetime for the Source of our Cosmic Day is 311 trillion, 40 billion years.

As you can see, everything is relative. To God this is like one half-breath in an infinite number of breaths. One begins to get a sense of how minuscule he/she really is in the whole scheme of things, yet still very important because God's plan will not be complete unless every cell is working properly.

There is a cosmic time relationship to everything. For example, what happens if one of Melchizedek's organs is not functioning as well as the rest of his organs are? Organs are again like galaxies. This is in a sense fouling up the timetable for the entire universal ascension. Melchizedek will then send one of his emergency teams from the Order of Melchizedek to rectify this situation. This is kind of what is going on with the Earth and our solar system. There is a big push to move it forward after 3.2 billions years of rather slow progress in the Cosmic Day. The Earth will make more progress in the forty-year time cycle from 1988 to 2028 than it did previously in 3.2 billion years. This is a mind-boggling concept and this accelerated progress is why it is such a blessing to be incarnated in this school at this time.

Each and every universe has to complete its cosmic theme whether through the infinite number of Cosmic Days or by being taken into the cosmic laboratory for completion. God's infinite universe is like a gigantic puzzle and if a particular universe is not completed, it is like a puzzlepiece is missing from God's divine plan. On a lower level this would be the same as thinking that the universe could ascend without one of its galaxies. On an even lower scale the galaxy can't ascend without all its solar systems, nor can a solar system ascend without all its planets ascending. Our planet can't ascend without every soul ascending.

In our planet there are 60,000 million monads in our school. This means 60,000 million times 144 to get the number of soul extensions or personalities in the process of incarnation. This is because each monad or mighty I Am Presence has 144 personalities connected to it in its monadic family, as I have explained in *The Complete Ascension Manual*.

Our solar system has two planets that have now ascended: Venus, which is the most advanced, and Earth, which has most recently advanced. Just as the universe deals with mahakalpas, or occult centuries dealing with one hundred years of Brahma, the Earth deals with smaller cycles that are connected with the seven root races. Each root race is connected with the evolvement of one chakra for humanity, beginning at the base.

We are currently in the fifth root race, which is the Aryan race. It has taken us 18.5 million years to work through just five root races. The Meruvian root race is just now beginning to cycle in. Each root race [see chart on p. 78] is also connected to a certain soul quality. The Aryan root race, which we have currently been in, is connected with mental development. In the Atlantean time it was emotional development. Personality development and intuition are now coming in on a mass scale.

The advanced initiates on this planet are much further ahead of the mass consciousness, which (of course) is good. Helios is the Solar Logos and is in charge of the ascension process of the solar system. The Planetary Logos of each of the nine planets in our solar system work for Helios and are like chakras in his body.

Helios works for Melchior, who is the Galactic Logos, and is in charge of helping the galaxy to ascend. The most advanced civilization in our Milky Way Galaxy is Arcturus. This is why the Earth is now beginning to work so closely with the Arcturians.

In regard to our solar system there is a term called a "sacred planet status." A planet in our solar system achieves this status when it takes its third initiation, or soul merge. So one can see that planets take initiations the same way humans do. This initiation process also applies to solar systems, galaxies and universes, but of course with different standards for achieving their initiations.

Melchizedek, who runs our universe, reports to the Source of our Cosmic Day and sits on one of the councils of the Cosmic Council of Twelve, which runs the infinite universe. Just as our solar system, for example, is a

The Seven Root Races

Root Race	Continent	Attunement	Chakra	Yoga
1. Polarian	The Imperishable Sacred Land	Physical	1st chakra	Hatha yoga
2. Hyperborean	Continent of Hyperborea	Physical	1st chakra	Hatha yoga
3. Lemurian	Continent of Lemuria	Physical	2nd chakra	Hatha yoga
4. Atlantean	Continent of Atlantis	Emotional	3rd chakra	Bhakti yoga
5. Aryan	Europe, Asia Minor, America	Mental	4th chakra	Raja yoga
6. Meruvian	North America	Personality	5th chakra	Agni yoga
7. Paradisian	Tara	Soul	6th chakra	Unknown

second-ray solar system and our planet a fourth-ray planet, our universe on a macrocosmic level is made up of one of the cosmic rays.

The elder who Melchizedek reports to is the member on the Cosmic Council of Twelve in charge of the cosmic ray (not planetary ray) under whose auspices our universe falls. Remember that each one of the twelve members of the Cosmic Council of Twelve, which runs God's infinite universe, is in charge of one cosmic ray.

In this sense the infinite universe is divided into twelve sections. We see this on a microcosmic and planetary level in the study of astrology, which has the twelve signs of the zodiac, in the twelve major archetypes, in the twelve planetary rays and in the twelve planets, nine exoteric and three hidden. Even though Melchizedek said there are an infinite number of sources for Cosmic Days and universes, they all fall under one of these twelve cosmic rays. Now, there might be a process of exploring one of the other cosmic-ray externalizations after we return to Source and achieve our cosmic ascension. But we will each achieve our cosmic ascension on *one* cosmic ray.

There might be an aspect of the ultimate cosmic plan in which one would take twelve different cosmic ascensions, one on each ray. This would give one a complete experience of God on all twelve cosmic rays and levels. I am not completely sure on this; however, we did receive information on such a concept. This would deal with the future inbreaths and outbreaths of God.

The nature of these other cosmic ascensions would be very different from our experience here, for we would be on a different cosmic-ray theme. It would also be a more evolved understanding and experience because of already having achieved one cosmic ascension. I received information that the core group and I are working on our third cosmic ascension.

To put this in perspective, if this is true, that means I have only 345 more initiations to go (352 all together, but I have completed seven) to achieve cosmic ascension through this cosmic ray, and then nine more cosmic ascensions to go. Nine times 352 equals 28,512. This total plus the 345 to go in this cosmic ascension equals 28,857 initiations to go until completion. This should only take me about 500 trillion occult centuries, so I am almost home! (Rather a humbling thought.)

What we are really dealing with here is cosmic astrology, not planetary astrology. One would be taking cosmic ascensions in the twelve cosmic signs, or twelve cosmic rays. Then one has achieved ultimate cosmic ascension and can serve at full God potential, capacity and maturity on all cosmic rays in all cosmic zodiac signs. God's divine plan will not be complete until all souls achieve this. When this is all complete, knowing God, He/She will probably create a new cosmic divine plan. So what we are dealing with here is a new concept of what I am now terming ultimate cosmic ascension.

Melchizedek also told us that just as monads group together in their work on this planet, universes also group together. In this sense we have neighboring universes. I have spoken of this as the forty-three christed universes from the Source of our Cosmic Day in *Beyond Ascension*. (Melchizedek tells me that number might not be right, but the concept is sound).

Besides the fact that we are connected to all the universes by the Source of our Cosmic Day, we are also connected to all the universes by the Cosmic Council of Twelve member who is in charge of our particular universe and cosmic ray. There might also be a grouping of cosmic rays and cosmic members of the Council of Twelve in a particular quadrant, so to speak, of the cosmos.

I know that on a more microcosmic level this concept applies in terms of our galaxy. Our galaxy, under the guidance of Melchior, is divided into four quadrants. I intuitively believe that this same principle applies on the cosmic levels as well. If it is true that there are in a sense twelve cosmic ascensions prior to full ultimate cosmic ascension, then I am sure there is a certain grouping of cosmic-ray ascension masters first.

Metaphorically, like a pie divided equally four ways, each quarter of the pie would have three cosmic ascensions in it. So in a greater sense we would also be connected to all universes in each cosmic quarter. This gets complicated however, because we are not just dealing here with the material universe, but also with multidimensional realities. But this might be one good model for looking at this.

I spoke of extraterrestrial visitation; however, there can also be soul and spirit travel visitation by us to other universes and other universal beings to ours. I wouldn't do this without the help of Melchizedek and without a good spiritual reason for doing it. If going there is not helpful to your spiritual progress, then why go? Leave this up to Melchizedek to decide, for this is obviously beyond each of our comprehensions to know at this level of development.

The three cosmic rays and cosmic ascension paths that are grouped together may share similar cosmic themes as to their expression. This is much like an astrological horoscope, with the three forming a type of trinity.

Just as people on Earth, once achieving and fully realizing their ascension have the potential to ultimately be able to raise their body by dematerialization into light, the same is true for the planet, solar system, galaxy and all galaxies in Melchizedek's universe. It still has existence but at a higher dimension of reality as it evolves upward.

This applies to the physical planet as well as the beings living on the planet. Arcturus is an example of this. It was once a planet like ours, but now exists at a much higher level of density because of its evolvement. (I suggest reading Norma Milanovitch's book, *We, the Arcturians*, as well as my books, *Beyond Ascension* and *Hidden Mysteries*, in which there are chapters on the Arcturians.)

Melchizedek commented humorously on the incredible amount of time of these cosmic cycles when he said, "What else do you have to do?" He then said, "You can rush to get it done and all God is going to do is breathe you back out again." The point was obviously to keep it all in perspective and to enjoy ourselves.

One other interesting point that Melchizedek made about this process is that even though we are only at the seventh initiation of 352 initiations for total completion, there is a simultaneity to the initiation process. He said that with all the spiritual work we are doing with him and on the inner plane in meditation and sleep time, we are picking up many different energies simultaneously. We are also anchoring and activating higher chakras, bodies and light quotient, as I have mentioned earlier in this book. Because of this, in truth, it is more than seven initiations.

We are laying the foundation in a profound way to make future initiations much easier, even though we haven't taken those initiations yet. I was happy to hear from Melchizedek that for our process we might triple or quadruple this number to get a true sense of the current intensity. While reassuring, this would still be only twenty-eight out of 352.

The guidance that comes to me as I say this is that the first seven initiations are the slowest because they are tied to material existence. The fact that the rest of the initiations will not be tied to matter will speed things up enormously and nonlinear space and time realities will be the norm. So in a sense there is the possibility to work on many initiations simultaneously, for the process is not quite as linear as we conceive it now from the Earth-sphere perspective and phase that we are currently in.

I again asked Djwhal Khul about this issue of the existence of previous solar systems. This question arose because of his statement in the Alice Bailey book *The Rays and the Initiations* in which he said that the Jewish race was the most advanced root race from the previous solar system. I have never fully understood what this meant. What Djwhal Khul seemed to indicate is that a new solar system begins when the evolutionary process of the seven root races has been completed. In the back of my mind I can't help but think that there might be more to this statement than this.

This whole subject of the globes, the rounds, the schemes is an area of understanding that I have not yet been able to decipher. Sometimes I need to understand a subject more clearly before the masters can bring through more obscure information. (If any readers have more information on this subject or can explain how this works, please call me.) The old theosophical books that were supposed to have information on it were not all available anymore.

The conclusion that I have arrived at is that one day of Brahma equals one round. One week of Brahma equals seven rounds, which make up one scheme. One year of Brahma equals seven planetary schemes, which is somehow connected to the seven chains. One hundred years of Brahma equals an occult century, which is the period of a solar system.

In going through this I think I might have answered my own question. Each solar system is one hundred years of Brahma. Therefore, what I first said about the seven root races is not true, as my intuition was telling me. I think the seven root races would be more like one hour of Brahma. Even though one hour of Brahma might not seem like a long time, in truth, this could translate to 30 or 40 million years of our time. What we have here are cycles within cycles, within cycles, within cycles. My mechanical mind would love to figure out how this all works. Yet in this moment I am getting this with my intuitive mind; however, my left brain is not yet completely satisfied.

I will continue to research this concept and if any readers have a book that explains this that they would let me borrow, I would appreciate it. What I now realize is that the information I received from Djwhal Khul refers to the completion of a *planetary* cycle. This is what he thought I was asking, but the completion of a whole solar system is a much, much, much longer cycle made up of millions of planetary cycles, or the completion of seven root race cycles.

So to go through seven solar systems, which is another longer cycle, would take 700 years of Brahma. Again remember, just one day of Brahma is 4.3 billion years. It would take seven occult centuries to complete a solar system cycle, which again is a smaller cycle within a larger cycle of the evolution of a galaxy. As we evolve and become masters on solar, galactic and universal levels, this is the cosmic science we will study. As planetary masters we are currently focused mainly on the planetary cycles. Once we fully master this we will be ready to contemplate the solar system, the solar science and on upward, until eventually understanding the cosmic science of the entire infinite universe.

The Sacred Planets

I mentioned earlier the fact that a planet is termed sacred once it has attained the third, or soul merge, initiation. The following is an updated look at our solar system in terms of which planets have attained at least this initiation level. This gives us a sense of the evolvement level of our solar system. The following chart is from Alice Bailey's *The Rays and the Initiations*.

Sacred Planets and Their Rays

Earth	Ray IV
Vulcan	Ray I
Mercury	Ray IV
Venus	Ray V
Jupiter	Ray II

Saturn	Ray III
Neptune	Ray VI
Uranus	Ray VII

The Nonsacred Planets and Their Rays

Mars	Ray VI
Pluto	Ray I
The Moon (veiling a hidden planet)	Ray IV
The Sun (veiling a hidden planet)	Ray II

I mentioned earlier that Earth and Venus were the only planets to have taken their ascension in our solar system. Djwhal Khul told me that Jupiter was the next planet that was getting close to taking its ascension, which I found very interesting, as Jupiter has to do with expansiveness and transcending the negative ego.

A Footnote from Melchizedek

After completing this chapter I was running a few last things by Melchizedek when he asked me to put one footnote or qualification on the information I have presented regarding the twelve cosmic ascensions leading to ultimate cosmic ascension. What he told me is that this was most definitely the model he wanted me to present as representative of his teachings; however, he wanted me to add to this model that God is not limited.

He gave the example of the twelve major archetypes, which each have hundreds of subarchetypes. For categorization purposes and clarification we have divided them into the twelve subarchetypes. Melchizedek said that in a similar way the twelve cosmic ascensions could have such subdivisions, given that there are twelve cosmic rays and twelve elders who sit on the Cosmic Council of Twelve. The number twelve is the most accurate model for mapping the cosmos. He said however that God is infinite and cannot be limited by any model. Melchizedek definitely wanted me to present this model, but who knows, there might be 144 cosmic ascensions through other universal ascensions or six million or infinite numbers of them.

I say "infinite" in the sense that even though there is definitely a cosmic ascension that is achieved, just as there is a planetary ascension, there is no ceiling on evolution. Maybe the twelve cosmic ascensions are the ultimate completion of the ascension process, but growth still continues after this point. There are always higher and higher levels of refinement and purity that can be focused upon.

We must be open to the fact that there could be more then twelve cosmic inbreaths and outbreaths of God. There is some kind of completion point between the fifth and seventh cosmic plane. There will be a place of basic total completion; however, refined growth and service will continue.

I also asked Melchizedek about how our galaxy was evolving in terms of all the galaxies in our Melchizedek universe. The only thing I could get out of the grand master was that our Milky Way galaxy was neither the most advanced nor the least advanced in his universe, but somewhere in the middle. I was glad to hear that at least we aren't a backward galaxy holding up the progression of the universal ascension. (As one shifts to a cosmic-citizen focus, thoughts such as this enter one's mind.)

Melchizedek and Djwhal Khul also said that in regard to ultimate cosmic ascension, which is indeed a reality, there might be a way of absorbing these other cosmic inbreaths and outbreaths connected with the cosmic rays in a way that is different from going back into physical existence. There is a possibility that they might just be integrated from the Source level. Once cosmic ascension is achieved, absorption of other cosmic ascension paths most probably may not be done in the incarnational process we have just experienced.

Djwhal Khul said that this school or universe we are in is the "hardball" school. That is why the theme of this Cosmic Day is *courage*. It is one of the hardest schools of all. The most important thing to understand here is that there is a point of attainment of comic ascension; however, growth, expansion, creativity and service is infinite.

6

Ultimate Monadic Ascension: The Next Step

Unification with Your Soul Extensions

This next soul-extension technique is very important and is one of the keys to achieving and completing your ascension. As with so many things on the spiritual path, the key is to ask: "Ask, and it shall be given you; . . . knock, and it shall be opened unto you" [Matt. 7:7]. Ask to unify first with your eleven other soul extensions. After taking your ascension, or sixth initiation, also ask to unify with your 144 soul extensions that make up your monadic family (see *The Complete Ascension Manual* for an in-depth discussion on this). Ask to be released from any lower-dimensional psychic charges, which are fourth dimensional and separate you through the veils of glamour and illusion.

This issue is very important, for even though you might be walking the straight and narrow path, one of your soul extensions from your oversoul who is living on another planet or another dimension might be carrying on a pattern that is divisive. You must realize that if you are seeing things really clearly, you are not working for yourself. You are working with your eleven other soul extensions from your oversoul for the evolution of your oversoul and later, at higher stages, for the monad or mighty I Am Presence.

Each soul extension from the oversoul functions like a finger on one of your hands—the only difference is there are twelve fingers instead of ten. Do your ten fingers cooperate with your physical body? Your physical body is metaphorically likened to the oversoul here. Our little ego tells us we are the center of the universe, which in truth, we are not. We are working with the first twelve and then 144 soul extensions in our oversoul and monadic family.

In taking on the responsibility for ascension you are taking on the responsibility for being a teacher for and helping your eleven other soul extensions from your "greater body," so to speak. After first getting your self psychologically integrated and cleansed in terms of all your subpersonalities, archetypes, past-life aspects, thought forms, feelings, emotions, intuition, instincts and so on, the next step is to integrate and help cleanse your other soul extensions.

You must first understand that all your subpersonalities, archetypes, past-life aspects, thought forms, feelings, emotions, intuition and instincts are also like a family. They are your subconscious, superconscious and four-body-system family. This inner family must first be integrated and cleansed before you are really in a position to be truly helpful to your other soul extensions from your oversoul.

It also must be remembered that your soul extensions have free choice and you cannot order them around or you will create karma for yourself. You wouldn't want one of your other soul extensions who lived on another galaxy ordering you around, for example. Remember, do unto others as you would have them do unto you. Make your prayer request to your mighty I Am Presence, your oversoul and the ascended masters and frame it, or end it, as "God's will." If you ever call your other soul extensions forward for a meeting or for any purpose, *ask* them to come—don't order them.

You can order your subpersonalities, archetypes, thoughts, feelings, emotions, instincts and images. You must be a strong and loving president of your personality. Other people—which is what your soul extensions are—must be asked. On a larger scale, Sanat Kumara and the Buddha, functioning as the Planetary Logos, don't order us around even though we live in their body. They respect our free choice. If they interfered with our free choice, they too would create karma for themselves (which, of course, they would never do).

Eventually, if our other soul extensions aren't cleared and integrated, they will create lack of clarity and cloudiness coming toward our consciousness, just as an injury to one of our fingers effects the full functioning of our whole body. Djwhal Khul said that one cannot join with the full power of one's monad until this work is done. In later stages of evolution this same principle will apply on the group-soul level, group-monadic level, solar, galactic and universal levels.

At every stage each person is taking responsibility for a larger expansion, integration and cleansing. In our core group, we are currently working on this at the beginning stage of the solar level, having installed and activated the group-soul and group-monadic levels, which correspond to the eighth and ninth levels. This is the work one will be doing after he/she completes his seven levels of initiation. Even though one is not allowed to take his eighth initiation, he can be doing the continual dimensional installation, integration and cleansing work I have spoken about in other chapters.

Therefore it must be understood that the soul extensions from one's oversoul and monadic family will either assist in or interfere with the planetary and cosmic ascension process. If one really wants to make progress on his/her path of integrating the twelve bodies and 200 chakras, planetary and cosmic light-quotient building and twelve strands of DNA activation and actualization, she must get her entire oversoul and monadic family working on the same page. As within, so without; as above, so below.

Look what happens if your mind, emotions, body, subpersonalities, archetypes and past-life aspects don't cooperate in your own consciousness: You become completely conflicted, confused and, basically, dysfunctional. The same is true in your larger body that spans your planetary, solar, galactic and universal bodies. All soul extensions that you are connected to must cooperate and be playing the same piece of music. You can greatly help in this process by asking your oversoul, monad and the ascended masters to help your twelve, and then 144, soul extensions become clear, integrate and unify for the greater purpose of the mighty I Am Presence. Just because a person has taken his/her sixth initiation and has become a "kindergarten" ascended master doesn't mean he has done this work.

The 144 soul extensions from your monad don't impinge on your consciousness in the same way that the eleven other soul extensions from your oversoul do. As I mentioned in *The Complete Ascension Manual*, one soul extension does ascend for the whole oversoul. At a higher level, one soul extension or more will do the same thing on the monadic level. Each level you move up, in truth, is like an ascension. In this regard, there is a type of higher monadic extension, group-soul extension, group-monadic ascension, solar ascension, galactic ascension and universal ascension. This might not be the best way to describe this; however, each of these integrations is incorporating another dimension of consciousness, so you are ascending.

All these miniascensions through the forty-eight dimensions makes up what again might be called "cosmic ascension," our planetary ascension being only one-tenth of this process. It is in the integration of the soul extensions and the clearing work done here that the work of clearing and integrating the archetypes is also done. It must be remembered that when this clearing work is not done on the psychological level and soul-extension level, it tends to attract alien implants, negative elementals, parasites, negative imprints and astral entities.

This is why traditional counseling as it is practiced on Earth often doesn't work. The counselors and psychologists do not have any understanding, perception or knowledge of these other factors that are impinging on the consciousness, so only a partial healing can take place. In reality you are not just responsible for yourself. You are responsible for the first twelve, and then 144, monadic family members. You are functioning almost as an oversoul or monad for your soul and monadic family.

So what we have here is a new concept of ascension. After you achieve your ascension for your oversoul, you must remember that there are twelve oversouls that make up your monad. The next level of ascension is where the entire monad ascends. I am not speaking here of just your personal merger with your monad. For ultimate monadic ascension all twelve oversouls with their twelve soul extensions from each of the twelve oversouls must all ascend.

One master can take on this responsibility for ascending the entire monad and this is the work that the core group and I are currently attempting to do in our evolutionary process. It is the next step after attaining planetary ascension. This works in conjunction with the process of integrating and activating levels eight through twelve after achieving one's seventh initiation. Just as one person ascended for the oversoul family of twelve, one can be the master to ascend for the entire monad, which is 144 soul extensions in the entire monadic family from all twelve oversouls.

There is a similar process that continues all the way up the cosmic evolutionary scale. The solar system, galaxy and universe can't ascend until each person achieves his/her planetary, and then higher, monadic ascension. Every part is a cell in the body of God, for God's divine plan of supreme ultimate cosmic ascension is for everything to return home. The following is a prayer request that people can use if they wish to be this master to take on this responsibility.

Ultimate Monadic Merger Prayer Request

Beloved presence of God, my mighty I Am Presence, Melchizedek, Lord Buddha, Lord Maitreya, Vywamus and Djwhal Khul, I hereby call forth a divine dispensation from the Karmic Board and that it now be written into the soul records that I wish to be the soul extension and master from my monad to ascend not only for my eleven other soul extensions but for my 144 soul extensions from my monad.

I now hereby request as God and the masters now stand as witness that I hereby take on this mantle of responsibility in service of my greater monadic family if this be God's will. So let it be written, so let it be done. Amen.

My beloved subconscious mind,

I hereby ask and command that you take this thought-form prayer with all the manna and vital force that is needed and necessary to manifest and demonstrate this prayer to the Source of our being through Djwhal Khul, Lord Maitreya and Melchizedek. Amen.

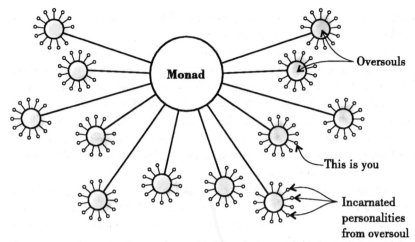

Diagram of Monad, Oversouls and Soul Extensions
Planetary ascension: merger of one oversoul and soul-extension family
Ultimate monadic ascension: merger of all twelve oversouls and soul-extension
families back with their monad

Walk-in Soul Extensions

It must be remembered that from the perspective of spirit and not the
personality on Earth, the focus is first, the evolution of the oversoul and second, the evolution of the entire monad. Sometimes one soul extension from
an oversoul, or from any one of the twelve oversouls, might be holding up
the program, so to speak. What can happen is that one of the soul extensions from your oversoul or from another one of the oversouls from your monad might "walk-in" and exchange places with the existing incarnated personality.

This is no different from a normal walk-in experience (see *Hidden Mysteries* for more detailed information on this subject), except that the exchange of physical bodies is occurring within your own soul or monadic
family. This can occur as a soul braid or as an actual walk-in situation.
This is one of the options your monad has in speeding up its ascension process.

A Higher Level of the Ascension Process

This new higher understanding of the ultimate monadic ascension process that occurs far beyond the achievement of one's seven levels of initiation really forces one in a very positive way to embrace group consciousness. There will be one master or higher-level initiate from each of your
twelve oversouls who will have to achieve planetary ascension. Then that
master will need to let go of his/her single focus and work for the good of all

twelve oversouls and 144 soul extensions. All of a sudden you see how interdependent you are on your entire monadic family.

You can choose to ask to be the one who leads this process. However, if your other soul extensions don't cooperate you are not going anywhere. This in truth is really how things work on Earth. In any organization or group, if all people don't do their part, the work doesn't get done and the goal is not achieved. When President Clinton runs for president it is his entire organization down to the grass roots' help that makes it happen. Now, the fact is, everyone wins in his organization if he is elected. The same is true in ultimate monadic ascension.

All twelve oversouls and 144 soul extensions are lifted up when the whole monad ascends. Do you see why getting rid of the negative ego is so important? You are no longer working for yourself anymore. You are working for something much greater than a puny personality. You are working for the evolution of first, an oversoul and second, an entire monadic consciousness.

At more advanced stages you will work for the solar, galactic and universal ascension of groups of monad, not just your own monad. Eventually you will work for the evolution of all monads of God. Each one of these steps is your true self. One's true self is not the personality, but first, the oversoul, then the monad, then groups of monads at the solar, then galactic, universal, Paradise Sons' and elohim consciousness levels, leading up to the cosmic ascended level.

One must actualize this in steps and stages however. This idea of working for the evolution not of yourself but of your oversoul and monad, is a revolutionary shift of consciousness. This shift needs to be made if you are going to fully embrace the consciousness of the anointed Christ overself body, or universal being, integrating all twelve dimensions and all twelve bodies.

The term "transpersonal psychology" comes to my mind here. Transpersonal psychology is spiritual psychology that is beyond personal. It is *trans*personal. It is beginning to see life from the perspective of spirit instead of personality.

7

The Importance of Integrating One's 144 Soul Extensions

One of the recent insights I have had in my discussions with Djwhal Khul and Melchizedek is the incredible importance of integrating and cleansing one's soul extensions. In the previous chapter I began to discuss this; however, as this book has unfolded, I have come to realize that integrating and cleansing soul extensions is as important as anchoring chakras, bodies, strands of DNA, light quotient and initiations.

In my books I have offered literally hundreds of ascension activations that can help accelerate spiritual growth. In my opinion the above-mentioned principles, along with integrating and cleansing one's soul extensions, are the "keys to the kingdom," so to speak. The insight of integrating and cleansing soul extensions is a new one. I had been skirting around it because I did not have a solid handle on what is actually to be done. Now I do, and the repercussions are mind-boggling.

As mentioned in the previous chapter and in my first book, *The Complete Ascension Manual*, each person's monad has twelve oversouls ("higher souls" or "souls" in Alice Bailey language). Each oversoul has twelve soul extensions, or twelve personalities, that incarnate into material existence, although not necessarily just on this planet. In more recent times I have decided to use the word "oversoul" instead of soul or higher self because it seems to be a more fitting description of how the process works.

In using the word "oversoul" one can then also use the word "souls," instead of soul extensions of personalities. In this context one could say that each person's oversoul incarnates twelve souls into material existence.

The twelve souls, or soul extensions of one's oversoul, work for the development of the monad or mighty I Am Presence.

Djwhal Khul told me that to achieve one's ascension one must integrate and cleanse the twelve soul extensions from the oversoul. This would be the taking of one's sixth initiation, which is the beginning of the ascension process. The key question here is, what does this mean, to integrate and cleanse a soul extension?

Each of your soul extensions is a person (just like you) who is either incarnated on another planet in this galaxy or universe or working on the inner plane. These twelve people make up your soul family—just like on a larger level each of your twelve oversouls has twelve soul extensions, so you have 144 in your monadic family.

To integrate a soul extension means to unify or blend spiritually with its energy body. This creates a greater electrical circuiting in your field and energy body, helping to build your light quotient. In a sense it also makes you a larger, more expansive being in terms of your auric field. This also allows you to incorporate the knowledge, wisdom and abilities of these other people in your soul family. It serves to have a very positive effect on them, given your spiritual development (which I am taking for granted given your interest in reading this kind of book).

Not all soul extensions are necessarily developed. Some can be unconscious and unevolved. The goal is for you to become like an oversoul teacher for first, your soul family and second, your monadic family. One of the biggest and most fascinating effects of integrating and cleansing your soul extensions is the balancing of your karma.

In *The Complete Ascension Manual* I spoke of the requirement to balance 51% of your karma to achieve ascension. This issue of integrating and cleansing your soul extensions is one of the keys in achieving this. This 51% requirement is not just for your own soul extension but for your entire oversoul. You must balance 51% of the karma from your soul family of twelve to achieve ascension. This is why it is required to integrate and cleanse the twelve from your oversoul to take the sixth initiation.

Djwhal Khul and Melchizedek both told me that in order to fully complete the seventh initiation you must integrate and cleanse all 144 soul extensions from your monadic family. This was a totally new, revolutionary concept to me that I just recently learned.

I immediately asked Djwhal Khul about how the core group and I were doing in this process. This is something I had never asked before because I never knew it was a requirement. I think there are only a handful of people on Earth who do because this is such a revolutionary new understanding of how spiritual evolution actually takes place. It has only been since the 1990s that initiates have even really been allowed to move into these higher levels, as I have mentioned previously.

In the past most masters left, or ascended, their bodies after the sixth initiation. Djwhal Khul told us that we had integrated and cleansed about two-thirds of the 144, or approximately one hundred of them. I found this fascinating. This led to the next insight: that it was possible to do this process without actually knowing you are doing it. I had only a vague notion of how this process was working.

Djwhal Khul told me that often this is done through one's own psychological and subpersonality clearing work. It is happening spiritually and is then filtering through the subconscious mind for cleansing.

We had been doing a lot of work with our soul extensions, however, I had never targeted our work so specifically on this point. I am sure the enormous amount of work we had done in this area even without this targeted focus had helped.

I then asked Melchizedek what the negative effects of this could be. For as I mentioned before, one is balancing karma by doing this. He gave an example of a person who was in very good physical health and then all of a sudden comes down with the Epstein-Barr virus. This could be, he said, from the integration of a soul extension. An integration of a soul extension is not a small-time thing. It has an enormous impact on one's four-body system (physical, emotional, mental and spiritual). This example would of course be an extreme case.

In merging with that soul extension you are in a sense absorbing its karma and cleansing it. Its karma is your karma because you come from the same oversoul and monad. Remember, you must stop thinking of yourself as a separate soul extension, but rather understand that you are an oversoul and monad made up of many aspects. This idea of being a separate soul extension is an illusion of the negative ego. You are not working for yourself but for the oversoul and monad, just as your fingers work for your physical body. There must be a change of perspective here.

I then asked Melchizedek how much karma one balances from the time one takes the beginning of the sixth initiation until that person integrates and cleanses all 144 soul extensions. He said this is an individual thing, but as a ballpark figure, if one is at the 51% level at the beginning of the sixth, one might be at the 65 to 75% level at the full integration of all 144 soul extensions. Isn't this amazing! The movement from integrating the twelve soul extensions from your oversoul to integrating and cleansing the 144 from your monad balances approximately 20% of your overall karmic debt from your entire monad.

I then asked Melchizedek how long it would take for the core group and I to integrate our last forty-four or fifty soul extensions. He and Djwhal Khul said it would take about a year if we asked for a divine dispensation.

This, of course, would be moving at lightning speed because of our overall development and leadership responsibilities we have been given. I figured this out mathematically and it works out to be integrating one soul extension every week or two.

Before you get too gung ho on this process, remember the example I gave from Melchizedek about Epstein-Barr. If you try to go too fast you might burden yourself with karmic lessons that could debilitate your physical, emotional, mental and spiritual bodies beyond your ability to cope effectively. The good news is that you can always ask that the process be slowed down or speeded up. The stronger you are in all your bodies and the clearer you are psychologically, the less the karmic repercussions in your four-body system. The group body that the core group and I have formed together as a service vehicle also provides an enormous strengthening effect that allows for a greater acceleration.

As I tune in I think a safe speed, but one that will allow you to move very quickly would be to request for an integration and cleansing of your soul extensions at a rate of about one every two weeks. This is enormously fast and might never have been done so quickly until recently. I recommend doing a prayer to Melchizedek, Lord Maitreya, Djwhal Khul and the Karmic Board for a divine dispensation for this to take place under the direction of your mighty I Am Presence at this rate of speed, if this prayer is in harmony with God's will for you. Basically ask that this process proceed as fast as possible without debilitating your four-body system too greatly. Melchizedek said that it is also possible to request an energy field to be placed around you that will help to ease any karmic implications.

The other superkey to this process is to always request not only for integration but also for cleansing of your twelve, or 144, soul extensions. In requesting the cleansing, much of the karmic implications can be short-circuited. I also don't want to make this process sound like every soul extension is going to create an illness or be debilitating. This process will be unique for each person depending on the overall karmic history. I would venture to say that once most initiates are very solidly on the path and fundamentally strong in their four-body system, they will not even significantly notice the effects of integrating soul extensions.

This work, Melchizedek said, is usually done while one sleeps, or in group settings where a lot of energy is available to help in the integration process. In integrating soul extensions there is an electrical charge that is put in place and a greater electrical wiring that is added to one's field. There is definitely a need to have integration time after a soul extension is added to one's field. It takes a good two weeks or more to integrate and absorb all the energies. The fact is that certain soul extensions will be easier to assimilate than others. This is why the speed of the process should be left up to spirit and the masters.

Two weeks is just a very general ballpark figure to give a sense of how the process works. Some soul extensions might be done in a week; others might need three months to integrate. Put your mighty I Am Presence in charge. Having integrated all 144 soul extensions from your monad and/or mighty I Am Presence along with the various other key factors I have mentioned in this book, such as initiations, chakras, bodies, light quotient and so on, will give you the complete merger with the monad in all its ramifications.

Another interesting aspect to this whole process has to do with how it relates to initiations and dimensional-anchoring levels. As I have mentioned previously, Djwhal Khul and Melchizedek told us that we had installed and activated our fifty chakras and nine bodies, completed our seven levels of initiation, built our light quotient to the 99% level and were now moving on to the cosmic light-quotient scale.

The interesting insight here is that even though we were operating out of the ninth level in terms of chakras and bodies being installed and activated and had completed the integration of all our soul extensions, we still had not completed the seventh level. This discrepancy was interesting to me. I think it was probably in part due to the fact that I was conscious of the need to anchor chakras, bodies, light quotient and initiations, but was not aware of the need to integrate and cleanse soul extensions.

When I am conscious of a growth focus, I am relentless in terms of achieving that level of realization. It just goes to show the importance of being conscious of these various aspects. In being conscious of these aspects and working with them, divine dispensations can be obtained to accelerate the progress. This is how we moved so quickly through these other factors. The fact is that very few people are aware of initiations and the need to build light quotient, to anchor one's fifty chakras and to anchor the twelve bodies, let alone soul extensions.

This is why this whole process is so revolutionary. It has always been available; however, no one knew they were supposed to do these things. In truth, this entire subject comes down to one simple point: Ask and you shall receive; knock and the door shall be opened. Our core group has moved so quickly because we have uncovered the key principles of God that need to be asked for in order to accelerate spiritual growth. What we have done you can do, for God loves all His sons and daughters equally.

God and His infinite universe is governed by laws. My entire life has been dedicated to discovering these laws and I have been relentless in this pursuit, like a Sherlock Holmes of the spiritual world. My relentless mission has been to discover these laws and make them easy to understand and very practical and easy to use. By the grace of God, I feel like I have succeeded in this task and this is why this series of books is so important.

In concluding this subject of soul extensions, after one has integrated and cleansed the 144 soul extensions from one's monad, the process continues. The next step is integrating and cleansing one's soul extensions at the eighth level. This would be, as I talked about in the previous chapter, working with the six monads of one's group-monadic vehicle. This entails integrating the twelve oversoul leaders of the six monads.

The ninth level is the integration and cleansing of soul extensions of the entire six-monad configuration (which means 864 soul extensions). The tenth level involves the integration and cleansing of soul extensions from the solar-monadic grouping, the eleventh level is the integration and cleansing of the galactic-soul-extension monadic grouping and the twelfth level is the universal-monadic grouping. As you can see, we all have our work cut out for us. Melchizedek told us that in actuality very few people on the planet have integrated as many as one hundred of their soul extensions as we have, and that is why we are functioning as prototypes.

The fact that I had uncovered the importance of this was now allowing for an even greater acceleration of the process. For the first time I feel like the whole puzzle of planetary and cosmic evolution is really starting to come together and make sense.

It really doesn't need to be that complicated. It is the same basic core principles being repeated over and over again at higher and higher octaves of spiritual evolution. Once one understands the mechanics and laws that underlie spiritual growth, it is amazing how fast one can work through these levels. What I have learned in my planetary ascension is exactly what will be carried over to my cosmic evolution, for the concepts are exactly the same, except much larger and more expansive.

Again, as within, so without; as above, so below. Initiations, chakra anchoring, body anchoring, light-quotient building, soul-extension integration, just keep continuing dimension after dimension, octave after octave, until one eventually returns to Source. One soul extension being integrated might not seem to have that big of an effect. Day after day, week after week, month after month, year after year, however, the electrical charge, light quotient, dimensional anchorings and the dispensation of karma continues. Sometimes it seems like it is moving very slowly, but in actuality, it isn't.

The key point here is to keep asking, because God and the masters cannot turn down any sincere request for spiritual growth and acceleration. Not only can they not turn down any sincere request, but they don't want to. Remember their growth is dependent upon your growth. They cannot move to their next level until we move to their level. This is the way the universe works.

The other key point for integrating these soul extensions is, in a sense, holding up the process of full actualization of the solar level. Our chakra and body anchoring, light-quotient and initiation development is more advanced than our soul-extension-integration development. This is kind of strange to say when Melchizedek said that we were serving as prototypes in this area.

However, from my perspective, I can see the effects of what happens when a piece of the puzzle is not completely understood. In a sense it slows that piece down because that piece has not been understood nor has it been consciously invoked. We were basically told that by Wesak of 1996 we would have integrated our 144 soul extensions from our monad. Melchizedek was teasing us that we were rushing forward to finish this level off so we could then invoke the eighth-dimensional level—after that only forty more dimensions to God!

The key is having the "map" and the understanding of the process. At each level the exact same principles will be applied. The exact same things will be quickly invoked and then one's total focus will be placed on world service. Once the dispensation has been asked for and given by the masters and the Karmic Board, you are in a sense riding a wave that has a certain timetable, and only service really needs to be focused on.

As one goes higher and higher in his/her cosmic evolution, there is always a module or grouping of monads. I am not able to get beyond the ninth level in terms of numbers, for they begin to become astronomical. One does this incorporating, however, through a group-monadic module, which is very important to understand. For example, on the solar level one doesn't have to integrate all the soul extensions in the entire solar system, just a certain number that make up the group-monadic module to which one is connected.

One integrates the solar system this way just as on the eighth and ninth levels—the integration is achieved through just six monads. On the solar level the number of monads is much larger. As one moves to the galactic level, the principle is the same and this is also how one incorporates solar systems into one's being. At the universal level this is how one incorporates galaxies into one's being. The same process happens at the multiuniversal level. Can you imagine incorporating universes?

The principles and concepts are the same. It is like writing a check but simply adding more zeros. At the actual Source level one is incorporating multi-Source levels into one's being through this same massive group-monadic module concept. The key point that must be emphasized over and over again is that we each, in truth, are not an individual consciousness. This separation is illusion. We are each a group consciousness and individual identity simultaneously.

At the highest God level we are in essence incorporating all the soul extensions of God's infinite universe through the vehicle of our group module to which we are connected. The honeycombed effect of modules being connected into the overall latticework just keeps getting larger and larger as you go up each step of the evolutionary. program ladder.

8

Self-Realization and the Issue of Accountability

This chapter, in my opinion, is one of the most important chapters in this book. It is a subject I feel extremely passionate about, maybe more than any other. What I have come to understand through personal experience is that there is a state of consciousness and spiritual goal that is really beyond ascension and beyond the seven levels of initiation, but is prior to and a prerequisite of cosmic ascension.

This state of consciousness and spiritual goal is called self-realization. This can also be called full monadic realization, spiritual realization or I Am realization. The reason for this distinction is that there are a great many lightworkers on the planet now who are taking their ascension initiation (sixth initiation) and even their seventh initiation, but are still very unclear emotionally, mentally, psychologically and physically.

This realization came as a very great shock to me in recent years as I began to meet extremely high-level initiates, some who had completed all seven levels of initiation, who were total egomaniacs, extreme emotional victims, totally lacking in self-love and self-worth, mentally unclear in the philosophy, chronically physically ill—in essence psychologically unclear.

I mean this as no judgment but rather just as a point of observation. This applied even to many of the "leadership" people in the field. I found this to be quite disturbing and had many discussions about this with the core group. They were running into this same experience themselves, so one day we sat down and did a deep meditation asking about this. Interestingly enough it was Sanat Kumara who came through and explained what the problem was. Later we did further meditations and Djwhal Khul, Lord Maitreya and Melchizedek added to this discussion.

The masters said that the actual passing of one's seven levels of initiation and achieving one's ascension has more to do with spiritual development and the anchoring of spiritual energies than it does with complete mastery of the mental, emotional and physical bodies. It has more to do with the building of one's light quotient and invoking the merger with the soul and monad than anything else.

When I first read the Alice Bailey books and read about the three initiations—first, physical mastery; second, emotional mastery; and third, mental mastery—I thought at the time that a person would legitimately have to master these bodies and functions to pass those initiations. It turns out that this is not true. I might clarify this by saying it is true in the sense of needing to master 51% of that body.

Because of the extraordinary times we are all living in being incarnated now, the potential for spiritual advancement is enormous. Lightworkers are completing initiations in two or three years that once took the most advanced masters on this planet whole lifetimes to do just one. Sanat Kumara told me that this is one of the great dangers of this time: Lightworkers are advancing incredibly fast spiritually, but their mental, emotional and physical bodies are not keeping pace.

By this I mean their mental body and philosophies might still be unclear or not integrated properly. The emotional body might still be victimizing the disciple or initiate to a great extent. The person might also not be taking proper care of the physical body in terms of diet, exercise and the raising of its vibration to keep pace. Hence, we have the potential here for a very high-level initiate to be extremely controlled by the negative ego.

I asked the masters if there was ever a time of accountability. They told me that in the past the ring-pass-not, so to speak, before one was allowed to move on without doing this clearing was the fifth initiation. Interestingly enough, this was changed as recently as 1990. A special dispensation was given to humanity to allow it to take the seventh initiation and even just about complete it before accountability was required.

The masters were very firm, however, on the point that no lightworker would be allowed to completely finish the seventh initiation and move on to anchor the fifty chakras and the twelve bodies, including the solar, galactic and universal without doing his/her psychological clearing work. By psychological clearing work I am referring to the mastery of the mental, emotional and physical vehicles, the controlling of the negative ego, the balancing of the four bodies, the proper integration of the three minds and the proper parenting of the inner child.

It is a very common practice among lightworkers to be more interested in spiritual and esoteric things and not to be as interested in doing the real work. An analogy could be a three-story house. The first floor is the physical level; the second floor, the psychological level; and the third floor, the spiritual level. All three levels must be mastered and integrated properly. Each level is a distinct and separate level with a unique set of lessons that must be learned and mastered.

In my opinion the most important is the psychological level. If this level is not mastered there will be a "cancer" in your program. Think about it. So what if you achieve your ascension and pass your initiations if you don't have inner peace, you are physically ill all the time, in poverty, fighting with your partner, fearful and worried, filled with negative thoughts, haven't found your service work, lack self-love and self-worth, or you are on an ego trip after passing your initiations and achieving your ascension.

This can happen and is happening more than you think. You will run into this as you meet many of the leadership people in the field. You will see them being brilliant in one area and on a personality level extremely unclear. I know that every one of my readers knows what I am talking about here.

This is why I have said that there is a step beyond ascension that lies between planetary ascension and cosmic ascension, which I am calling self-realization. Self-realization and/or the true completion of your ascension process will not come until you go back and clear, master and properly integrate this psychological level. The masters told me that lightworkers will be held at the seventh sublevel of the seventh initiation and not allowed to go further until they do this.

I emphasize again, you will not be allowed to anchor the solar, galactic and universal levels until you learn to master the negative ego. It is also common for the lightworkers to say, "Oh, the negative ego. I mastered that in the spring of '72." In my experience, ninety-nine percent of the time this is not true. The negative ego is so devious and there is so little training about how to master it that most lightworkers don't even realize how much it is running them.

I would like to share some signs that the negative ego is getting in: any negative emotions, lack of inner peace and calmness at all times, lack of happiness and joy at all times, physical illness, negative thinking, alien implants, negative elementals, parasites, negative imprints, fear or worry, astral entities, negative archetypes, etheric mucus, philosophical imbalances, superiority, inferiority, competitiveness, selfishness, separation, guilt, judgmentalness, grudges, attack thoughts, self-righteousness, insecurity, self-doubt, anger, sadness, depression, laziness, procrastination, jealousy, moodiness, over/underindulgence, lack of balance, just to name a few.

If you can read this list and in a devastatingly honest manner say you have not one of these, then I say, congratulations! You have done your homework. I have never met anybody who has, including myself, so you would be the first. The point I am trying to make here is that even masters such as Sanat Kumara and Vywamus admit that they have small fragments of negative ego to clear. If you think that you don't on this plane, then you are deluding yourself, which is another quality of negative ego.

It is always easier to see other people's stuff rather than your own. The game of the negative ego is always to tell you that you are either the best or the worst. It will tell you that you are superior to everyone else or inferior to everyone else. The truth is that neither are true and that is one of the keys of transcending negative-ego consciousness. In *The Discourses of Sai Baba*, Sai Baba said that the true definition of God is: "God equals man minus ego."

It was the Master Jesus who in *A Course in Miracles* [textbook] states, "Perfect love casts out fear." Jesus also said that there is one problem in the world that is the core of all other problems and that is separation—separation from God and/or separation from self or from others, in truth, is all the same thing. Get rid of separation, which is the essence of ego, and all your problems or challenges will be solved.

The idea is not to have to be perfect in your clearing, but to get as clear as you possibly can. In this world, with the amount of environmental and psychic negativity floating around there is the constant need to have the tools to continually clear yourself, as we all must learn to deal with mass consciousness all the time. Now, the key question is, how do I get the proper training, tools and education I need to do this?

The masters have guided me in between my three major ascension books, *The Complete Ascension Manual*, *Beyond Ascension* and *Cosmic Ascension*, to write other books to help lightworkers clear the psychological and physical areas. *Soul Psychology* is one of these books, which offers suggestions on how to achieve the mastery and balance that I have addressed in this chapter. *Soul Psychology* offers the reader the tools and information needed to accomplish the clearing and integration to achieve self-mastery on all three levels, not just the spiritual level.

In discussing this subject further with Djwhal Khul, he said that the ring-pass-not is really determined by one's own soul. A person can be focusing on the spiritual level doing all kinds of spiritual work, light-quotient building and ascension techniques, but the fact is, if he/she is not clear psychologically and in control of his negative ego, it is not going to be absorbed and integrated properly.

It is not necessarily that only the masters will be less likely to help if they see the negative ego and emotional body not under control, but also one's own monad and mighty I Am Presence will hold him/her back until this psychological cleanup work is done. Djwhal Khul also said that a person who has completed his ascension and/or seven levels of initiation can also fall back and lose this status if his negative ego really takes over.

This has happened before and is not beyond the realm of possibility. This process usually begins with any given initiate put on probation on the inner plane for inappropriate behavior of an extreme nature. If the behavior continues, the actual energy current he/she is receiving can be cut back or cut off. I personally know of one actual case where this was in motion. This usually occurs when the issue of power is not clear and/or when the understanding of negative ego, which is a specific type of training and education, has not been developed.

The key to this whole problem is that even the "experts" don't have training in this. Your basic psychologist, psychiatrist, social worker, marriage and child counselor, minister and even spiritual teacher, channel and mystic, do not have a solid understanding of the difference between negative ego and Christ thinking. If the experts don't have this except in rare cases, how are humanity and the up-and-coming disciples supposed to learn? In my opinion the biggest thing this world needs more than anything else is qualified spiritual counselors who can work with people on themselves, relationships, children and life lessons.

Most counselors are traditional in their orientation and do not integrate the full perspectives of the soul and monadic realization, orientation and philosophy into their practice. One's entire philosophy or psychology completely changes when one moves from personality identification to soul and monad identification. I often see a great many counselors still teaching personality issues. They have made the bridge on the spiritual level, but have not learned how to fully translate this into the psychological level (see *Soul Psychology* for a deeper explanation of this subject).

If the negative ego is in control of the high-level initiate this will prevent the proper absorption of the light. So in other words, light quotient is just not built; it must be integrated. Djwhal Khul referred to this ring-pass-not as a state of "dormancy" that certain lightworkers will be held in until the negative ego and emotional body are under control. The four-body system must be balanced and a proper relationship with the inner child and the conscious, subconscious and superconscious minds must be developed. Djwhal Khul also said that there is too much focus being placed on passing initiations and not enough focus on total self-realization on spiritual, psychological and physical levels.

In summary, he said that the boundary for this understanding used to be the fifth initiation. Now the boundary is drawn by one's own soul and monad at the seventh initiation. This is the ring-pass-not where all will be held in a state of dormancy until these lessons I speak of are totally addressed and mastered. Djwhal Khul said the reason that this was switched from the fifth initiation to the seventh initiation was to bring more vehicles of light into the planet to add to the planetary light. He then said, "For the self-evolution or self-realization there cannot be any more progression until there is the balance."

Djwhal Khul said that this is the true understanding of the initiation process. Otherwise it is steeped in glamour. Without this understanding, Djwhal Khul said, one also sees many initiates who observe these discrepancies and inconsistencies among the so-called high-level initiates and they develop a disbelief or mistrust in the whole process.

Djwhal also said that in the initial stages there is the fascination with the ascended masters, higher dimensions, archangels, extraterrestrials, elohim, inner-plane ashrams and so on. However, at some point in the maturing process of the initiate this must ground into one's self and into the real world. The danger is to stay stuck in the glamour and fascination of the heavenly worlds and not bring heaven to Earth on the mental, emotional and physical levels.

One must be grounded physically and psychologically with what it means to be a truly God-realized being. Djwhal Khul also said that, "It is very easy to become enamored with the beauty of consciousness and dismiss the responsibility of consciousness, seeking the ephemeral and unconsciously avoiding the work."

He went on to say (rather eloquently, I might add) that "this ephemeral fascination" is absolutely of no value whatsoever if it isn't used to break down the barriers of separation between the self and others. If the self is lost in projection (negative-ego interpretation of life) and self-importance, then the barriers continue to grow. Djwhal spoke of this as "character development," which really struck a chord of truth within me.

This is what the teachings of Sai Baba as the Cosmic Christ emphasize so strongly. Sai Baba does not even focus his teachings on initiation but rather on the development of a pure and refined character as the highest goal and expression of the self. Character reaches its highest refinement when all traces of negative ego are cleared and only the soul and monad guide all expressions and interactions with self and others.

This is the real work of the spiritual path: to harmonize all mental, emotional, intuitive and instinctual functions with self and others, so only godliness is extended at all times, in all circumstances on Earth.

Melchizedek chimed in at the end of this discussion, referring to the seventh initiation as the accepting of accountability, because we have accepted the responsibility of self-mastery in taking this step." Melchizedek went on to say that "the responsibility of self-mastery is to be totally and always in tune with oneself on all levels, to be able to again keep the balance. The balance is most important." Melchizedek continued by saying, "We, as masters in our own right, are not holding up our end of the deal, so to speak, when we do not pay attention to our human qualities. It is about being impeccable, especially as we stand representing the Spiritual Hierarchy. So impeccability, responsibility and integrity go hand in hand here."

9

Spiritual Leadership and World Service: The Next Step

What I am about to say here might be a new and revolutionary concept: Leadership and world service come after ascension. Most of our fantasies about ascension hold that it is the other way around. Given that we are in a new dispensation in the ascension process where lightworkers are taking these higher initiations on a massive scale never before known on this planet, there is a need for this new concept.

Most lightworkers, even though they have taken their fifth, sixth and even seventh initiation, have not moved into true leadership and world service. This, in truth, is what the ascended masters are preparing them for. The ascended masters are probably more focused on this than even the initiations. However, ideally both go together.

The purpose of life isn't just to ascend and break the wheel of reincarnation. It is also to serve and help others. Once one takes the seventh initiation there really is no other reason for being here. I recommend to all lightworkers to spend time in El Morya's ashram, who specializes in the first ray, which is connected with fully coming into your personal power and world leadership.

There are a great many seventh-degree initiates I know who still haven't found their service work. Many lightworkers spend so much time focusing on initiations that they don't serve at all. This is not the ideal. Once you move into your sixth and seventh initiation it is really time to forget about spiritual evolvement and focus completely on the highest level of service work you are capable of performing. It is time to put yourself out there and go beyond your fears and excuses. In truth, it is time to become a spiritual leader and use all the gifts and light that you have been given in service to humanity.

The form this takes does not matter, as long as you are doing something. You all don't have to be famous or write a book or be a great channel or psychic. This is not everyone's destiny. Just do the part that God has designed for you—your puzzlepiece. Ask El Morya for help in really putting yourself on this path. The quickest path to evolving from this point on is to immerse yourself in service work. The ascended masters of the inner plane are not focused on personal evolution; they are so immersed in service that they don't have time for anything else.

Let this be a lesson to us all. It is now time to take up the rod of power and step forward and not let all the excuses of the inner child, subconscious mind or negative ego stop you anymore. Do not wait until you feel comfortable. If you wait until you feel comfortable or until you can dematerialize or raise the dead, you might actually never serve this lifetime.

The masters are not really very interested in helping you evolve if you are not willing to take the risk of putting yourself out there by serving. This service can be in the form of volunteer work or a type of work that not a single other person in the whole world knows you are doing except God. Also, do not wait for God to tell you what to do. Take creative action on your own first, and God will help you as you move your feet. The negative ego has a million excuses why it is not time to really take the reins of spiritual leadership and world service. These excuses are all illusion. You now have enough knowledge, wisdom and love to put yourself out there.

Jesus lived in the marketplace, not in a cave. It is now time to just own your personal power and, as the Nike commercials say, "just do it." Fake it until you make it. I see and know thousands of lightworkers who keep waiting for some unknown miracle to happen to make them ready to take their power, leadership and the risk to serve. I am here to tell you that the unknown miracle is not going to happen. It is our job to own our power and use our creative abilities to figure out a way we can be of service. Many lightworkers get stuck on the negative ego's need to be glamorous in this work or to be famous or the best or to do something new. As Sai Baba has said, "Hands that help are holier than lips that pray."

The two requirements that must be in place for you to move on to your cosmic ascension are: (1) the requirement of clearing your negative ego and developing psychological clarity and balance and (2) the requirement of service.

The service form does not matter; it is the *intent* of your consciousness. Not everyone is meant or supposed to be well-known; that is meaningless to God. It is intent and a pure heart that He looks at. Whatever your profession, use that to demonstrate godliness and service to others. If you want to change jobs and move into the healing profession, then set about to do so. Take action. A great deal of all our service is not about our professions, but how we go about our daily lives: how we treat strangers, praying for people, sending people light, doing world-service work in our meditations.

Just make up your mind that every moment of your life you are going to be of service in your every thought, work and deed; that you are not on this planet anymore for your own selfish needs but rather to help others. Sometimes the service is a smile or a kind word or a dollar for a homeless person. Most of the time it will be just the emanation of love to every person you meet, whether you know him/her or not.

Pray to God to help you find the ways you can best serve. Maybe it's helping people to read or being a Big Brother. Maybe it's giving to a charity. If you just make up your mind that every moment of your life, for the rest of your life, you are going to serve as your main focus, you will be amazed at how many creative ways you can come up with. Ask the ascended masters for help in coming up with creative ideas of how you may be of service. Sometimes your service will be your example or your silence or just your energy in a room.

As long as the ego is not getting in the way, this is fine. It is the intent more than anything else that the masters are looking at. Everyone has love to give, so everyone can be of service. Some people will serve through being a lawyer, doctor, comedian, secretary, politician, businessman or woman. What you do doesn't matter, but rather the knowing that you are doing this type of work to be of service, not to make money.

The irony or paradox is that those who take this attitude are the ones who truly become successful financially and, more importantly, rich in their soul. God and the creative power of your subconscious mind will guide you how to serve, if you are constantly praying and affirming your sincere desire to serve. It is the small things that God looks at, not the big things. I know you all know what I mean.

Again, the real purpose of ascension is to prepare you for spiritual leadership and world service. As we move through ever-expanding levels of initiation, all this really means is that slowly but surely we are serving at more and more expanded levels. When we leave here, we will serve on the inner plane. When we graduate, we may go to the Great White Lodge on Sirius and continue our service. After that we will serve on universal levels. Even after we complete our cosmic ascension, we will continue to serve. God's creation is one eternal everlasting service mission. This is why the Master Jesus said in *A Course in Miracles* [textbook], "True pleasure is serving God."

It is when we are serving every moment in our intent that we know all is well and we are in tune with God. Ascension demonstrates ideally the attainment of self-mastery, which is the state of consciousness of now being able to give rather than take. One has become whole in the highest sense of the term and can now dedicate his/her life to giving back to all those who have not attained this wholeness yet. Serving or giving is what allows you to keep your own God-consciousness flowing properly. You need the blessing as much as your brothers and sisters. I often feel more grateful than the people receiving my service. What a great blessing it is to find a means of service to God and humanity, which are one and the same. Never forget that every person you meet is God visiting you in physical form.

10

Cosmic Golden Nuggets

This chapter is a potpourri of extremely important cosmic golden nuggets that do not deserve a whole chapter each, but put together form one of the most interesting chapters in the whole book.

The first golden nugget is a chart I developed listing a cosmology of cosmic and planetary ascended masters who are most well-known and who are available to work with.

Cosmology of Ascended Teachers

Source Level

Elohim Councils

Hyos Ha Kodeish

Paradise Sons'

Multiuniversal Level

Melchizedek

Universal Level

Melchizedek

Metatron

Archangel Michael

All Archangels

Adonis

Atlanto

Sathya Sai Baba

Lord of Great Bear Star System

Galactic Level
Lenduce
Vywamus
Sanat Kumara
Lord Buddha
Lord Maitreya
Averan
Melchior
Lord of Arcturus
Lord of Pleiades
Lord of Sirius
Allah Gobi
Saint Germain
Kuthumi

Solar and Planetary Masters (Beginning Galactic)
El Morya
Serapis Bey
Paul the Venetian
Djwhal Khul
Hilarion
Lord Sananda
Isis
Virgin Mary
Lord Ashtar
Quan Yin
Lady Nada
Babaji
Yogananda

This list is pretty self-explanatory, however, I would like to make some comments on a few of the masters or groups of masters listed. At the Source level I have listed the elohim, who are the creator gods. I asked Melchizedek recently if the core group and I would eventually become elohim and he said we would. Just as we are each Melchizedeks, eventually we will also become elohim.

Now, one level below elohim in evolution are what I called the Paradise Sons. He said we would also eventually become Paradise Sons, just as we would become elohim. Then one level slightly above the elohim are the highest servants of God or YHWH, which are the Hyos Ha Kodeish. These beings seem to represent cosmic stages of evolution. I found this to be extremely interesting. The word "elohim" has always been my favorite mantra. As we move down the list to the universal level it is interesting to me that

Melchizedek said the archangels work out of a universal level.

Communicating with the Masters

If one was to gather all the lightworkers on the planet, very few communicate with the masters directly in a clairaudient fashion. There is a percentage of lightworkers who communicate through clairvoyant means. However, the majority communicate intuitively. It is very common for those who use and have a more intuitive connection to often desire to be more clairvoyant and clairaudient and have direct communication. This can be developed by some, but for the larger majority this will probably not be your destiny.

I am writing this little section to say that those who are not clairaudient or clairvoyant don't need this type of psychic faculty to achieve all the things I have talked about in my books. If you have this ability, that is great; however, you don't need it. There are a great many psychics who have great mystic vision, but have very weak occult vision.

Usually the people who are more intuitive have much better occult vision. This means they are more mentally, emotionally, intuitively and psychologically clear. Occult vision is most definitely a type of vision, which most lightworkers don't recognize as a type of inner sight in and of itself.

For those who are not clairvoyant or clairaudient there is another type of communication you have with the masters that all lightworkers can work with. This deals with communicating with the masters through energy. For example, when you call on the Arcturians for light-quotient building, everyone—and I mean everyone—can feel the subtle flow of energy through the crown chakra and through the entire body. One doesn't have to be clairsentient to feel this.

When anyone requests to sit in the ascension seats, there is a very physical, tangible feeling. When you call on any one of the twelve rays, you can definitely feel this energy. When you call on Metatron, you can definitely feel his energy.

The energy is the key to the ascension process. It is running this type of spiritual energy that accelerates your initiation process. Even if you can't hear the masters speak directly to you clairaudiently, you can always hear them speak to you directly through the experience of their energy. As you work with processes you will see that the ascended masters will respond to you instantly with each of their unique energies, which will bring you confidence as to your constant, unwavering connection. There is no better feeling in the world than establishing this connection and recognizing you are a part of them and they are a part of you.

Interviews with the Masters

It is possible to request to have an interview with one of the masters. Unlike channeling or telepathic rapport, which can occur on a regular and quite friendly basis, an interview is a more serious meeting with a member of the Spiritual Hierarchy. The most important meeting or interview you could have is with Lord Maitreya and Lord Buddha to share with them your vows and specific commitments regarding your service work. Also ask for their help and blessings.

When Melchizedek mentioned this he also gave a very strict warning to lightworkers not to waste the masters' time. Just as you wouldn't schedule a meeting with the President of the United States without a pretty good reason, do not request an interview with the president of the Spiritual Hierarchy, Lord Maitreya, for example, without a very good reason. It is appropriate to request an interview if there is something extremely important you want to talk with the masters about, especially in regard to how you can be of service.

To request a meeting, just call forth the master with whom you want to talk. Even if you are not clairvoyant or clairaudient this can still be done. Request the meeting and just start talking. I have done this many times myself, especially with Sanat Kumara, Lord Maitreya, Djwhal Khul and Melchizedek. I have been extremely careful to be well-prepared before I do this and always to have some important agenda to discuss when I do. You must realize that when you do this, you are pulling their focus away from other important work in which they are involved.

You might also request an interview with Sai Baba in a similar vein and request his help in your mission. Now it must be understood that the masters could be busy and on rare occasions might not grant an interview. An interview with one of these masters is a very sacred thing. Just like everyone who wants one is not going to get an interview with the President of the United States, the same is true on a spiritual level. In my opinion, the masters are more available than the President, however.

The one thing I will tell you is that if they are not available, they will grant you an interview with one of their senior initiates on the inner plane. They will never turn you away completely. It is also important to be appropriate in terms of with whom you ask an interview. As a fourth-degree initiate you really have no business asking Melchizedek for an interview. If you are in junior high school, you don't schedule an interview with a college professor in the Ph.D. program.

There are many lightworkers who try and skip levels, and from the viewpoint of the ascended masters this is a sign of great immaturity and you risk annoying them. The idea is to work with the planetary masters first, then when you are ready, the solar masters, then when you graduate to the next level, the galactic masters and then, the universal masters. You can determine which masters to ask an interview with by your level of initiation and your degree of cosmic activation.

Cosmic Light-Quotient Building

In my previous book *Beyond Ascension* I wrote a very important chapter on how to raise your light quotient. I would now like to share twenty of what I consider the most effective methods of building your light quotient. They are all pretty straight forward and I will let this list stand on its own.

Cosmic and Planetary Light-Quotient Building

1. Metatron: Directly or Metatron's ascension seat
2. Mahatma: Light-quotient building
3. Melchizedek: Directly or Golden Chamber of Melchizedek
4. Lord of Arcturus and Arcturians: Directly or with their ascension seat
5. Melchizedek yod spectrum: Directly or yod spectrum ten lost rays ascension seat
6. Lord of Sirius: Great White Lodge light-quotient building or ascension seat
7. Elohim: Light packets of information activation for pure light-quotient building
8. Use of any and/or all of the ascension seats
9. Request of Vywamus for help in electrical rewiring to prepare for carrying a greater voltage
10. Request to Hyos Ha Kodeish for light-quotient building
11. Request to Paradise Sons for light-quotient building
12. Request to Melchior for light-quotient building or sitting in his ascension seat
13. Request to Helios for light-quotient building or sitting in his ascension seat
14. Request to Archangel Michael for light-quotient building or sitting in his ascension seat
15. Sitting in Djwhal Khul's light synthesis ashram and requesting activation of light drip light-quotient building program
16. Cosmic treasury of light, anchoring light packets of information from tablets of creation, cosmic ten commandments, cosmic book of life, Melchizedek scriptures, Metatron scriptures and the Torah Or
17. Anchoring of lightbody of Metatron
18. Anchoring of Microtron by Metatron
19. Anchoring and activation of fire letters, key codes and sacred geometries from the twelve dimensions of reality

20. Call forth the decadelta light encodements for the Ten Superscripts of the Divine Mind.

The Great Central Sun Cosmology

The next cosmic golden nugget deals with the understanding of what
has esoterically been called the Great Central Sun. I know in my studies I
never quite knew what this meant. Was this the solar, galactic, universal,
multiuniversal or Source level?

According to Melchizedek there are a whole number of what might be
called Great Central Suns: the first of which is the galactic core; second is
the universal core; third is the multiuniversal core; and fourth is the actual
Source Itself. The following chart lists them using this terminology.

The Great, Great, Great Central Sun =	Source level
The Great, Great Central Sun =	Melchizedek's multiuniversal level, our Source of the Cosmic Day for our forty-three christed universes
The Great Central Sun =	Universal Core and Central Sun for our specific universe
The Central Sun =	Galactic Core and home of Melchior, the Galactic Logos

The Cosmic Council of Twelve Cosmology

The leadership group of God's infinite universe is broken down into
five subdivisions. God is at the top and there are twelve cosmic beings who
run God's infinite universe. At the multiuniversal level there are twelve
more beings who make up our Cosmic Day. It must be understood that
there are infinite numbers of sources and cosmic days, so possibly there are
infinite numbers of cosmic councils of twelve for each source.

At the universal level there is another council of twelve for each universe, and again there are infinite numbers of universes. At the galactic
level there is another cosmic council of twelve for each galaxy that exists
within every universe, of which there are infinite numbers. Then there is a
council of twelve within every solar system within every galaxy in God's infinite universe.

This is the basic cosmic governmental structure. There are infinite
numbers of other councils that exist; however, all these other councils take
their orders from the cosmic councils of twelve. This can be likened to federal government, then state government and then city government, in terms
of councils within councils. The cosmic councils of twelve are federal government, so to speak.

Activation of the Solar, Galactic and Universal Sun

The next ascension technique and tool is to call forth to Helios and Vesta, Melchior and Melchizedek for the permanent anchoring and activation of the solar sun, the galactic sun and the universal sun. After making this initial request this must be worked with on an ongoing basis. It is connected with the process of anchoring and activating your solar body and solar chakras.

This particular technique is ideally begun after the completion of your seven levels of initiation. If you want to request it before, it will not hurt. The real work of building this bridge begins when the seven levels of initiation are complete and the fifty chakras are anchored and activated. This work is the true beginning of cosmic ascension. Up to this point one has really been focusing on planetary ascension. This might more succinctly be called the "solar ascension process."

The Importance of Sending Light

One of the key tests of the spiritual path for the high-level initiates who the masters watch is our willingness to send light. The concept here is that whenever and wherever there is a situation of need or of suffering, the lightworkers either immediately call to the mighty I Am Presence or the masters to heal it, as is God's will. The second possibility in this regard is to do an affirmation of healing, or a visualization of healing. The third alternative is to just send light through your heart or third eye.

If you prefer, you can pray to your mighty I Am Presence or to the masters to send light. It doesn't matter how you do this, just that you do something. By doing this you keep your own consciousness in a state of perfection. It is not just for others, but is, in truth, also for yourself. This is the appropriate response to those who are suffering and those who are caught in the negative ego. It is not to judge them, but to pray, affirm or send light to them, or all three if you like.

The idea is to walk through life as a blessing, praying and light-giving machine. I do not mean "machine" in a mechanical sense, but in a steady, committed, focused, compassionate, sincere, sense of this term. This is why your very presence in every situation is an automatic healing force of the highest regard. The light you give will also bless you immeasurably, for what we sow, we reap and what we put out comes back to us. Many others will be helped way beyond our possible knowledge of the results. As the Bhagavad Gita says, the results of our service are unimportant. What is important is that we give it at every opportunity or as much as we can. In truth, it is just a matter of remembering to do this.

Becoming a Mystical Traveler

One of the interesting byproducts of working with all the ascension seats, different ashrams, planetary and cosmic masters, is that there is a feeling that develops of truly being a cosmic citizen. In the flash of an eye, by the power of the spoken word, you can move around God's infinite universe.

In the past, it was usually only those who could consciously soul travel who could do this. Even those with this ability did not have the conscious knowledge of the cosmos and cosmic ascended masters as is coming forth in this most extraordinary time we now live in. To be a mystical traveler you don't even have to be clairvoyant or clairaudient. This feeling of being a mystical traveler and cosmic citizen is a most wonderful feeling, and I suggest that you cultivate and enjoy it.

Lightworkers and Physical Health Lessons

Living on planet Earth in a physical body, no matter what one's level of spiritual development, just about guarantees lightworkers to have physical health lessons at one time or another. For each lightworker it will obviously be different. Some of the health lessons are karmic in nature and some have to do with the enormous speed of personal and planetary evolution going on during Earth's evolution at this time.

Each octave change in frequency can present a whole new set of health lessons and purification that is needed. No one can escape this completely. It is the nature of having a physical vehicle. It is also common for every lightworker to have at least one area in his/her physical body that is a little bit weaker than the rest. This can also be the case in one's four-body system. In the latter case, it is usually the emotional or psychological vehicle, although again it is different for each person. The higher one goes on the spiritual path, the greater the need for self-discipline and self-mastery and, hence, the quicker the karma if one does not hold the proper focus.

When you are going through health lessons, be it a cold, flu, virus, bacterial infection, headache, digestive problems, organ weakness, endocrine weakness and so on, I would make the following suggestions. It is of the highest importance to keep the physical vehicle as healthy as possible. My suggestion for getting through health lessons is not to focus as much or at all on ascension seats and ascension activations. Instead, make your meditations focused on healing your physical body. In essence I am suggesting that your meditations be working with the: (1) ascended masters and the angels of healing; (2) the Arcturians; and (3) the synthesis ashram of Djwhal Khul.

The ascended masters and the angels of healing are a group of healers.

Call them and tell them what area needs work. Then take an hour to relax and let them work on you. This can be done in a meditation, watching television or just relaxing. You have your own personal healing team anytime you need it. I cannot tell you how much money this type of healing team has saved me. You can call on them as often as you need them—they are happy to be of service.

The second suggestion that is equally valuable for physical health problems is to work with the Lord of Arcturus and the Arcturians. They have been an absolute godsend in my life. For physical health concerns I would suggest working them in three ways. First, directly ask them for what you need. Second, request a 100% light-quotient increase and then request the focus of where you want the increased light channeled. Third, request to be taken to the mechanism chamber on the Arcturian mothership, to be placed on their computer and worked on.

What is unique about the Arcturians is their advanced extraterrestrial technology, which they use to help in this regard. There is not a single physical health problem in the universe that they are not equipped to help with. They will scan your physical and etheric bodies with their advanced computers and can see energy blocks on the screen. You will immediately feel the increased flow of light and will experience a change in that area.

Their work has an immediate strengthening effect, which is more significant than with any group of beings I have ever worked with on a consistent basis. They are most wonderful service-oriented beings. Their technology allows them to do some things over a more prolonged period of time than other more metaphysical-type beings.

The third suggestion for physical health problems is to ask to go the interdimensional synthesis ashram of Djwhal Khul. Call forth Djwhal Khul and the matrix-removal program. Ask very specifically here for a complete clearing of all implants, negative elementals, parasites, and imbalanced energies—in a general sense and specifically in that area you are having problems.

For chronic health lessons it is a good idea to do this twice a week. It is in our physical weak areas that the implants and elementals often seem to congregate. Djwhal Khul and Vywamus will sweep your fields and clear away any form of negative energy or etheric mucus that is in the area causing problems.

Another suggestion in regard to this is sometimes to not do any formal meditation and just rest. Let the natural inflow of energies come in as needed. After working with this process of ascension-activation work for a period of time, you will find energies coming in and working with you that you are not formally asking for. You have asked so many times in the past that permission has already been given. Sometimes the natural flow of your own body's natural energies is what is needed.

I find the ascension seats to have a very healing effect on my physical body when everything is functioning well. However, when I have specific health lessons, I lay off and let these other types of processes be my meditation. I feel good because I am still meditating and an enormous amount of light is still coming in; however, the purpose is for physical healing. Because some of the ascension seats take you out of your physical body to a great extent, there is the need to get grounded after doing a lot of this work.

The other Arcturian process that can be very helpful in regard to physical health problems is the prana wind-clearing device (mentioned in *Beyond Ascension*). It is lowered into the body and clears away, or blows out like a fan, all etheric mucus from the chakras and meridian system. It is important to make sure that there is a free flow of energy circulating through your veins, arteries, etheric nervous system and nadis. This process will help any type of physical health problem and is a good idea to use once a week as a preventative process and/or any time you feel contaminated by the lessons of life—which is quite easy in this world.

These simple techniques will have an enormously positive effect and will save you tons of money going to healers. I am not saying that you should never take advantage of other healers. However, these healing teams are there any moment you need them, twenty-four hours a day.

Eat to live (don't live to eat), drink lots of fresh water, exercise and get fresh air and sunshine every day if you can. This should collectively have an enormously strengthening effect on your physical and etheric physical bodies. Ask the etheric healing team to repair any etheric damage you might have. Call to the aura healing team to repair any holes or leaks in your aura. This should do the trick.

In some cases this focus for your meditation work might last for three days, a week or two weeks. Many lightworkers have chronic health lessons of various kinds. There might be a need in more extreme cases to make this focus for an entire year. You will still be building light quotient in the process by working with the ascended masters and the healing angels, the Arcturians and the synthesis ashram.

The main point here is that you don't want to do spiritual work at the expense of your physical vehicle. Each person will have to find his/her own balance in this regard. I do also want to mention that physical health lessons will not impede your ascension process. You do not need perfect health to ascend or complete all seven levels of initiation.

Also, you *will* be dealing with health lessons even after you ascend and complete the seven levels. You don't become superman or superwoman and become invulnerable to physical imbalance. Any areas of physical, emotional, mental or spiritual weakness you had before your ascension will still be there after your ascension.

One last golden nugget on this subject, which might be one of the most important, has to do with the Arcturians. A great insight I have discovered in working with the Arcturians is how helpful they can be in working with physical health lessons. Their energy, in my opinion, is the most substantial and effective I have found in dealing with physical health weaknesses. The best way I can explain this is to use myself as an example.

Because of a case of hepatitis in my distant past, my digestive system is a little weaker and more sensitive than it should be. I am now in the process of realizing my mayavarupa body. However, until that process is complete I need to be careful in this area in terms of diet, stress and not overworking.

What I have discovered is that Arcturian energies can be used as sort of an "electrical brace" to support this area of my body. For example, every morning before I start working at my desk, I call in an increase of light-quotient and a strengthening of my pancreas and liver. I am immediately hooked up with their starship and master computer. They electrically strengthen my entire field, liver and pancreas, as requested.

I have done experiments, and when I don't do this, my system conks out much sooner. I also use the Arcturians as my first line of defense any time these organs start getting electrically out of balance. The Arcturians immediately put them back in place. It really is quite amazing!

The fact is that all lightworkers have some area of their four-body system and/or their physical body that is their weak spot or Achilles' heal—the weak link in their chain. What I am suggesting here is to call on the Lord of Arcturus and the Arcturians to strengthen this weak link as a part of your daily program. I often do it before I go to bed at night. I do it before all big events to ensure my physical strength.

If a person's weak link is his/her knee, then I suggest calling for an 100% light-quotient increase and strengthening of the knee before walking or running. If your weak link is your immune system, then simultaneously call forth an 100% light-quotient increase and a specific strengthening of your thymus gland. If it is bladder infections, then have them clear and strengthen that area. This will serve as an electrical brace, so to speak, just like a physical cast or physical brace on the material level.

If your area of weakness is your emotional body, then have them strengthen this area when you first get up and throughout the day. If it is a soul quality you are weak in, such as joy, then have them beam you joy all day long. There is no problem or lesson that they cannot help you with.

The Arcturian energies are the core energies I run most of the time to keep myself physically strong. I have tried thousands of other types of energies in this regard and nothing, in my experience, works as well as the

Arcturians. Maybe it is because they are extraterrestrial and use advanced technologies.

The nice thing about this is that using this method is helping to build light-quotient while simultaneously strengthening your etheric and physical body in whatever area needs help. You are killing two birds with one stone, so to speak. The Arcturians can help you with all kinds of other spiritual stuff; however, they are an absolute godsend in dealing with physical health lessons.

After your ascension you will be operating out of the perfect monadic blueprint body, or mayavarupa body, and will be carrying much more light and spiritual current. The process, however, of realizing the monadic blueprint body and mayavarupa body is a gradual one. There is a misconception among many lightworkers that it happens instantly. It doesn't. You will be much healthier after your ascension, but not completely invulnerable. Give in to your lower self and as the Bible says, "After pride cometh the fall." The same clearing work, self-mastery and self-discipline that got you to achieve your ascension will still continue to be needed afterward.

Why Don't We Have Superhuman
Abilities after Ascension?

This is another misconception about the ascension process that just about all lightworkers have had, including myself. We are now living in an entirely new age with an entirely new set of rules. Masters in the past took at least fifteen years or even whole lifetimes to do one initiation, and these were the most advanced initiates of the planet.

Your average committed lightworker is now completing initiations in two or three years. It is much easier now. This has a lot to do with the current time period in Earth's history and the fact that we are living in the beginning of the Aquarian Age and in a period of mass ascension. We are very lucky to be incarnated at this time. Masters in the past had much more time to practice between initiations. Masters in the past also usually lived in the Himalayas and not in big cities.

There is a new dispensation in the ascension process since the examples of Jesus, Saint Germain, Djwhal Khul, Kuthumi and El Morya. The new dispensation is that lightworkers are being allowed to accelerate spiritually sometimes way beyond their mental, emotional or even physical development. It is like the spiritual body is moving ahead of the other bodies.

The advanced ascended-master abilities will come, however, not until all seven levels of initiation are complete, all fifty chakras are anchored and activated and all twelve bodies are installed and activated. Remember what I said previously about there being three steps: anchoring, activation and actualization. Once the initiations, chakras and bodies have all been installed and activated, then the final step of actualization occurs, which will bring in the advanced ascended-master abilities such as teleportation, materialization, dematerialization and so on.

Because of this new dispensation the masses are now being allowed to take their ascensions and complete their seven levels of initiations first and then work on developing the advanced abilities. Again, there is this misconception that all the advanced abilities come instantly the moment you ascend, which is not true. They need to be developed. Personally, I have met all the requirements and still have not developed the truly advanced abilities.

Melchizedek told us that they will come with installation, activation and actualization of the twelfth body, or universal body. For our core group this is still about five years away, which puts us at the year 2000, before they become feasible to really practice.

Your main goal, in my opinion, should be to get to the seventh initiation, which is the true liberation from the wheel of rebirth. There are many advanced psychic and spiritual abilities that can be developed before this. However, I am speaking here of those advanced abilities dealing with the transcendence of physical laws, such as teleporting and materializing physical objects.

In this new dispensation it would seem that the passing of the initiations and achieving ascension is much, much easier than in the past, but achieving the advanced ascended-master abilities is a little harder. Given how many initiates are taking their higher initiations now, this is probably a good system. Again, initiations have more to do with spiritual development and the building of light-quotient than with mental, emotional or physical development. This might seem surprising, but it is true.

Loneliness and the Spiritual Path

Often lightworkers comment about feeling alone or not having enough spiritual companionship and community on their path. It is true that the higher and higher you move on the path, the fewer people, in terms of numbers, you will meet with whom you can really relate. The first remedy, I would say, is to come to our Wesak celebrations every year and you will meet literally a thousand people from your greater spiritual family. Another remedy for loneliness is working with the different ascension techniques in my books.

Anytime you want, you can talk to, see, travel to or energetically connect with thousands of different masters and spiritual locations around God's infinite universe. Again, even if you are not clairaudient or clairvoyant, just connecting with the energies is extremely comforting. It is like energetically blending with these different masters and your own monad and higher self. You begin to sense more clearly how thin the veil is between you and the spirit world and how readily available all the masters are for the asking. You begin to see that you have literally a thousand different masters who you can spiritually call up on the inner-plane phone and connect with anytime you want.

My books contain an incredibly eclectic, universalistic and wide range of tools and techniques to use. You will never get bored. You can literally, anytime you want, not just read about God, but experience God in all His/Her infinite manifestations. I encourage you to experiment and not limit yourself. Travel to Sai Baba's ashram and experience the succor and sweetness of Sai Baba in his "love seat." Travel to the Golden Chamber of Melchizedek and experience the all-embracing love of the grand master himself. Call forth Metatron and experience his profound light frequencies. Travel to the different ashrams of the masters and sit in meditation, communing in their energies, and ask for their ascension blessings.

As you experiment and practice you will soon experience how you are never alone—never have been and never will be. It was all an illusion from a veil that the recognition and practice of what I speak of here will truly bring you a "peace that passeth all understanding."

Ganesha Ceremony

In the Hindu religion the name *Ganesha* refers to the Hindu god who is the "remover of obstacles." He is depicted in Hindu literature as an elephant god. Even though to the Western mind there is the tendency to believe that Ganesha is mythological or fantasy, this is far from the case. He has appeared to us many times in meditation and is an enormous ally for the purpose of removing obstacles in any form.

To begin this ceremony you will need to buy a coconut. Stand before your altar with the coconut in a large bowl, with a hammer in hand. Call forth to Ganesha in a reverent, meditative state. Then crack the coconut with the hammer and let the juice spill into the bowl. Break apart the coconut and place it at your altar as an offering to Ganesha. Then recite the following Hindu mantrum: *Jai Ganesha, Jai Ganesha, Pariman. Sri Ganesha, Sri Ganesha, Rokshaman.* (Repeat three times.)

Call to Ganesha and pray that he remove the unwanted obstacle. Do not underestimate the power of this brief ceremony. You might consider going to a metaphysical bookstore and selecting a greeting card with his picture for your altar. This ceremony along with the Huna Prayers [see *Beyond Ascension*] are a "can't miss" spiritual practice to achieve the victories you desire in your life in service to God.

Our New Planetary Logos

About four days prior to the Wesak Festival of 1995, the core group and I received some information from a friend in Seattle who is connected to another major planetary hierarchical ashram. This friend, whose name is Peter, told my friend that their organization had received some extraordinary information regarding the status of Sanat Kumara and the Buddha. They had received inner guidance that Sanat Kumara was now moving to a higher position in his cosmic evolution and that Gautama Buddha was now taking over the position of Planetary Logos.

The core group and I meditated and were told that this was indeed true and that Sanat Kumara was now going to be responsible for two other planets as well as overlighting Buddha in his new job as planetary logos. So Sanat Kumara is in charge of three planets now—ours and two others—and Buddha is now holding the position of Planetary Logos and will work with Sanat Kumara very closely.

Just as humanity was about to begin its first wave of ascension, Sanat Kumara was going through his next step in his cosmic ascension process. The Buddha was coming back from the Great White Lodge on Sirius and teaming up with his brother Lord Maitreya again, as they had done many times in the past to help enlighten humanity. Quite a team: Sanat Kumara, Lord Maitreya and the Buddha! This is also why the Wesak celebration we hold each year takes on even more significance. While there was some confusion regarding this at the Wesak in 1995 because of the newness of the information, the core group and I have checked it out thoroughly since then, and it is indeed true. Sanat Kumara is still very much involved with Earth's evolution, as he has always been. However, by the grace of God, Buddha is back with us again. The Buddha officially took over the position of Planetary Logos at the Wesak 1995, which I personally feel is quite extraordinary.

Clearing the Seven Veils and the Twelve Veils

Call forth in meditation for the clearing of the seven veils connected with the lower expression of the seven rays. Then call for the clearing of the twelve veils connected with the lower expression of the twelve archetypes. Then call forth for the clearing of the twelve veils connected with the lower expression of the twelve signs of the zodiac from Metatron, Melchizedek and Archangel Michael.

Cancer-Removal Activation

Call forth to the Lord of Arcturus and the Arcturians for the removal of all cancers in the brain and all cancers in the entire etheric-, astral-, mental- and physical-body matrix. Then request this for all the soul extensions in your oversoul and for all your 144 soul extensions in your monadic family. Finally, call forth a genetic clearing of all diseases of all kinds from your entire genetic line.

The Etheric Webbing

This next insight from the ascended masters will be extremely important to a great many lightworkers. Every person, of course, has an etheric body, or webbing, which is the perfect mold or blueprint for the physical body. In many cases this webbing is either too open and loose, or too restricted and tight.

A person who is too open and psychically sensitive and who takes on too much of other people's and life's energies needs to have his/her etheric web tightened. On the other side of the coin, someone who is too controlled and possibly not psychically open enough might need to have his/her etheric web loosened.

Call to the ascended masters, especially Djwhal Khul and Vywamus, and have them, in conjunction with your own mighty I Am Presence, find the perfect webbing tightness that is right for you.

Atomic Bomb Testing

One day I asked Melchizedek about the effects of the testing of atomic bombs that is currently going on with Communist China and France and that took place in the past in the United States and some European countries. Melchizedek told me that the atomic bombs cause gaping holes in the aura (mental, astral, etheric) body of the Earth. This is very similar to the type of gaping holes humans develop in their auras from being raised in abusive environments.

The holes in humans' auras allow for energetic leakage and psychic bleeding as well as allowing opening for negative extraterrestrials and astral entities. The exact same thing takes place on a planetary level. We were also told that almost every time there is an atomic test, within a few days there is a major earthquake someplace in the world.

The military industrial complex of the world doesn't realize how everything in life is interconnected. There is no such thing as an "isolated" atomic test, and add to this the fact that of all the substances in the infinite universe, uranium is at the top in terms of being detrimental to human life. There is really no safe way to store this substance. Then add to this the effect of the atomic bomb being dropped on Nagasaki and Hiroshima in World War II. Can you imagine the effect it had on the etheric bodies of the Japanese people who lived in these cities?

Remember, the etheric body can most definitely be damaged from any kind of past-life trauma. Here we have an actual case of a meltdown of the etheric body. I am not saying that it is beyond repair, but the damage is enormous. It is the worst possible kind of death. This is a type of energy that we should not be messing with. This is a form of energy that humankind does not understand and, in truth, doesn't need. Even atomic energy plants, as we all know, are not safe, and in the future it will be possible to obtain energy from the universe that can destroy. This is still third-dimensional thinking. Eventually burning oil, coal and even electricity as we know it will be outdated. We will be able to tap into free energy as spoken of by Nicola Tesla.

I was surprised to hear that there was one seemingly positive effect of the atomic testing. The masters said this has to do with the hole that was created between the third and fourth dimension. This gaping hole has very definite negative effects, but the positive side is that it allowed for greater communication between the third and fourth dimension.

All Christed-Universes Activation

Call forth to Melchizedek, Metatron and Archangel Michael for an anchoring and activation of all christed universes from the Source of our Cosmic Day.

Strange Humming Sound in New Mexico

Recently I watched a television show called *Sightings*, which reported that tens of thousands of people in New Mexico and around the world were hearing a strange humming sound that seemed to be emanating from the Earth. The main focal point seemed to be New Mexico. It was not a sound that everybody could hear, but rather those who were more sensitive.

I asked the masters about this and they told me it was a fourth-dimensional, not a third-dimensional sound. They also said it was coming from the underground extraterrestrial base in New Mexico that was shared by the Grays and the United States Government.

The Bermuda Triangle

Recently I saw a fabulous documentary on the Bermuda Triangle, which, in conjunction with some channelings of the ascended masters, gave me a much greater insight into what is actually going on there. In my previous books I spoke of the great crystal in Atlantis that sunk to the ocean floor, which was part of this phenomenon. I knew this was true, however, I never completely understood what happened to the people and ships. Now I do.

Basically, what is happening in the Bermuda Triangle is that there is a fourth-dimensional vortex that comes and goes depending on a number of factors, one of which is this great crystal on the ocean floor. When a ship or plane moves into this vortex it literally disappears into the fourth dimension. The people are not killed; they are just in another dimension—much like when one dies, but in this case their physical bodies, ship or plane have gone with them. This is kind of like an ascended master teleporting to the inner plane. In this case though they are in the fourth dimension, not the fifth.

In this documentary there were a number of amazing stories that showed how this worked. In the most amazing one a ship was dragging a barge with a very strong rope or chain. The ship moved into the Bermuda Triangle and the barge just disappeared, right in front of the crew members' eyes—almost like the Philadelphia Experiment.

The fascinating thing is that the rope or chain was still taut and dragging the barge. The ship was in the third dimension and the barge was in the fourth dimension. Ten minutes later the barge reappeared out of nowhere.

In another example, a ship with very advanced radar equipment detected on the radar screen a gigantic land mass in the middle of the ocean where no land mass existed. They moved right to the edge of it, but there was nothing there. As soon as they started to enter it, their radar and other equipment started to malfunction; therefore they decided to turn around. They actually saw the Bermuda Triangle on their radar!

In another amazing case, a plane was flying around in circles over a certain island around the Bermuda Triangle. The woman flying the plane said over the communication system to the tower that her equipment was malfunctioning and when she looked down on the island all she could see was a deserted empty island with no buildings or inhabitants. In actuality, on the third dimension this was a resort with lots of people and buildings. The people on the island could see her flying in circles and didn't know what she was doing.

The masters told me that she was in the corridor or hallway, so to speak, of the Bermuda Triangle. She was half in the third dimension and half in the fourth dimension. It was almost like she was seeing the past Earth two hundred years ago, even though the people on Earth were seeing her in the present. Later she disappeared and was never seen or heard of again.

The same exact thing happened to six airplane bombers. The tower reported that they were right over inhabited cities, but the airplane bomber planes could only see deserted desolate islands. They were also in the corridor between two dimensions. They later disappeared never to be seen or heard from again.

I asked the masters about this and they said that they were living in the fourth dimension and continuing their lives there in most cases. It must be understood that the fourth dimension looks like this dimension. These planes and ships just began traveling in the sky, ocean and Earth of the fourth dimension, rather than the third. This is why in some rare instances they were able to come back into the third dimension.

In one case an ocean liner disappeared off the radar screen for ten minutes and then reappeared. The ship was traveling in the fourth dimension and probably didn't even realize it except for the fact that all the ship's equipment was going crazy.

This idea of dematerializing is, of course, one of the ascended-master abilities. In this case it is a vortex on Earth that allows for this transformation. As many are aware, in the Philadelphia Experiment (which I spoke of in *Hidden Mysteries*) the United States Government had and used the technology to make battleships disappear at will using advanced extraterrestrial technology.

The only problem was that even though they were able to do this, they were not able to control it to the degree of it being safe for the crew members. Crew members dematerialized and came back, but many were rematerialized inside the hull of the ship.

In one last example of happenings in the Bermuda Triangle, ships would move into it and just the crew would disappear. It could be that the crew got off the ship in the fourth dimension and the boat eventually floated back into the third dimension. The other possibility is that the vortex just dematerialized the people but not the ship.

I asked the ascended masters whether there were other such vortexes such as the Bermuda Triangle on Earth and they said there most definitely were. Some people crashed or died in their planes in the fourth dimension and others have just continued their lives without the ability to contact their third-dimensional lives.

Can you imagine being on a cruise or flying in a plane and then all of a sudden being in the fourth dimension? It could be like Earth in the past or Earth in the future. It would be like dying, but you are not dead. This reminds me of a very good science fiction movie that might not actually be fiction. An aircraft carrier went through a vortex and was projected back into Earth in 1945 just prior to the bombing of Pearl Harbor by the Japanese. This led to the ethical dilemma of whether they should use their advanced fire power to destroy the Japanese fleet and change history. This might be a little far-fetched, but you never know.

Initiation Process for Fundamentalist Christians

In one of our group meditations one day I asked Djwhal Khul about the initiation process for Fundamentalist Christians. I was not asking this in a judgmental sense, but rather really curious about how their often dogmatic, confused and self-righteous belief systems affected their spiritual progression.

What Djwhal Khul said was that it had a great effect. As a general rule their religious doctrine and program seemed to be able to take them to the third initiation, which is the soul-merge initiation. This is where they as a whole seemed to get stuck. Djwhal said there were exceptions to this. However, on the whole, this is what seemed to take place.

The 64 Sacred Letter Grid of the DNA and RNA Activation

Call forth to Metatron and Melchizedek for the anchoring and activation of the sacred letter grid of the DNA and RNA. This is connected to the twelve strands of DNA, but is the actual grid that underlies this process. Again we have the process of installation, activation and actualization. Full realization of this process will not come until the twelve bodies (solar, galactic and universal) and two hundred chakras are installed and activated.

All these processes work together synergistically. Do call for this installation and activation, for it will set the process in deeper motion. Djwhal said this grid is the code that unlocks the DNA principle. The strands are activated four sacred letters at a time.

The Ban of Noninterference

This next golden key might be one of the most important in this entire book. One of the things that all lightworkers will run into in their service work is the negative ego of other people. This is especially true as one moves into the greater and greater leadership responsibilities. It is human nature, as opposed to godly nature, for the negative ego to be in power struggles, be critical, bad mouth and sabotage other lightworkers in an attempt to obtain self-esteem.

Many lightworkers are not in control of their negative egos and others are actually in the category of being twilight masters, which I have already mentioned. This means that they are being used by both the Dark Brotherhood and the ascended masters.

The core group and I have run into certain people at times who because of their jealousy and competitiveness, overall insecurity and lack of clarity can create a lot of havoc on the inner plane. They can basically stir up a lot of false gossip and trouble. I am sure you are all familiar with this. There is not a single lightworker on this planet who will be able to avoid this because the negative ego is so rampant.

The key question is, what is the appropriate response from a spiritual perspective. The first lesson is not to react and sink to that level. The lesson is to remain neutral, detached, forgiving, loving and maintain divine indifference.

Sometimes communication of some kind is in order. However, many times any form of communication will exacerbate the problem. What is a lightworker to do then? The masters have given these three suggestions:

1. Report this person to Lord Maitreya and the Buddha on the inner plane in a loving and nonjudgmental way. Sanat Kumara said there is a system in place for these kinds of circumstances. First, the person is given a warning, then placed on probation and in extreme cases, his/her energy is shut off to a great degree.

2. Most important, you must ask for a ban of noninterference from Lord Maitreya, Lord Buddha and the Lords of Karma. The invocation of the ban of noninterference will invoke on a spiritual level the powers that govern this planet to step in and prevent the Dark Brotherhood attack on your lightwork from taking place. Anytime a lightworker on this planet is getting into his/her negative ego and trying to sabotage your program, this ban should be invoked.

3. Ask for a ban of protection for yourself, your operation, your books, your tapes and your entire program. These things should be asked for in total forgiveness and unconditional love. It could be called "tough love." It should be asked for in each individual case where this is taking place.

I would also recommend that you do this one time on an entire planetary level, to all people and lightworkers on the planet. This is a form of preventative medicine. It must be understood that many lightworkers, although well-intentioned, are often taken over by their negative ego and the Dark Brotherhood. This is how the Dark Brotherhood tries to sabotage and block God's divine plan. These three tools will create an enormous force field of protection both on the individual and on the collective level.

An Expanded View of Projection

We are all aware of the concept of projection. When a person is really run by the negative ego, this process of projection can also translate into one's clairvoyance and visual perception. In one recent case I observed a clairvoyant woman seeing astral entities being attached to the project and person of someone with whom she was competing.

I checked this out with Djwhal Khul and he said that actually she herself was the astral entity. She was seeing clairvoyantly the projection of her own unclear subconscious negative-ego material on her competitor. This lady was totally unconscious of the degree to which her emotional body and negative ego had taken over her personality. She was unconscious of the degree to which her clairvoyance was contaminated by the negative ego. I bring this up, for lightworkers very often give their power to channels and psychics and don't realize the degree to which the negative ego contaminates these processes.

Another time during a small workshop this same woman channeled one of the great masters. She proceeded to fill the channeling with her own agenda, which I know for a fact was not what the masters really believed. I honestly think that this person was completely unconscious that she was channeling her negative ego, which was parading as one of the great masters. Her channeling sounded just like the ascended masters, and I'm sure everyone in the audience believed that.

Lightworkers need to be much more discerning about the psychic's or channel's personality. If anyone ever tells you any differently, it is his/her negative ego talking. Even the Alice Bailey books and Edgar Cayce were colored by the personalities of the channels involved. This is not meant as a judgment, but rather as just the nature of channeling and psychism itself. There is no channel or psychic who is completely clear of this. However, some are more clear than others, which is the ideal. Remember, just because someone channels something from the masters or clairvoyantly sees something doesn't mean it is true or really there.

Misconceptions About Initiations and Ascension

There is a common misconception among lightworkers that when a person ascends and/or completes his/her seventh level of initiation, that everyone will have similar abilities. The fact is, nothing could be further from the truth. Using an extreme example to demonstrate this point, take two make-believe people who have just completed their seventh sublevel of their seventh initiation.

Let's say the first person is a world teacher and leader in the spiritual movement, who is a clairvoyant, clairaudient channel traveling around the world doing workshops. The other make-believe person is a housewife with three kids and is not a psychic, whose life is focused around her husband and family. She has not moved into spiritual leadership or world service. One is not better than another, for everyone follows the beat of a different drum and each person has a different mission and puzzlepiece to fulfill.

The point I am trying to make here is that too much emphasis is being placed on initiations. People can be at the same level of initiation and yet vastly different in their abilities and the form these abilities take. Some people are meant to take leadership positions, some to take a supporting role. All are meant to serve, but each in his/her own way. For some, fame will come their way; for others, they are supposed to serve humankind from behind the scenes without anybody's knowledge, except God.

The initiation status is merely an indication of the amount of light you are carrying. In the above example, the light quotient is equal. Initiation status says nothing about your abilities, spiritual gifts, psychological clarity, character development, spiritual leadership, world-service capabilities or purity of heart. Very often in the qualities mentioned above, there might be a fourth- or fifth-degree initiate more developed in these abilities than a completed seventh-degree initiate. This is why it is never wise to judge a person by his/her initiation level.

Take a person like Gandhi, who I don't believe was at that high a level of initiation. However, look what he was able to do in his life. Too much focus is put on initiation and more should instead be put on overall self-realization. I know many fourth- and fifth-degree initiates, who, in my opinion, are a thousand times clearer than some seventh-degree initiates I know. This gets back to the understanding that initiation level does not have a lot to do with psychological clarity and character development. Wherever you are in your life and whatever role you find yourself in, be the best you can be, of greatest possible service in that role and let God take care of the rest.

Djwhal Khul also spoke of another misconception about initiations that has to do with lightworkers looking at this process as a "self-serving honor as opposed to an honor of serving." The higher you go, the more is expected of you at all levels, for you are now considered a master. The work load does not become easier but much increased, for there is an inherent expectation of service responsibility that goes with becoming an ascended master. Maintaining this new level as a representative for the Spiritual Hierarchy on Earth with all your service responsibilities will require as much vigilance and effort as it did to get to this level. It is not like you have made it to heaven and you can sip lemonade and sleep on a pink cloud.

Everything we have gone through was just preparation for the real work that now begins. If you lose your focus and commitment, you can fall back just as easily as you did before you achieved this level of initiation. So what I am trying to say is that nothing really changes once these higher initiations are taken, except that more is expected of you because you are now considered a master. You still have to monitor your thoughts, emotions and physical body in the same way you always have.

People have this fantasy that when you ascend, some magical process happens where you become like superman or superwoman and you don't have to work as hard to keep yourself in balance. I am sorry to say, but this is not true. In many ways I don't feel that much different than I did as a fourth-degree initiate. The only difference is that I am holding much more light, have a much greater sense of purity and a much higher level of spiritual attunement. Besides these factors I am pretty much doing the exact same spiritual practices, diet, physical exercise, journal writing, meditating and service work I have been doing.

The only other difference I notice is much greater and more expanded service responsibilities. One has to work to develop the advanced ascended-master abilities. They do not come automatically, which of course, seems different than what we have all been led to believe from past literature on the subject. We are living in an entirely new dispensation of Earth's history in this regard. From what the masters have told us, one must get to the twelfth dimension or universal level in terms of installation and activation before one can realistically begin to practice these advanced abilities.

This again deals with the twelve bodies, two hundred chakras and forty percent cosmic light-quotient level. That is why this book is not as esoteric or far-reaching as one might initially think. To develop the wide range of advanced ascended-master abilities such as teleportation, dematerialization, turning water into wine, raising the dead, walking on water and so on, all the advanced lightworkers on this planet must integrate the things spoken of here.

The fastest path to achieving advanced ascended-master abilities is to live a life of supreme balance and godliness in one's daily life, without any sense of negative-ego infiltration. The advanced abilities will come as a natural result and byproduct of practicing the presence of God in one's daily life. If a person is focused in this state of consciousness, he/she will not be concerned about the advanced ascended-master abilities and powers. It will not be her focus. What is more important, the powers of siddhas, or godliness? When one is developed in godliness, she has mastered the art of living and so, in truth, doesn't even need these abilities. The irony and paradox of life is that it is when this state of consciousness is achieved that the advanced ascended-master abilities come.

Djwhal Khul spoke of this as the need to let go of the "glamours of ascension." There might be some lightworkers who will fall away from the path of ascension and initiation because without the glamours and the siddhas, they are not interested. These souls are still young and will have to be molded and purified by the fires of life and the reincarnation process. True ascension is for those who are truly pure of heart in the highest sense of the term and who have no other desire but to dedicate their lives to the service of humanity.

The Six Types of Soul Incarnations

In my first book, *The Complete Ascension Manual*, I spoke of this, however, I have received some updated and more in-depth information. The six types of souls in incarnation are:

1. Lemurian souls
2. Souls from Atlantis
3. Souls who came in through the Moon chain
4. Souls from other planets

5. Souls who have come in through the Aryan race

6. Rare and advanced souls awaiting incarnations.

This list has to do with where souls first entered the Earth school. Some souls came in or had their first incarnation during the Lemurian root race. They were at that time, Earth and feeling primarily focused. Other souls came in first during Atlantis, which was Earth, feeling, mental and psychically focused. The next group of souls came in during the Aryan root race and were more mental, causal and higher-mind focused. This was different from the mental aspect of the Atlantean root race, which was not higher mind or a cause of their reality as Aryan souls were.

I want to make it clear, one is not better than another. It is just that the further you go back, the less humanity was evolved as a whole. Souls who came in during Lemuria and Atlantis incorporate all these higher abilities as their reincarnation process into these later root races continues.

There is another group of souls which came into the Earth school by first stopping on the Moon in fourth-dimensional, or astral, form, dealing with an astral aspect of creation and also differentiation of light and dark.

Then there is another group of souls which came from other planets, possibly not even in our solar system, before coming to the Earth school. This is very common. The last type has to do with avatars and world teachers who come in at certain unique times or cycles of Earth's history.

Spiritual Artery-Connection Activation

Call forth to Melchizedek and the masters of your choice to connect your spiritual arteries to all the inner-plane ashrams and masters to which you are connected. For example, I am personally connected through Djwhal Khul's ashram, to Kuthumi's ashram, to Lord Maitreya's ashram, up through Shamballa with Sanat Kumara and Lord Buddha. From here, I am connected to the Ashtar Command, then up to the Great White Lodge on Sirius and the Lord of Sirius, to the Lord of Arcturus and the Arcturians. Then I am connected to Melchizedek's Golden Chamber, then to the Multiuniversal Chamber of Melchizedek, then back to the Source, or godhead.

This is my ascension lineage and spiritual artery system, as well as the core group's. Study the cosmic maps in my books *The Complete Ascension Manual* and *Beyond Ascension* to figure out yours. Ask with the help of the masters that your spiritual artery system be officially established and activated.

Just as you want your arteries and veins flowing in your physical or microcosmic body, you want the same thing in your macrocosmic, or God-body, which is just as real. Your macrocosmic body, or God-body, hence, will feed your spiritual body and four-body system just as your microcosmic physical body is fed by your microcosmic arteries and veins. As within, so without. As above, so below.

Soul-Braid Activation

The soul braid is a very positive thing that all lightworkers should ask to have installed and activated. It is the weaving together of your eleven other soul extensions from your oversoul, soul or higher self into your state of consciousness. This an essential step in the ascension process.

Monadic Braid

After taking your ascension initiation, then request the next step in the process—the installation and activation of the monadic-braid process. This is the cleansing and integration of your 144 soul extensions from your monad. Each initiation is another expansion of consciousness and consti-tutes a greater and larger merger, integration and cleansing.

The Issue of False Godliness

The ideal of life is that each and every one of us practice godliness, or practice the presence of God in our daily lives. One of the glamours or traps of the negative ego is the demonstration of a godliness that is contaminated by the negative ego. It could be an air of superiority. It could be a coun-selor who is full of grace and love as long as he/she is getting paid; however, as soon as the hour is over, his negative ego returns. It could be one who goes to church every Sunday and then lives a life counter to what she/he is being taught. Examples include: a person who goes to confession in the Catholic Church, but continues to repeat the same sins; a New Age person who puts on a false sense of holiness and is truly not coming from the heart and soul; a person who has completed his/her seven levels of initiation and thinks she is God's gift to humankind and has forgotten her humility.

False godliness is acting holy, but underneath this there is no sub-stance. This might manifest in a spiritual teacher who leads or channels a wonderful workshop and then goes home and abuses his/her spouse or child after he has been "holy" all day. It might be a minister who preaches fire and brimstone and then gets caught having an affair. No one is immune to such glamours. It might be a spiritual New Age teacher who is a wonderful channel or teacher and then goes around criticizing and judging all the other spiritual teachers. It might be a psychic, channel or spiritual coun-selor who is spiritual while he/she works, but when the session is over, she falls back into depression, anger and negative emotions.

This pattern, when it manifests, is seen as a performance that the spiri-tual teacher or leader is putting on, and once the performance is over, he/she goes back to the real self, which in truth is his false self. A great number of people don't even realize they are doing this. Another example might be leading a wonderful spiritual workshop and having lots of fame and recognition in the New Age community and then being rude to the bank teller or gas station attendant. Even worse is being indifferent, like they are just peons or strangers; this is false godliness.

In the ideal state of godliness, the demonstration is the same whether you are giving a workshop, doing counseling, talking with your spouse, washing dishes, meeting the grocery clerk, passing a stranger on the street or going to the bathroom. The true test of one's spirituality actually comes when you are not on stage and simply involved with the marketplace of mass consciousness. If you really want to see how you are doing, see how you deal with the stranger you walk by on the street or a stray dog, or how you treat your neighbors. The true expression of godliness is practiced all the time with the same intensity, every moment of your life, for everyone and everything is God.

The true test of your godliness is how you deal with people who attack and criticize you. Do you love your enemies as Christ said? Do you respond with love and forgiveness and innocent perception, or with victim consciousness and defensiveness, attacking back? This is a twenty-four-hour-a-day job. It is even a bigger job once you take your higher initiations, for you are now representing the Spiritual Hierarchy and operating for and influencing the collective.

At these higher levels of initiations one is affecting mass consciousness with every thought he/she thinks, with every word she speaks and with every action she takes. As children, many people were in a sense victimized by the collective consciousness. As masters, many have now reversed this process, however—hopefully doing it with true godliness. Everyone has always had this power within them, but the attainment of the higher initiations has truly allowed individuals to realize this energy and power.

Our job now is to be as pure, as loving and as refined as we can in the use of this enormous gift. Most lightworkers do not realize the enormous effect we have in holding the amount of light quotient we are speaking of in this book. To create this positive effect on the world we must maintain absolute mastery and balance within ourselves.

The Issue of Good and Bad

In all my books, which I have collectively titled *The Easy-to-Read Encyclopedia of the Spiritual Path*, I have never addressed the duality or polarity of using the terms "good" and "bad." To be honest, I wasn't sure if this terminology was a spiritual concept or a negative-ego concept. Then one day Melchizedek spoke in a channeling of the need to release this type of thinking of good and bad, light and dark.

The issue of developing the quality of spiritual discernment is essential to living effectively and spiritually on this Earth plane. A spiritual discernment is not a judgment however. It is a discernment or an observation with love. A judgment is a discernment or discrimination without love. It is obviously preferential to ascribe to a philosophy of being spiritual rather than egotistical in one's viewpoint and living. It is not, however, good to do one, and bad to do the other. This way of terming it is an interpretation of the negative ego and not the spirit.

This is how the Fundamentalist Christians frame it. You are "bad" and "sinful" and will go to hell if you don't follow the teachings of Christ. This, of course, is not true. It is not bad, it is not sinful and you will not go to hell. A person choosing the path of the negative ego is just unconscious and in glamour, maya and illusion, and is learning a lesson. In truth, he/she is still the Christ, but in her own thinking she is not. This is her right, with her free choice.

Framing things in the terms "good" and "bad" is judgmental, clear and simple. The same is true of using the terms "light" and "dark." Whatever happens in life happens for a reason, and in that sense everything that happens is perfect. A given person who acts unconsciously or out of the negative ego is coming into our sphere of awareness to teach us something. He/she is not bad but instead is our master teacher. He might be teaching us how not to be, or teaching us forgiveness, unconditional love, patience, humility, compassion, understanding, looking at things as lessons and many other similar qualities.

As the Master Jesus said on the cross, "Forgive them, Father, for they know not what they do." Words, attitudes and semantics such as these are very important, for it is our thoughts that cause our reality. As *A Course in Miracles* says, "There are no neutral thoughts." All thoughts have either an egotistical or spiritual charge.

This insight as to not framing reality with the words "good" or "bad," "light" or "dark," is also connected to what Melchizedek calls the blessing system. It is a tool and perspective of life that helps us to perceive life as the anointed Christ overself body perceives life. The idea is to bless everything that happens in your life. Sai Baba teaches this in a similar way when he says to welcome adversity. The idea is to say, "not my will but thine, and thank you for the lessons" to everything that happens. This is a chance to look at everything that happens as a spiritual test, in a sense, and as a stepping stone for soul growth. Every experience and every contact with another human being, no matter what the form, is a chance to practice the Christ consciousness rather than the egotistical consciousness. Every circumstance or word a person says to you is a teaching, lesson, challenge or opportunity to grow spiritually.

As I said before, it might be teaching you to be a master not a victim, a cause not an effect, to respond rather than react. In essence you are being given the opportunity to practice being God in all circumstances. When someone does something negative or life does not go according to your preferences, it is an opportunity to practice evenmindedness, nonattachment, inner peace and equanimity amidst the storms of life. One of the premiere qualities of God consciousness is to be able to retain your inner peace, inner calm and joy even when the outer world is in turmoil.

The negative ego will tell you to curse your brother and sister or the given situation that is not going your way. The spirit will tell you to bless the person or situation and welcome the adversity and thank them or it for the opportunity to grow and practice the presence of God. Your higher self might have actually, purposely placed this person or situation there as a spiritual test to see if you have passed that initiation.

Every person and every situation is your master teacher, even if the person or situation is negative according to your preferences. The true nature of preference is that you are happy either way. Do you see now why calling someone "bad" or "dark" is a misperception?

In truth, they are God teaching you a lesson you need to learn, and if you didn't need to learn it, this would not be happening, for there are no accidents. The lesson might be a product of your personal karma or just a product of mass karma, which we all take on when we incarnate into this school. Either way, it is there to teach and the ideal is to bless this opportunity to practice all the Christ qualities that are called for. One sure sign that you are not practicing this way of thinking is cursing and getting angry. This is a sign that you are fighting the universe instead of working with it and learning from the lesson.

As Melchizedek states, you want to learn to flow with life. There is no bad, but only opportunities for spiritual growth, which are good if you will look at them this way. You can't change what comes into your life, but you can change your attitude toward it. It is your attitude that creates your feeling and emotional response, so in this sense you have great control.

By looking at life in this positive perspective you will attract and magnetize more positive things toward you. It is okay to have a preference for things to go the way you want and to not want to deal with negative people. The key is to be happy either way and to use whatever life (God) deals you as an opportunity to practice godliness and the Christ consciousness.

This is a major shift in perception from the way the world, mass media and mass consciousness interpret reality. The key question is, what do you want? Do you want the full merger with your anointed Christ overself body? *A Course in Miracles* says, "Choose once again." Every moment of our lives on Earth we are confronted with this choice. Do we choose God, or do we choose our ego in any given situation? It all comes down to what you want and how committed and focused you are to realizing your goal. Do you want God 50%? Do you want God 75%? Do you want God 100%?

The true measure of this question is determined not by just what you say in this moment, but rather the degree of the vigilance and focus for this purpose that you are willing to demonstrate in your daily life. It only takes twenty-one days to cement a new habit into the subconscious mind. The subconscious mind is as happy to interpret life from the spirit's perspective as it is the negative ego's perspective, given that it has no reasoning.

At first this switch of perception might take some real effort, and even some battling with the negative ego. After twenty-one days it will begin to become a positive habit to think in this new way. Vigilance however will continue to need to be maintained because of the pull of mass consciousness. Most people live on automatic pilot. A true ascended master is alert, aware, conscious and focused at all times. Do you want God as much as a drowning man wants air? If you do on a continual basis, you shall find Him. Namasté.

In regard to the concept of light and dark, there is a slight variation on this theme. The concept of good and bad has no redeeming value. This is not the case with light and dark, which has some redeeming value when not applied to interpreting lessons having to do with relationships. When used in this way it sounds judgmental, and third-dimensional people might even interpret it as racist. When applied in other areas such as differentiating the Great White Brotherhood from the Lodge of the Dark Brotherhood, it is a very useful concept.

When you apply the word "dark" to a person, it has a strong negative stigma. This isn't appropriate for addressing a son or daughter of God regardless of how conscious or unconscious he/she is. Melchizedek said that what we are really dealing with here is moving from a third-dimensional consciousness to a fourth-dimensional consciousness, and then to an ascended fifth-dimensional consciousness and beyond. There could almost be a slightly different language for each level, depending on one's level of development.

The Issue of Spiritual vs. Egotistical Ambition

Recently I had an insight as to the psychological concept of ambition. Ambition is usually thought of as a negative-ego term. A person who is ambitious is thought of as power-, fame- or money-seeking in a materialistic or egotistical sense.

I have come to understand from the masters, however, that there is a spiritual type of ambition that is a very important quality to develop. Ambition seems to be very connected to desire. There is lower-self desire and higher-self desire. Spiritual ambition is connected with your personal power, motivation, spiritual goals and enthusiasm. When spiritual ambition is highly developed, one has great motivation to achieve ascension, to complete the seven levels of initiation, to serve the masters and to serve humanity. It is like a commitment to excellence, perfection and God realization.

It is good to be spiritually ambitious as long as the negative ego doesn't taint the purity of such a divine quality. I have seen many lightworkers who do not have this quality, who are very gifted in different ways, but don't take advantage of these gifts because of lack of ambition. Probably the single most important factor to achieve ascension is to have the ambition and desire to do so.

Once ascension is achieved, this transfers to ambition for greater leadership and service manifestation. On an evolutionary level it then transfers to a spiritual ambition to achieve cosmic ascension. Do you remember how excited you were when you first got turned on to metaphysics and the newer understanding of spirit and the ascended masters? The idea is to keep that same level of motivation or spiritual fire and enthusiasm flowing as you had in the beginning.

Many lightworkers are like the story of the tortoise and the hare: They start out fast and then lose their spiritual ambition. Their spiritual fire goes back down to a match stick, instead of a raging bonfire. This spiritual ambition is connected to properly integrating the spiritual-warrior archetype and the wisdom archetype and blending them together. Those who will take the leadership positions in the Spiritual Government will have developed this quality of spiritual ambition, spiritual motivation, spiritual desire and spiritual enthusiasm that never ceases. In actuality, it builds greater every day. Yogananda's famous quote seems fitting here: If you want to realize God, you must seek God "like a drowning man wants air."

Jesus said the whole law could be summed up in the words, "Love the Lord Thy God with all thy heart, and soul, and mind and might, and love thy neighbor as thyself." Every day you should cultivate this spiritual fire and divine ambition and give literally one hundred percent, never wasting a single moment or piece of energy. This type of motivation will also help in regard to overcoming temptations of the lower self. As the saying goes "an idle mind is the devil's workshop." Be filled with spiritual ambition to serve God and the masters. Become one of the spiritual leaders in your community to pave the way for the next millennium. This does not mean, however, competition with other lightworkers. This spiritual ambition must be done with a sense of complete egolessness to retain the purity of the Christ.

The Issue of Integrity and Your Word

One other little golden nugget I would like to address here is "your word." By this I mean the verbal statements you make to other people. One of the most disturbing things I see happening in the spiritual path is how people's words mean nothing. You must realize from the perspective of the masters, your word is law and your word is God.

There must be a consistency between your words and your actions. Lightworkers say they are going to call someone and they don't. They say they are going to do something and they don't. They give a time commitment and they don't meet it. They say they are going to be somewhere and they don't show up. They say they are going to be someplace at a certain time and they are late.

If a person cannot trust your word, what can they trust? In essence, you should never, and I mean never, say anything that you are not going to follow through on. This is an issue of integrity. The key lesson here is if you are not going to follow through on what you say, then just don't say it. The problem is not an issue of not doing something but of saying you are going to do something and not doing it. What if God did not keep His commitments? If you don't want to do things you don't feel like doing, then keep your mouth shut and don't make commitments.

The issue here is also one of people being run by their emotional body. They commit to something that feels right one minute but later doesn't feel right. Well, I have news for you. Feelings mean nothing in this case. If you make a commitment, you keep it, for your word is law and your word is God. Now, occasionally emergencies do come up. In those cases you call the person and tell him/her that you have to break your commitment, if it is even spiritually appropriate to do this.

Jesus summed up this principle when he said, "Do unto others that which you would have others do unto you." Every person you make a verbal commitment to is God, in truth, whether he/she realizes it or not. When I make a commitment to call or be someplace, I don't care if it is ninety years from now, I will be there at the exact time I said, even if I had no contact with the person for ninety years. Every word you speak and every thought you think is God communicating with God.

Another tremendous weak area among many lightworkers is time commitments. The people who don't keep time commitments always have a million excuses and rationalizations, but it comes down to selfishness, insensitivity, inconsiderateness. If you have a problem keeping time commitments, then just don't make time commitments, or give yourself much more leeway. If you are late, then have the consideration to call. The key words are integrity and consistency at all times between your thoughts, words and actions. This is the behavior of a true ascended master.

Twilight Masters

The term "twilight master" is one every lightworker should be aware of. A twilight master is a lightworker who is working for both the light and dark side of life. We have heard the saying, making a pact with the devil. Well, this is making a pact with the Dark Brotherhood. It is much more common than lightworkers realize, although most of the time it is happening unconsciously, as I have already stated.

The basic cause of this is the negative ego. The lightworker might be very gifted in some aspect of healing or teaching and is often very powerful. Not being clear on a personality or psychological level or in terms of the negative ego, the lightworker draws and attracts a member of the Dark Brotherhood, which overshadows him/her in a similar way that ascended masters do.

This can be clearly seen clairvoyantly, and you would be amazed at how often we see this. In my opinion, the issue of learning to control the negative ego is the single most important lesson on the spiritual path bar none. Unfortunately, it is also the single biggest area of weakness among lightworkers. Be very discerning of this phenomenon, for it usually occurs in spiritual teachers and healers who are the most dynamic, but the power has gone to their head. I am sure every single one of you who are reading this book know what I am speaking about here.

Evolution Beyond the Seven Levels of Initiation

As I have mentioned previously, the seventh initiation is the highest level of initiation that one can take while still in embodiment. What I have come to understand from Melchizedek, however, is that with all the working at anchoring the fifty chakras, and potentially two hundred chakras, anchoring and activating the twelve bodies, the potential for building the cosmic light quotient even beyond the 99% planetary light quotient, using all the other ascension techniques, soul and spirit travel techniques—one can evolve far beyond this level.

As I said previously, it is like being in high school but taking college, master's degree and even Ph.D. courses at times. One remains in high school (seven levels of initiation); however, enormous growth continues to be made. In one meditation with the core group and myself, we were joking around and commenting about how we only had nine cosmic ascensions and 345 initiations in this universe to go to truly return to Source. The point is, we have barely even made a dent in achieving what true God realization really is.

Then Melchizedek said something surprising. He told us that even though, indeed, we were only at the seventh initiation, with the anchoring and activation work we were doing and with spiritual exploration and work with him, the Arcturians, Metatron, Lord Maitreya and Djwhal Khul, in truth our level of evolvement was three or four times higher than this. More accurately, we would be at the twenty-first to twenty-eighth level.

This, of course, was very encouraging, and I share this not for ego purposes, but rather to point out to the great many lightworkers who either are or will soon take these higher initiations that there is a world of opportunity for spiritual growth. It doesn't stop just because you are not allowed to take the eighth initiation until you pass on to the spirit world. In this sense I feel like the process of working on initiations in a less sequential and more multidimensional manner has begun.

One other interesting point on the initiation process: I always thought that it was totally up to Sanat Kumara (now Buddha) and Lord Maitreya to decide when a person was ready to pass a given initiation. Basically this is still true, for they do have the final say. What I have come to understand, through my conversations with Djwhal Khul, is that the chohans of the seven rays and Djwhal Khul, as head of the synthesis ashram and given full authority by Kuthumi, have much more control over the passing of initiations than I realized.

Each of the chohans, El Morya, Kuthumi, Serapis Bey, Paul the Venetian, Hilarion, Sananda and Saint Germain, as well as Djwhal Khul, keep detailed profiles and charts of the disciples under their care. They have the most fantastic holographic-type computers that give detailed analysis of just about every aspect of disciples' and initiates' growth. They can see brainwaves, really just about everything. It is these ray masters who send reports to Lord Maitreya and Sanat Kumara (now to the Buddha) as to when they think any given disciple is ready to take another initiation.

I asked Djwhal Khul if Lord Maitreya, Sanat Kumara or Buddha ever turned down his recommendation for a disciple to take another initiation. He said just about one hundred percent of the time when the ray masters make a recommendation, it is put into effect and the disciple or initiate receives the rod of initiation, which is the official ceremony of taking the next step. All the disciples and initiates on Earth are in one of these seven ashrams of the Christ. The ray masters have much more power and control of this process than I previously realized. (I share this because I think that lightworkers would appreciate having this information.)

If you want to pass your initiations, then have a chat with the master who is in charge of the ashram to which you belong. This will have to do with the ray of your monad and soul. All of us, of course, work freely in all the seven ashrams. They are not separate, for they are really all one ashram of the Lord Maitreya. If you don't know what ashram you are connected with, give me a call to find out resources for scheduling a ray reading, which will provide this information.

The Emerald Tablets

In my continuing research I came across the exact translation of the famous Emerald Tablets of Thoth/Hermes, the great Egyptian master, a former incarnation of the Buddha. As the legend goes, the Emerald Tablets were originally carved by Thoth/Hermes on tablets of emerald and placed in the King's Chamber of the Great Pyramid of Cheops in Egypt. This has been known throughout history as one of the keys to the primary mysteries of God and nature.:

> Truly and without deceit, certainly and absolutely: That which is below corresponds to that which is above, and that which is above corresponds to that which is below. In the accomplishment of the miracle of one thing, and just as all things have come from One, through the mediation of One, so all things follow from this One thing in the same way.
>
> Its Father is the sun; its Mother, the moon. The wind has carried it in his belly. Its nourishment is the Earth. It is the father of every completed thing in the whole world. The strength is intact if it is turned toward the Earth. Separate the Earth by fire: the fine from the gross, gently and with great skill. It rises from Earth to Heaven, and then it descends again to the Earth, and receives power from above and from below. Thus you have the glory of the whole world. All obscurity will be clear to you. This is the strong Power of all power, because it overcomes everything fine and penetrates everything solid.
>
> In this way was the world created. From this there will be amazing applications, because this is the pattern. Therefore am I called thrice greatest Hermes, having the three parts of the Wisdom of the whole world. Herein have I completely explained the operation of the sun [excerpted from *The Kyballion*].

It is truly by the application of this great law, "as above, so below; as within, so without" that cosmic ascension may be understood.

11

Past Lives of Some of the Well-known Ascended Masters

Djwhal Khul
- Confucius
- One of the Three Wise Men (Caspar)
- Kleineas (assistant to Pythagoras)

Jesus
- Amilius
- Adam
- Melchizedek (not Universal Logos, Melchizedek, but another)
- Enoch
- Zend
- Ur
- Asapha
- Jeshua
- Joseph
- Joshua
- Apollonius of Tyanna
- Incarnation in a Syrian body in this century

Godfre Ray King (author of *The "I AM" Discourses*)
- George Washington

John Kennedy
- Abraham Lincoln

Sai Baba
- Shirdi Sai Baba
- Kabir

El Morya
- Abraham (father of Jewish race)
- One of the Three Wise Men (Balthazar)

Kuthumi
- Pythagoras
- Saint Francis
- Architect of the Taj Mahal
- John the Beloved (disciple of Christ)
- John of Penial (incarnated now)
- One of the Three Wise Men (Melchior)

Buddha
- Orpheus (father of Greek mystery schools)
- Arjuna (disciple of Krishna in Bhagavad Gita)
- Thoth/Hermes (Egyptian mystery schools)
- Vyassa (scribe for Bhagavad Gita)
- Zoraster (Persian avatar)

Lord Maitreya
- Bhagavan Krishna

Saint Germain
- Joseph (foster father of Jesus)
- Christopher Columbus
- Prophet Samuel (Jewish religion)
- Francis Bacon (William Shakespeare)
- Merlin
- Prince Racgozi

Mohammed
- Bartholomew (disciple of Jesus)
- Patrick Henry

12

The Twelve Planetary Festivals

The ascended masters and Spiritual Hierarchy under the direction of Sanat Kumara, Lord Buddha, Lord Maitreya and the chohans of the seven rays celebrate twelve festivals each year, all occurring on the full moon. The full moon functions like a window or magnifying glass for the intensification and downpouring of planetary and cosmic energies to disciples and initiates and to the Earth. Of these twelve festivals there are nine lesser festivals and three major festivals. The three major festivals form the high-water mark of the year.

The following information in this chapter is based on the writings of Alice Bailey, in particular her two compilation books, *Ponder on This* and *Serving Humanity*. The three major festivals are: (1) the Festival of the Christ (at the Aries full moon); (2) the Festival of Wesak (the full moon in Taurus, which is usually in May); (3) the Festival of Humanity or Good Will (full moon in Gemini).

The nine lesser festivals and full moons function to build the divine attributes into human consciousness. The three major festivals function to establish the divine aspects. The divine aspects have to do with the qualities of the first three rays: power, love-wisdom and active intelligence. The divine attributes are the qualities of rays four through seven: harmony, concrete science, devotion, ceremonial order and magic.

These twelve festivals are ideally used as a means of service through meditation to receive the higher transmissions of energies that I mentioned earlier. In the future when the externalization process of the Spiritual Hierarchy is complete, all of humanity will celebrate these universal festivals regardless of religion or spiritual path.

The Festival of the Christ (Easter)

This is the Festival of the Living and Risen Christ. In truth, this is not referring to the Master Jesus, but rather to the Lord Maitreya, who over-lighted Jesus and shared his body the last three years of his life.

Lord Maitreya is the Planetary Christ, head of the entire Spiritual Hier-archy, teacher to all the ascended masters and is currently physically incar-nated on this planet, living in London. He is a galactic avatar. This festival celebrates the life of Jesus and the resurrection example that the Master Je-sus and Lord Maitreya set then and have built upon during the past 2000 years. Lord Maitreya is the perfect embodiment of the love expression of God. This is the great Western and Christian festival that honors the recog-nition of his embodiment on Earth now as head of the externalization pro-cess.

The forces of restoration are particularly active at the time of the Festi-val of the Christ. These restorative forces emanate from the mind of God and are connected with the principle of active intelligence. This energy stimulates the birth of form and stimulates mass intelligence. It makes peo-ple think, plan and take action along spiritual lines. On a planetary level this time of energy will eventually lead to a reorganization of planetary life. The effects are primarily physical, with the object of creating heaven on Earth.

The keynote of the festival is *love,* in the highest sense of the meaning of this term. The second keynote is resurrection. The third keynote is con-tact. This refers to a closer relationship with Lord Maitreya and his disci-ples and initiates and between the Spiritual Hierarchy and humanity. This festival lasts for three days and prepares the way for the Wesak Festival. At this time Lord Maitreya sounds forth the great invocation, first alone and then with the united Spiritual Hierarchy.

The Festival of Wesak

The Festival of Wesak is the most important of the three major festi-vals. It is the time of the year at the full moon in May when humanity re-ceives the highest level of transmission of light frequency. The Wesak Fes-tival is the Festival of the Buddha. The Buddha is the perfect expression of the wisdom aspect of God. He is the embodiment of light and divine pur-pose.

The festival is the great Eastern festival and serves to show the solidar-ity of East and West. The term "Wesak" refers to the Wesak Valley in the Himalayas, where every year all the ascended masters gather both on the inner and outer planes to share in a very sacred ceremony. At the precise rising of the full moon in May, the Manu Allah Gobi, Lord Maitreya, the bodhisattva and Saint Germain, the Mahachohan, stand in a triangular formation around a bowl of water that sits on a crystal. Buddha appears and hovers above this bowl of water and transmits cosmic energies into the water and through Lord Maitreya, then to be disseminated to the Spiritual Hierarchy and the initiates, disciples and new group of world servers.

At the end of the ceremony the water is shared by all those in attendance. Wesak is also the time when all initiations are given to the disciples and initiates on Earth by Lord Maitreya, Lord Buddha and more recently also by Melchizedek, the Universal Logos.

The Wesak is a time of great renewal and celebration. At Wesak the quality of energy that is prevalent is the force of enlightenment. This force-of-enlightenment energy emanates from the heart of God. It is related to divine understanding and the love-wisdom aspect of God. This force on a planetary level initiates the new world education.

This affects the educational movements, values, literature, publishing, television, radio, newspaper, magazines, writers, channels, speakers across the board. This force of enlightenment that is so prevalent at Wesak is why the coming together of large groups at this time can be such an awesome experience. Wesak is the pinnacle each year where the greatest window for mass enlightenment can occur on a planetary level.

During the ceremony Buddha sounds forth a great mantra and becomes an absorbing agent of the first-ray force. Buddha then uses the magnetic power of the second ray to attract this force to himself and holds it steady prior to then redirecting it to the Lord Maitreya, who is the receiving agent of this energy. This energy is then disseminated to the seven chohans and their ashrams for a sevenfold expression and direction into the world.

All the disciples and initiates on Earth are invited to come to the Wesak Valley and attend this sacred ceremony and join in the festivities. This is also a time to come and stand before Lord Maitreya, Lord Buddha and Sanat Kumara to give your vows of service and to receive special blessings.

If you can't make it to the Wesak celebration in Mount Shasta, mentioned previously, then I would recommend gathering with your lightworker friends wherever you are and traveling in one of the ascended master's group merkabahs to the Wesak Valley right at the time of the full moon. Go before the masters as I suggested and then explore the Wesak Valley and/or just enjoy the energies. I might suggest after returning home that as a group you do the meditation in the last chapter of *The Complete Ascension Manual*. This will really pull in the energies.

It is important to note that this is also an actual physical event. At the hour of the full moon a stillness settles upon the crowd and all look toward the Northeast. Certain ritualistic movements take place under the guidance of the different masters and their ashrams. Certain chanted words and esoteric phrases are also sounded forth at this time.

The expectancy and excitement begins to build as all wait on the inner and outer plane for Buddha's arrival. A few moments before the exact time of the full moon, in the far distance, a tiny speck can be seen in the sky. This tiny speck gradually grows larger and the form of the Buddha seated in a cross-legged position appears. He is clad in a saffron-colored robe and bathed in light and color, with his hands extended in blessing.

While hovering above the bowl of water, crystal and rock, a great mantra is sounded that is only used once a year at Wesak. This mantra is sounded by the Lord Maitreya. The entire group of people in the valley fall upon their faces. This invocation sets up an enormous vibration of spiritual current. It marks the supreme moment of intensive spiritual effort of the entire year. It releases a massive downpouring of cosmic energies from the cosmic hierarchy.

Buddha then slowly recedes into the distance from whence he came. The entire ceremony takes only eight minutes; however, its effects last an entire year. This is Buddha's annual sacrifice for humanity. This is changing in recent times because the Buddha has now taken a much more active involvement in Earth's evolution, after spending a great deal of time in the Great White Brotherhood Lodge on Sirius.

The Wesak Festival has been regarded by the knowers of the world as of paramount importance in world affairs. Through the two representatives of deity upon our planet, the world of spiritual realities and human affairs are being brought closer and closer together. I also want to mention here that though the Wesak Festival usually falls on the full moon in May, on rare occasions it does fall on the full moon in April, so it is important to check this out each year. This can occur because the actual timing is the full moon in Taurus. Wesak is a living event based on current astrological cycles, not past events that occurred centuries ago, as most religions celebrate.

Many people have dreamed of this event, but have not known of its spiritual significance and where or why they were doing what they were doing in the dream. It is at Wesak that a type of channel is opened for humanity that allows disciples and initiates to contact certain energies that are not normally available or as easily accessible. This allows great expansions of consciousness to take place.

In Alice Bailey's *The Externalisation* [sic] *of the Hierarchy*, Djwhal Khul stated that, "it is the intention of the Buddha and the Christ that in each country there shall eventually be someone who will act as their representative of the time of the two festivals, so that the distribution of spiritual energy from the first great aspect or ray will be directed from the Buddha to the Christ and then from the Christ to those initiates in every country who can be overshadowed and so act as channels for the direct current of energy." This is referencing the Festival of the Christ and the Wesak Festival.

Djwhal Khul, in the Alice Bailey book *Ponder on This*, also said about the Wesak, "No cost is too great to pay in order to be of use to the Spiritual Hierarchy at the time of the full moon of May, the Wesak Festival. No price is too high in order to gain the spiritual illumination which can be possible, particularly at that time."

The Wesak has four basic functions:
1. To substantiate the fact of Christ's physical appearance on Earth;
2. To physically prove the solidarity of the Eastern and Western approaches to God;
3. To form a rallying point and meeting place for those who annually in synthesis and symbolically link up and represent the Father's house, the kingdom of God and humanity;
4. To demonstrate the nature of the work of the Christ as the great and chosen intermediary and leader of the Spiritual Hierarchy and disciples and initiates on Earth.

In his person he voices the recognition of the factual existence of the kingdom of God, here and now (Alice Bailey, *Ponder on This*, pp. 422-423).

The purpose of the Wesak Festival is as follows:
1. The releasing of certain transmissions of energy to humanity, which will stimulate the spirit of love, brotherhood and good will.
2. The fusion of all men and women of good will into a responsive, integrated whole.
3. The invocation and response from certain cosmic beings if prior goals are achieved.

I would like to end this section with one final quote from Djwhal Khul on the Wesak from a passage in Alice Bailey's, *The Rays and the Initiations*, Book II: "If you have faith as a grain of mustard seed in what I have told you. If you have a staunch belief in the work of the Spirit of God and in the Divinity of Man, then forget yourselves and consecrate your every effort, from the time you receive this communication, to the task of cooperation in the organized effort to change the current of personal and world affairs by an increase in the Spirit of Love and Goodwill in the world during the month of May."

Through the Buddha, the wisdom of god is poured forth. Through the Christ Maitreya, the love of God is made manifest to humanity. This festival links the work of the Buddha and the Lord Maitreya in symbolic and literal form. This is a time of enormous blessings being poured forth to the disciples, initiates, new group of world servers and humanity on Earth. As the masters, initiates and disciples leave the ceremony, they are filled with a sense of renewed strength to undertake another year of world-service work.

The Wesak Festival is the single greatest event upon our planet from the perspective of the ascended masters and the one that has the greatest effect upon the human race. It is also at this time period that the Lodge of Masters meet on the inner plane for the following three reasons as outlined by Djwhal Khul in the Alice Bailey books: "To contact spiritual force, which is transmitted to our planet through the medium of the Buddha and the Christ; to confer together as to the immediate necessity and the work to be done for humanity; to admit to initiation those who are ready and to stimulate their disciples to increased activity and service."

Can you imagine the effects on this planet when all of humanity is celebrating the Wesak Festival consciously? In recent times a call has been sent out by the entire Spiritual Hierarchy of ascended masters to all initiates, disciples and new group of world servers to prepare themselves each full moon of May for an intensive holy month of accelerated service. This intensive effort is to increase the receptivity of humanity to the new spiritual forces that are released at this time.

The actual Wesak focus has recently been extended to cover five days for work and service: the two days prior to the full moon, the day of the festival itself and the two days after the actual Wesak ceremony. The two days of preparation are called the Days of Renunciation and Detachment, the day of the festival is called the Day of Safeguarding and the two succeeding days are called the Days of Distribution.

This demands five days of the most intensive service. This is why the masters have guided us to hold our celebration for Wesak at Mount Shasta for three days and one day each side for traveling, which prepares and then integrates the collective-group experience.

In our ceremony we will travel as a group in Lord Maitreya and Lord Buddha's merkabah to the Wesak Valley and participate as I described in the section above. We as a group will receive blessings from these great masters. In the auditorium we will have the bowl of water that will be blessed in synchrony with the actual ceremony and from which people can drink and receive blessings.

This is not the first time that these great masters, Lord Maitreya and Lord Buddha, have joined together such as this. It should be remembered by those who have studied Eastern religion that Lord Maitreya was the great avatar Lord Krishna in a past life and Buddha was at that time his disciple Arjuna. Their work together continues now in a much more cosmic and expanded form.

The Festival of Humanity and Good Will

The Festival of the Spirit of Humanity aspires toward divinity, attunement to God's will and right human relationships. It occurs each year at the full moon in June. It is a day to recognize and honor the divine nature of humanity and aspire toward spiritual fellowship. This festival represents the effects in human consciousness of the work of Gautama Buddha, Lord Maitreya and the Master Jesus. This festival has also been recognized as World Invocation Day.

The force that is prevalent at this festival is the force of reconstruction. This is the force of the first ray, or will aspect of divinity, that is directly connected with Shamballa. This force is mainly effective between nations of the Earth. Its effect on any given nation is governed by the level of evolution of any particular nation. The two extremes are egocentric nations versus nations focused on world unity. The United Nations is one manifestation of this force in its more positive aspect. The three forces of restoration, enlightenment and reconstruction express the light, love and knowledge of God. The synthesis of these forces and the effects of these festivals consciously celebrated by humanity will produce the following results, as outlined by Alice Bailey in *Serving Humanity*:

1. Power will be given to the disciples and initiates so that they can direct efficiently and wisely the process of rebuilding.
2. The Will to Love will stimulate men of goodwill everywhere, gradually overcoming hatred. The inner urge in men and women to live together cooperatively already exists and is subject to stimulation.
3. The Will to Action will lead intelligent people throughout the world to inaugurate those activities which will lay the foundation for a new, better and happier world.
4. The Will to Cooperate will steadily increase. Men and women will desire and demand right human relationships as a natural way of life.
5. The Will to Know and to Think Correctly and Creatively will become an outstanding characteristic of the masses. Knowledge is the first step toward wisdom.
6. The Will to Persist will become a human characteristic, a sublimation of the basic instinct of self-preservation and self-centeredness. This will lead to a persistent belief in the ideals presented by the Spiritual Hierarchy and the demonstration of immortality.
7. The Will to Organize will further a building process which will be carried forward under the direct inspiration of the Spiritual Hierarchy. The medium will be the potency of the Will to Good of the New Group of World Servers and the responsive goodwill of mankind.

Summation

In the way the world is now organized, all the world's religions celebrate their festivals at different times. The Christian religion has certain holidays; the Hindu religion has certain holidays. Buddhists and Moslems and those of the Jewish faith each have yet another set of holidays.

In the future the disciples and initiates on Earth will all celebrate the same high holy days. One can clearly see that our current arrangement is a manifestation of negative ego and separation. It would be the same as the nations of the world all doing their own thing and not working together for the good of the planet. The celebrating of the same spiritual holidays will bring about a pooling of resources, united spiritual effort and much more powerful spiritual invocation.

The celebration of these three major festivals will create a unified spiritual approach that honors both Eastern and Western traditions. This will lead to a much greater spiritual unity on the planet. The remaining full moons will constitute lesser festivals, but will still be recognized as being of vital importance. This unified and more astrological approach will have a broad-based appeal to all religions of the world.

It must be recognized that on the inner plane the ascended masters all believe in a more universalistic approach. We, on Earth, are meant to do the same thing. The twelve annual festivals, in concordance with the study of astrology as to their meaning, will provide a complete revelation of divinity to humanity. This will also connect humanity to the understanding of the seven great rays, which underlay even the science of astrology. This approach will also connect humanity to the workings of the Spiritual Hierarchy and ascended masters, leading to the new world religion made manifest on Earth.

13

Comparative Overview of Eastern and Western Stages of Initiation and Meditation

The main theme of most of my books has been dealing with the seven levels of initiation and how to achieve ascension. I thought it would be interesting for my readers to approach this process from the Eastern tradition using the theoretical framework of the stages of *samadhi*.

In the Eastern tradition there are nine stages of samadhi, which are included in the fifteen leading to illumination. These fifteen stages, starting from the lowest to the highest are:

1. Wakefulness (becoming aware)
2. Sense withdrawal (turning inward)
3. Concentration (one thing focused)
4. Meditation (effortlessness)
5. Mind enstasis (beholding the void)
6. Sa-vitarka (gross ideas)
7. Nir-vitarka (gross and no ideas)
8. Sa-vichara (subtle ideas)
9. Nir-vichara (subtle and no ideas)
10. Ananda (bliss)
11. Asmita (aware of self)
12. Purusha khyati (atma and the world)
13. Asam-prajnata (relinquishment)
14. Dharma-megha (involution)

15. Kaivalya (touching ultimate reality)

The first five are the grosser stages. Numbers six through fifteen are considered the actual nine stages of samadhi.

Step One: Waking Consciousness

In this stage you experience Earth life. The struggle within this stage makes one aware that he/she is alive. This struggle makes one seek self-awareness and self-realization.

Step Two: Sense Withdrawal

This is the second step needed to achieve liberation in the Eastern tradition. This stage begins with the understanding that one cannot change the outside world, but can only change one's attitude and consciousness toward the outer world to maintain inner peace. This stage marks the movement inward toward becoming inwardly centered, rather than outwardly centered.

Step Three: Concentration

This next step in the process of self-mastery and liberation begins the process of focusing upon an object or ideal, which allows one to eliminate the rest of his/her mental universe that is not carrying her toward her ultimate spiritual goal.

Step Four: Meditation

In this stage the ultimate goal is to be able to hold onto the ideal or object of meditation effortlessly. One begins to let go of this object, with the ideal being to be able to hold onto it with less and less effort. The object begins to dissolve into your consciousness and then your consciousness into the object. The object could be a spiritual ideal, such as love, or the vision of a master, such as Krishna, Rama or Sai Baba. The person meditating, the object of meditation and the act of meditation become one and the same.

Step Five: Enstasis

In this stage you completely let go of or drop the object or ideal in your mind. There is now nothing except the mind in its pure unformed or voidless state. This is a state of superconsciousness. It is a state of pure consciousness without form. The mind perceives itself as the unformed and is the all-forming substance. The self beholds the self. This is the first stage of samadhi. Samadhi is then further divided into nine major stages, each of which is a progressive step toward God realization.

The Nine Stages of Samadhi

Stage one of samadhi. This stage of samadhi relates to a focus directed toward a *gross object* as its basis. This is the most basic form of samadhi and relates to certain ideations, but no thought. There is also a certain type of superconscious deliberation that is involved. There is a perception of the object as it was, as it is and as it will be.

Stage two of samadhi. In this stage one's focus is directed toward a gross object, but does not have the superconscious deliberation of the previous stage. The perception of the object of your meditation is *without ideation of any kind.* In this stage there is often a mixture of astral and causal sounds, lights and knowledge contained therein.

Stage three of samadhi. In this stage there is a focus upon *subtle ideas.* This is different from the previous two stages, which focused on gross ideas or no ideas. There is a differentiation here in Eastern religion upon ideas and thoughts, being of a grosser nature.

Stage four of samadhi. In this stage there is an even deeper movement to subtle ideas and no ideas. The mixture of sounds, lights and knowledge found in the previous two stages moves toward *transcendent knowledge.* Do you see that at each stage there is a gradual deepening from gross ideas, to subtle ideas, to no ideas? Each detachment takes one deeper to a more core level. This stage of samadhi is clear and truth-bearing.

Stage five of samadhi. This is the stage of samadhi focused upon *ananda,* or bliss. It is the withdrawal of all objective realities. *Atma,* or the self, cannot be found within form. Bliss arises as the supramental activities have been quieted. There is a stage, however, even beyond bliss. The metaphor often used here is that you can obtain the golden egg or the goose or gander that lays the golden egg, which is the "reality principle" behind the golden egg.

Stage six of samadhi. In this stage of samadhi there is a focus upon the awareness of the atma, or the self. In this stage of samadhi one is on the outer fringes of God consciousness. This stage is the last of the stages of samadhi, known as the *extroverted focus* with supramental cognition of matter. These last six stages of samadhi are called *sam-prajnata samadhi,* which means "transcendental knowledge."

Stage seven of samadhi. This stage of samadhi is total, complete, uninterrupted discerning vision between the universe and the atma (self). This stage, as well as the eighth and ninth stages to come, transcends supramental knowledge. This seventh stage of samadhi has also been called *viveka-khyati, vivekaja-jana* and *taraka-jnana.*

Stage eight of samadhi. This next stage of samadhi is focused upon and obtained by complete renunciation of all worldly objects. This state is devoid of any conscious impressions with only subconscious impressions. In Eastern religions these subconscious impressions are called *samskaras*. These samskaras, which are like one's mental karma, are burned up by remaining in this eighth stage of samadhi.

This stage reminds me of the fourth initiation in the ascended-master teachings, which also is focused upon renunciation. This is different in that these stages of samadhi are really stages of meditation realization. In Eastern religion these samskaras, or karmic thoughts, are also called "seed karmas." These seed karmas are what lead to future experiences and future rebirths. Classically there are considered to be two types of samadhi: *samprajna*, meaning "samadhi with a seed"; the second, *isasam-prajnam*, meaning "samadhi without a seed."

This eighth stage of samadhi is a samadhi without a seed. By remaining in this state all seed karmas are cremated or burned up. It is a state of consciousness beyond the ocean of this universe and thus all detachment from all seeds. Few souls ever attain this state. Again, I repeat, these are stages or depths of meditation and not initiations per se.

Stage nine of samadhi. This ninth stage is a focus producing an involution of the primary energies or qualities called *gunas* (*tamas, rajas, sattva*) [see *Hidden Mysteries* chapter on the Bhagavad Gita]. The ideal in Eastern religion is to be more sattvic than tamasic or rajasic. Being sattvic is being more Christlike in terms of the psychological qualities one emanates from his/her being. This stage of samadhi, according to Eastern religion, instantly leads to liberation from the wheel of rebirth. The fruits of karma and causes of bondage and limitation are dissolved. The self (atma/purusha) shines forth in supreme splendor. These nine stages, in truth, each have seven sublevels in a similar way that each of the seven levels of initiation have seven sublevels.

Stage ten of samadhi (final stage). God consciousness is achieved when the yogi attains *kaivalya* (emancipation). The previous nine stages were subtle techniques and stages. This is the ultimate experience. It is sustained God consciousness. This stage of awareness has been likened in Eastern religion to amorphous clay, or clay that has no real form. If water is added to this clay it can be made into an infinite number of material forms. This is the place where humanity gets lost, for it identifies with form instead of the formless. In approaching God consciousness, one is no longer concerned with form, but the essence that lives beneath the form. All form is made up of amorphous clay.

Sai Baba has demonstrated this ability to materialize instantly any object he wants out of this amorphous clay. This is our job to do with ourselves, to collapse all the forms we have created in all our past lives and this one, and to reshape them only into the Christ forms and learn to unceasingly sustain this. This is the consciousness of learning to live unceasingly in the reality of the eternal self.

School is then complete and one is ready to graduate and enter the next level of God's cosmic schoolhouse. Samadhi is the technique to become illumined so that one can attain kaivalya (God consciousness). If Samadhi is attained even for a second, it greatly improves and transforms one's existence. Experiences of samadhi reveal that ultimate God consciousness can be obtained. Samadhi is like little experiences of God consciousness, with the ultimate goal being living God consciousness at all times.

There are also stages of God consciousness. Full God consciousness cannot be realized in this earthly school. This would be the realization of cosmic ascension. It is possible to have a revelation of God, but not fully sustained God consciousness, for this would burn up the physical and etheric bodies instantly because it is such a high vibration.

The levels of God consciousness are: planetary, solar, galactic, universal, multiuniversal and cosmic ascension. This is the system that Melchizedek has guided us to use. Each of these are levels of God realization. Sai Baba has attained on this planet a universal level of God realization and is therefore an excellent example to use in this discussion. He is rather unique, however, for he is a true avatar. The true definition of an "avatar" is a person who is totally God realized at birth. Sai Baba is not part of the karmic wheel of this planet. He has come back for a special triple-avatar-service mission and nothing more. The incarnation of an avatar is a very unique and special circumstance, and there are only a handful on the entire planet, such as Lord Maitreya.

The highest level of God realization all others can ever attain on this planet is planetary and solar ascension, with a very beginning stage of galactic realization. One can anchor and activate the universal level on this planet, as I have already stated; however, this does not make a universal master. Full installation, activation and actualization of the universal chakras and universal body is at most only five-percent realization of that level in its full understanding and breadth of meaning.

So just as there are stages of samadhi, there are stages of God realization. God realization, or *daivalya*, as spoken of in Kriya yoga or the Eastern religion, is full realization of one's planetary ascension. There could be another book written entirely about the process of "cosmic samadhi," which I am actually attempting to do here in Western terminology.

The Eastern schools have been quicker to develop the advanced ascended-master abilities. As this chapter indicates, they are much more focused and trained in the science of meditation. The Western schools often offer more training in some of the other aspects. The ideal would be a greater blending of Eastern and Western traditions, which are so very rich and which I am attempting to do in my entire series of books.

Other Ideas on Samadhi

In his book *Autobiography of a Yogi*, Paramahansa Yogananda says that "samadhi is attained when the meditation, the process of meditation and the object of meditation, become one." In the initial states of God communion (*sabikalpa samadhi*), the devotee's consciousness merges in the cosmic spirit. His life force is withdrawn from the body, which appears dead or motionless and rigid. The yogi is fully aware of his bodily condition of suspended animation.

As he/she progresses to higher states (*nirbikalpa samadhi*), the yogi communes with God without bodily fixation and is in his ordinary waking consciousness, even in the midst of exacting world duties. Both states are characterized by oneness with the ever-new bliss of spirit, but the nirbikalpa state is experienced only by the most advanced masters. In nirbikalpa samadhi, the yogi dissolves the last vestiges of material or earthly karma. Nevertheless one might still have certain astral and causal karma to work out and therefore take astral and causal embodiments on high vibrational spheres.

In sabikalpa samadhi the body is in a breathless and motionless trance. In nirbikalpa samadhi one is irrevocably established in the Lord, whether one is breathless, breathing, motionless or active.

In Marshall Govindan's book *Babaji and the 18 Siddha Kriya Yoga Tradition*, he talks about Babaji entering a state of *soruba samadhi*, "wherein the divinity descended, merged with and transformed the spiritual, intellectual, mental, vital and physical bodies. The physical body ceased to age and sparkled with a golden lustre of divine incorruptibility." This soruba samadhi would then be likened to the advanced realization of the seventh initiation.

Swami Kriyananda in his book *The Path* (p. 427), also speaks of sabikalpa samadhi. He says, "In this state the body is immobile and one is in a trance state in God absorption." But it is a qualified absorption, a condition that is still subject to change. By repeated absorption in this trance state the ego's hold is gradually broken, until realization of what Yogananda called nirbikalpa samadhi, or unqualified absorption, is achieved. It is a condition or state of total realization of oneness with Spirit.

So even when one comes out of the trance state in nirbikalpa samadhi, it is no longer with the thought of separate existence from the ocean of spirit. This state is also called *sahaja samadhi*, or "effortless samadhi." Kriyananda said divine freedom comes only with the attainment of nirbikalpa samadhi. When this is achieved one becomes what is called a *jivan mukti*, or "soul liberated"—free even though living in a physical form.

This would be likened to passing the seventh initiation in the Western tradition, for one isn't freed from the wheel of rebirth until one achieves at least the beginning stage of the seventh initiation.

This ideal in Eastern tradition of nirbikalpa samadhi, or unqualified absorption in spirit, whether meditating, serving or living life, is a noble ideal all should strive for. It is easy to be spiritual while meditating. The real test is whether you can stay locked into this state of consciousness while living in the marketplace. This state of nirbikalpa can be achieved both through psychological means and spiritual means, and ideally, both. Eastern tradition stresses meditation; the West stresses more psycho-spiritual tools and methods. Both, in truth, are essential.

So we have here another system of understanding samadhi from Yogananda, Kriyananda and Babaji: stage one, sabikalpa samadhi; stage two, nirbikalpa samadhi; stage three, soruba samadhi.

The more one practices sabikalpa samadhi, the sooner nirbikalpa samadhi can be attained, which leads to the completion of one's seventh initiation, ascension and liberation from the wheel of rebirth. The consistent practice of nirbikalpa samadhi leads to soruba samadhi, which is the full realization of the seventh initiation and the development of the advanced ascended-master abilities and physical immortality.

Sabikalpa samadhi can and usually is practiced between the third to the fifth or sixth initiations. Nirbikalpa samadhi is fully realized at the seventh initiation. Soruba samadhi is realized at the full completion of the seventh initiation and/or the realization of one's planetary ascension in terms of installation, activation and actualization of the seven levels of initiation, fifty to two hundred chakras and twelve bodies, including the solar, galactic and universal.

These stages of Samadhi have a most definite relationship to initiations; however, they are not exactly the same thing. Soruba samadhi, for example, could occur within a range of higher chakra, higher bodies and dimensional anchorings. The attainment of this state of meditation has a most definite correlation with one's readiness to take initiations.

Again, it is your own mighty I Am Presence and the seven chohans of the seven rays, along with Lord Maitreya, Sanat Kumara, Lord Buddha and Lord Melchizedek, who decide when disciples and initiates are ready to take initiations. There is often a great discrepancy of abilities and gifts among those taking the same initiation. This is how it should be, for each person has a different purpose and puzzlepiece to play in God's divine plan.

Summation

This subject of the stages of samadhi has always been a subject of great interest to me. Eastern religion doesn't really focus on initiations in the same way that the Western mystery schools do. These stages are the closest counterpart to the Western tradition. I hope this comparative overview of the Eastern and Western traditions of initiation and meditative self-realization has been helpful.

I would like to acknowledge Julie Ray Kuever for her help in researching this chapter. Finding clear and concise information on the stages of samadhi is like looking for a needle in a haystack, which is why I am very happy to have written this chapter and attempted to bridge Eastern and Western traditions. For those interested in more information on the stages of samadhi, I would recommend reading Goswami Kriyananda's book, *The Spiritual Science of Kriya Yoga*. The essence of the first part of this chapter on the fifteen steps to enlightenment were synthesized from a chapter in his book. It is my hope and prayer that the Eastern and Western traditions may become even more integrated and blended in the future, forming a most divine spiritual marriage.

14

Planetary and Cosmic Discipleship

The following information in this chapter was synthesized from Djwhal Khul's teachings through Alice Bailey in her wonderful books, *Discipleship in the New Age*, Volumes I and II. For a more in-depth understanding of this subject, I highly recommend reading these books. The world owes Alice Bailey a great debt for the tremendous service she has rendered in disseminating this information.

Djwhal Khul, in his book *Discipleship in the New Age* through Alice Bailey, delineated six stages of discipleship. These six stages are esoterically called:

1. Little chelaship (the word *chela* means "student")
2. Chela in the light
3. Accepted disciple
4. Chela on the thread
5. One within the aura
6. One within his master's heart

The rest of this chapter will deal with coming to an understanding of these six stages of discipleship on the spiritual path.

Little Chelaship

This beginning stage is where a master contacts an up-and-coming disciple through a more advanced chela (student on the physical plane). The disciple is noticed by the master when light begins to flash out of the disciple's aura on certain occasions. This is a sign that the disciple is beginning to make soul contact.

In this stage the disciple begins to shoulder some of the burden of the group karma. When this begins to happen the soul or higher self comes out of its meditation and begins to "gaze downward at the soul extension in incarnation." The master, usually on the same ray as the soul, notices the downward-gazing soul, which serves to make the master interested in a newfound disciple.

The disciple is beginning to build his antakarana to his soul and spiritual habits are being stabilized. These activities also draw the attention of the master. The disciple's endeavors at this point, although admirable, are still weak from the soul's perspective. The personality still has a strong grip over the disciple at this stage.

The movement toward spirit is still a selfish one and there is no group consciousness developed yet. This is why the master does not contact the disciple directly and has an advanced chela perform the guidance. The more advanced chela, or disciple, guides the disciple gradually onward and provides him/her with the help she needs. The advanced disciple is closer to the newfound aspirant and in some ways can better relate to her than the master can.

During this period the master pays no attention to the aspirant. The responsibility is totally in the hands of the disciple. The disciple makes reports to the master at rare and widely separated intervals. When the aspirant can "enter into the light of the angel (soul)" is when the master takes over the training. This does not occur, however, until the third stage, called entitled discipleship.

All these stages of discipleship are related to the seven levels of initiation. This first stage of little chelaship is related to the first initiation. This initiation is connected to the physical plane. This is why this stage has also been referred to as the stage of Lemurian consciousness. The second stage of the chela in the light has been called the Atlantean consciousness. The third stage of accepted discipleship has been called the Aryan consciousness.

The stage of little chelaship is an elementary one of testing and karmic agitation. It has been referred to as the "stage wherein the roots of the disciple 'plant' are shaken." What is being shaken is a lifetime's worth of being consciously overly identified with matter and personality. The soul consciousness is now beginning the process of polarization from personality to soul.

The Chela in the Light

This second stage of discipleship is where a higher disciple directs the chela from the soul plane. This is different from the first stage where the aspirant was guided by a disciple on the physical plane. In this stage the chela is concerned with overcoming glamour and controlling his emotions, as this stage is related to the second initiation.

The master is still not involved at this level, for the masters do not work on the astral plane, which for them does not exist. It is for this reason that the chela is guided by a disciple, who is subject to glamour but at the same time aware of its illusionary nature.

It is at this stage that the aspirant makes a transition in consciousness from the astral to the mental plane. At this stage the aspirant learns to distinguish between the pairs of opposites. He/she also becomes aware of glamour as something that one must free oneself and the world from. Usually at this point the aspirant is still totally unaware of the master's interest in him.

The master receives regular reports from the senior disciple who has the neophyte in his charge. The aspirants of this stage are seen as the future world servers and are consequently of great importance to the work that needs to be done. The aspirant is taught to recognize members of the Hierarchy who are more advanced and those who are less advanced. This allows him/her to know who to learn from and to whom he can be of service.

At this stage the aspirant is working off his own karma as intelligently as possible. He begins to take on karma that would ordinarily be precipitated in a future lifetime. He also begins to shoulder some of the general karma of humanity and to comprehend something of planetary karma. It is only after the third initiation, however, and that of accepted discipleship when the disciple takes responsibility for planetary karma.

Djwhal Khul, in the Alice Bailey books, said that if the aspirant is earnest, this stage of chela in the light can be a short one. Two lives are sufficient to cover this period. I believe, however, that in the time period since these books were written this can be done even faster. Djwhal Khul recently told me that a disciple can move from the third to the sixth initiation in six years if he/she is one hundred-percent committed to his path of ascension. This is mind-boggling.

What took fifteen years of total commitment in the past can now be done in fifteen months. Many great masters (some of the greatest to have ever graced this planet) took whole lifetimes to pass through one initiation.

The stage of chela in the light is only difficult in that the emotional body and desire body must be mastered. This, for most people, is the hardest stage of all. Once this is done, one can move with lightninglike speed.

The chela in the light is one who treads the path of what has been esoterically called the "lesser revelation." It is lesser because it is focused more on personality integration, rather than spirit or cosmic revelation. In this stage the soul and advanced disciple attempt to reveal faults in character and conduct. What is most important to the master is not the results but the effort that is made.

From the charts that are kept on the aspirant's progress (three in number), the master can predict when the disciple is ready for the next stage of accepted discipleship. The disciple stays in the master's group until she passes the fourth initiation. At the fourth initiation the disciple has become a master of wisdom and lord of compassion. Remember, the initiate master still has two more initiations to achieve the beginning stages of ascension.

The most important point for each disciple in the master's ashram is whether he/she can step up his consciousness to the ashramic vibration so as not to hinder the planned activities of the ashram. The master's goal for his disciples is to stimulate within them the will to love. This could also be described as an effort by the master to unify love and intention, or will.

Accepted Discipleship

In this third stage of discipleship the master contacts the chela through: (1) a vivid dream experience; (2) symbolic teaching; (3) using a thought form of the master; (4) contact in meditation; or (5) definite remembered interview in the master's ashram.

The Master of an ashram and the senior initiates in his group are responsible for the relationship between Shamballa and the Hierarchy. "Accepted" disciples and the lesser initiates are responsible for the relation between the Hierarchy and humanity.

Initiated disciples, who are above accepted disciples, have no interest in anything but the vision and divine plan, and having it manifested on the Earth plane. Accepted disciples are in the process of learning this and in the meantime are reacting to this in a secondhand manner. Although not having the complete vision yet, they still are very much involved with the plan and with the distribution of the forces that will materialize it.

The keynote of this stage is the establishing of contact with the master. The master looks for an effort on the disciple's part to be "impersonal" with him, fellow disciples and people in general. "Impersonality" is seen as the first step toward the achievement of spiritual love and understanding.

The master also looks for an effort on the disciple's part to work on a larger and more generous scale with his work in the world of men. The type of work done is left up to the disciple, however, hopefully it is in line with the master's intentions and vision. The power of right focus and the ability to cooperate with fellow coworkers is highly encouraged by the master. The qualities of compassion tempered with divine indifference are essential at this stage.

The master's work with his disciples is to help them detach from the form side of life and to prepare them for great expansions in consciousness.

The master watches the disciple's note or vibration and then indicates where attitude and expression need to be changed. If the disciple becomes "ego sensitive" from the master's feedback, then this is a sign that the disciple is still steeped in personality reactions, which must be overcome. The master has assumed responsibility for preparing the disciples in his care for initiation.

The Chela on the Thread

This stage is where the disciple has shown wisdom in his work and appreciation of the master's responsibilities; hence, the chela is taught how to attract the master's attention in emergency situations. This allows the chela to draw on the master's strength, knowledge and advice. The thread in the phrase "chela on the thread" refers to the etheric telephone line that connects the disciple to the master. The disciple, under soul control at this stage, emits a vibratory call that can penetrate the ear of the master holding the thread.

This fourth stage, according to Djwhal Khul, is only possible to a disciple who has been an accepted disciple for more than one life and has demonstrated the ability to work selflessly and with great spiritual tenacity.

The disciple has succeeded in decentralizing himself. This means no longer making himself the center focus of his life, but rather making service to humanity his centralized focus. At this stage the disciple has developed the ability to be impersonal no matter how his ego might be reacting. This means that his own feelings, thoughts, likes, dislikes and desires are no longer the controlling factors. The disciple's priority is now for the good of the group.

The disciple has achieved the state of consciousness where he is more engrossed in the service work to be done, rather than his individual position in the master's thoughts. This reminds me of the ancient spiritual saying, "lose yourself, and you will find your *self*." It is the ability to transcend the negative ego.

In this stage the disciple has developed a good sense of proportion as to his work and the relative value of his contribution to the master's work and the ashram life in general. The disciple has achieved the ability to be in two states of consciousness simultaneously. He lives in the spiritual world and also in the focused sphere of activity of Earth life in service of humanity.

The disciple is only allowed to call for help from the master for the purposes of group service, never for his own personal benefit. This indicates the disciple's ability to handle his own life. It also implies that the disciple is filled with such devotion and selflessness that the ashram needs no protection from the disciple's vibratory activity.

At this point the disciple has most definitely passed the third initiation. The master knows that if the disciple calls it will be of great importance that he respond. At this stage, no matter what the master is doing or what his concern on the inner plane, he must respond to the call. The stage of chela on the thread is a reward for selfless service being carried forward at any cost.

The disciple makes the call to the master using a specific technique according to his ray type. This call is always sent out through the crown chakra and is made inwardly rather than vocally. This technique is taught directly to the disciple upon reaching this stage of discipleship.

The thread between the master and the disciple is not the antakarana. The antakarana is the thread from the disciple to his soul and monad. The thread to the master is made of living light substance and is the ultimate telephone line. The Huna teachings of Hawaii call these threads *akacords*.

The Chela Within the Aura

In this stage the disciple is permitted to know the method whereby he may send out a call to have an interview with the master. A disciple at this stage only uses the knowledge for selfless service and the great work that needs to be done.

This is a stage far advanced to that attained by most disciples. It indicates complete attunement between the disciple and the master's group. The disciple has now become a trusted agent of the master and the ashram. The disciple at the stage of chela within the aura can always be trusted to put the group good ahead of his individual good.

From the master's perspective, he knows that he has a disciple who is a totally dependable instrument and one who is no longer a drag on the life of the group. The actual assimilating of a new disciple into the group ashram of the master is a very slow, difficult process. The disciple slowly but surely moves from the periphery of the group toward the center. Only when the disciple has achieved what has been esoterically termed "occult serenity" can he/she be permitted to focus himself permanently within the group aura.

Djwhal Khul, in the Alice Bailey book *Esoteric Healing*, described the serenity in the following manner: "that deep calm, devoid of emotional disturbance" that distinguishes the disciple who is focused in a "mind held steady in the light."

At this stage the disciple's aura is becoming more and more like the master's aura. The disciple's consciousness continues to be trained, intensified and purified. The disciple's radiatory capacity is enhanced as the ashramic life plays upon his vehicles. The vibrations and auras of the disciple and master have begun to synchronize.

The initiate disciple carries forward his/her work in the outer world, while simultaneously standing in the radiant center of the ashramic group. The initiate disciple is ever vigilant over his own consciousness to protect the ashramic center from any quality in his own aura that is not in harmony with the qualities of the master.

When the initiate disciple has learned to intensify his vibration so that it is identical with that of the master and can hold that vibration as his normal radiatory quality, then he, himself, has become a master. In every ashram there is always one disciple who is being trained to take the master's place. This allows the master to move on to his cosmic level of evolution.

Djwhal Khul was Kuthumi's senior disciple. When he became a master this allowed Kuthumi to move on to even higher level work. As Djwhal Khul moved up the ladder of consciousness, another disciple took his place. He has said that two disciples becoming masters are needed to free the existing master from all ashramic duties. Djwhal Khul was the first to do this in master Kuthumi's ashram. At the time of his writing the Alice Bailey books, the other disciple had not yet made the grade. When this takes place there is a movement upward of every level of the group ashram.

As we who are reading this book evolve, we will eventually take the place of the members of the Great White Brotherhood and Spiritual Hierarchy as a whole as they move on to their cosmic evolution.

The master always has three disciples who are his closest cooperators and intermediaries. The biblical story of the Christ was a perfect literal and symbolic picture of the organization of an ashram. Christ had three disciples who were closer to him than the other nine. The twelve apostles made up the inner ashram. The seventy-two were symbolic of the ashram as a whole. The five hundred typified those upon the probationary path, yet still under the supervision of the master. The actual total number of disciples in an ashram varies constantly. However, the main three do not vary in number.

The chela within the master's aura comes to "know" the master's aura. He begins to be more aware of what is in the master's mind. He is telepathically in rapport with the master. The disciple initiate is past all inward discussion of what the master wants him to do. The initiate disciple knows his part and efficiently performs his part in the plan. The initiate is able to bring forth the master's plan on to the astral plane. He is also able to use the etheric force from the master's ashram and his own soul to produce results on the physical plane.

There are seven main ashrams, one for each ray type. All these ashrams together make up the ashram of the christ, the Lord Maitreya. The six stages of discipleship can also be related to the six schools of Indian philosophy.

The last three of these stages deal with *initiate consciousness*, for we have moved past the third initiation, which is the first major initiation from the Spiritual Hierarchy's perspective.

The Chela Within the Master's Heart

In this stage the initiate disciple can get the master's attention at any time. The initiate is definitely being prepared for immediate initiation, or being given specialized work to do in collaboration with his master. This is called one within his master's heart. There is one final stage after this that might be termed the seventh, called the blending of the lights.

An initiate at this stage has earned the right to be truly close to the master. His life and/or lives of service have brought him this just reward. The initiate has free access to the master in the closest possible and mutual relationship of loving understanding. The disciple has become an initiate of "high standing and elevated degree," and has a direct relation to the master of all masters, the christ Maitreya.

Discipleship

A disciple, above all else, is pledged to do three things:

1. Serve humanity;
2. Cooperate with the plan of the great ones;
3. Develop the powers and follow the guidance of the soul and not the three lower-nature bodies (physical, astral, mental).

A disciple is a person who is beginning to change his focus from self to the group consciousness. A disciple is in the process of fully realizing the "essence" side of life and is not interested in the form side of life except as it relates to the full realization of the soul and spirit. The disciple is one who has begun to know him/herself as an outpost of the master's consciousness. The disciple has moved from personal to an impersonal consciousness.

The difficulties for a disciple come from two main sources. One is the lower self, or negative ego, which is rebelling at being transmuted and repolarized to the higher self. The second source is family and friends who misunderstand the disciple's growing impersonality.

The disciple is one who takes responsibility for all that comes under his influence. He is able to discriminate between the real and unreal, truth and illusion, Christ consciousness and negative ego. The disciple has four basic aims:

1. A sensitive response to the master's vibration;
2. A purely demonstrated life;
3. A freedom from worry, which comes from detachment, divine indifference and attunement to the soul;

4. Accomplishment of duty.

The path of the disciple is a difficult one, filled with obstacles at every step. In staying on the spiritual path and overcoming these obstacles one realizes mastership and is a server of humanity.

There is a stage on the path of discipleship when the disciple might feel loneliness. This is a temporary transitory phase. The main work of the disciple is to control the lower self and eliminate material desire, so as to achieve an evenminded peace and joy at all times. The disciple achieves a point in consciousness where nothing can ruffle this inner calm because his consciousness is centered in the soul. The disciple also has great patience, perseverance and endurance.

The qualities that the disciple must overcome are selfishness, self-centeredness, material desire, personal ambition, pride, lack of integrity, separativeness, criticism, irritation, fanaticism, being too laissez faire, violence, suspicion, oversensitivity.

The qualities the disciple needs to develop are love, good will, forgiveness, sacrifice, responsibility, discrimination, free will, humility, simplicity, detachment, impersonality, acceptance, serenity, selflessness, courage, perseverance, sharing, giving, harmlessness, balance, stability, sense of humor, solitude, devotion, joy, esoteric sense, higher psychic development and sensitivity, ability to be silent, divine indifference and sincerity.

In the beginning stage of discipleship when a master is investigating the newfound aspirant, he looks at basically three things:

1. The light in the head of the striving aspirant;
2. The karma of the aspirant;
3. The aspirant's service to the world.

The disciple is subjected to the forces coming from three main sources:

1. His soul;
2. His master;
3. The group of co-disciples with whom he/she is connected.

I would recommend not discussing your level of initiation with others, except in rare cases, when you really feel it is appropriate. The reason for this is that the sharing of this information tends to create competition, jealously, criticism and claim-making. This information is between you (and maybe your spiritual teacher) and God.

The fact is that each person is the christ, no matter what his/her level of initiation, and that is how all should be seen. Using the term "disciple" for all levels of initiation creates this inherent equality, which is as it should be.

The masters are looking for aspirants and disciples who have a clear vision, uncompromising adherence to truth and an unceasing drive and focus to manifest this ideal. Most of all, the masters are looking for an enlarged channel from the soul or higher self, to the physical brain of the disciple via the mind. An enlarged channel indicates to the master that the aspirant can be utilized in the great work of redemption of humankind that needs to be done. The master is looking for the perfecting of the antakarana, or rainbow bridge.

The three qualities that are needed to bring about individual and group purpose in the disciple are: power, detachment and lack of criticism. The disciple also comes to realize the *one life* that pervades all forms and that there is no death, distress or separation. The disciple learns that the form life is just the veil that hides the splendor of divinity.

The soul knows no age and can use any incarnated personality of any age as long as the person makes him/herself a suitable instrument. Djwhal Khul has stated, however, that by the age of forty-nine the disciple's pathway of service should be clearly defined. The masters have stated that if a fusion between the soul and personality has not been achieved by the age of fifty-six, it is usually not achieved after this, although it has been done. When reached before the age of fifty-six, unfoldment on the path of discipleship is totally possible. The sixty-third year in the life of all disciples will be one of crisis and supreme opportunity, according to Djwhal Khul.

The disciple is usually one who is in transition between the new and old states of being. He/she is moving from form identification to compete soul and spirit identification. The path of discipleship is one of synthesis, hard work, intellectual unfoldment, steady aspiration, harmlessness, spiritual orientation and the gradual opening of the third eye.

The inner command of every disciple is to obey the inward impulses of the soul. The disciple is guided to pay no consideration to the self-righteousness of worldly science and conventional earthly wisdom that sees life as a half-truth, seeing only the form side of life. It is only when the disciple is willing to renunciate everything in service to God that liberation is achieved. When this occurs the body of desire has become transmuted into the body of higher intuition.

A great mobilization of disciples on this planet is needed now more than ever to help provide the final preparation for the reappearance of the Christ and the externalization of the Hierarchy. The disciple needs to focus all his energies, time and resources on behalf of humanity. This requires a renewed dedication and consecration of one's *Self* throughout life and forgetfulness of the *self.*

This forgetfulness of self leads to the letting go of all moodiness, personality desires, resentments, grievances and pettiness. This leads to an outer life that is totally focused on active service for humanity. It is through people on Earth who have taken these vows that the masters pour their love, light and guidance.

In the Alice Bailey book *Esoteric Astrology,* Djwhal Khul gave an interesting comparison of the three stages of the spiritual path that disciples have to move through. I think it serves as a good summation of the different phases of discipleship.

1. Path of evolution and probation
   a. Unfoldment of intellect and of sensory perception;
   b. Response to the center called humanity;
   c. The mind takes control; personality functions.
2. Path of discipleship
   a. Unfoldment of the love nature;
   b. Achievement of illumination;
   c. Response to the center called the Hierarchy;
   d. *Buddhi,* or the intuition, is in control; the soul functions.
3. Path of Initiation
   a. Unfoldment of the will;
   b. Achievement of synthesis;
   c. Response to the center called Shamballa;
   d. Dynamic purpose in control; the will-to-good, the monad functions.

In the beginning stages of discipleship, the disciple must do four things:

1. Inquire the way;
2. Obey the guidance of the soul;
3. Pay no attention to worldly concerns;
4. Live a life that serves as an example to others.

The disciple must also learn to distinguish between the following four polarities of the lower and higher self:

1. Instinct and intuition;
2. Lower mind vs. higher mind;
3. Desire and spiritual impulse;
4. Selfish aspiration and divine inceptive and group consciousness.

15

Evolvement of Nations

In continuing our discussion of cosmic ascension there is the need now to look beyond our personal evolutionary process and see how nations on planet Earth evolve and how humanity as a whole moves through the initiation process. I have synthesized the following information in this chapter from the writing of Djwhal Khul through Alice Bailey in her book, *The Destiny of the Nations.* For those readers who would like a deeper explanation of this subject, I would guide them to read this book.

Nations, in a sense, are a lot like individual people, but much larger. Just as people have a personality ray and a soul ray, so do nations. My attempt in this chapter is to bring forth the essential teachings from this work to give you an introduction to the subject.

To begin with, there are five great rays of energy manifesting in our world as a whole today:

1. The first ray of divine will;
2. The second ray of love/wisdom, which is always in manifestation because our solar system is a second-ray system;
3. The third ray of active intelligence;
4. The sixth ray of devotion and idealism;
5. The seventh ray of ceremonial ritual.

These five rays have an enormously powerful effect on this planet, just as they do when we have these rays manifesting within our monad, soul, personality, mind/emotional body and physical body.

The Five Major Ideas Manifesting in the World Today

According to Djwhal Khul, the five major ideas manifesting in the world today are:

1. The ancient and inherited ideas that have controlled the racial life for centuries;
2. Ideas that are relatively new such as Nazism, Fascism, Communism;
3. The idea of democracy, which is not particularly old or new, that ideally, the people govern and the government represents the will of the people;
4. The idea of the world state, divided into various sections;
5. The idea of the Spiritual Hierarchy, which will govern the people throughout the world through the best elements of all these above-mentioned systems.

First-Ray Influence in the World

The first ray influence in the world as a whole has only occurred two other times. The first was in Lemurian times, manifesting as the individualization of man. The second time was during the Atlantean root race during the battle between those who served the Laws of One and the Lords of Materialism, also known as the Sons of Belial.

The ray has a destructive quality within it in a positive sense of destroying that old form. This ray, in conjunction with the second ray, is part of the reason for the tremendous crisis in the world today. This destructive force can also be misused by man. An example of this is how, in the name of science, we have killed many of the forms in the animal kingdom. This is the destroying force manipulated by man's negative ego.

This ray also manifests as dominating first-ray personalities coming into the world picture. These figures are usually in the political arena. This force, depending on the individual, can manifest as a dictator or a supremely powerful, loving spiritual leader who has the good of the people enshrined in his/her heart.

This first ray also makes itself felt through the voice of the masses of the people throughout the world. This is manifesting in our world today as a mass voice crying out for values that focus on human betterment, peace and good will between people.

Second-Ray Influence in the World Today

This ray comes from the Spiritual Hierarchy, just as the first ray comes from Shamballa. This second-ray energy of love is seeking to blend its energy with the first ray. The first ray, in a sense, prepares the way for the second ray. The second-ray energy is primarily concentrated in the new group of world servers. This group has been chosen by the Hierarchy as its main channel of expression.

Third-Ray's Effect on Humanity

The third ray of intelligent activity finds its expression through the third major center of the planet, which is humanity itself. This ray calls forth a loving, intelligent response to the Shamballa and Hierarchical rays. According to Djwhal Khul this response is occurring in the world today.

The following diagram from the Alice Bailey book *The Destiny of the Nations* summarizes what has been said so far.

I. Shamballa The Holy City	Will or power Purpose, plan Life Aspect	Planetary head center, spiritual pineal gland
Ruler:	Sanat Kumara, the lord of the world The Ancient of Days Melchizedek	
II. The Hierarchy The New Jerusalem	Love-wisdom Consciousness Group unity	Planetary heart center
Ruler:	The Christ The World Savior	
III. Humanity The City, standing foursquare	Active intelligence Self-consciousness Creativity	Planetary throat center
Ruler:	Lucifer Son of the Morning The Prodigal Son	

Now, this next piece of occult information I think you will find absolutely fascinating. The ideology of the totalitarian government, although misinterpreted and confused by man, is a response to the first-ray force from Shamballa. The ideology of democracy as a form of government is a response to the second-ray influence from the Hierarchy.

The ideology of communism as a form of government, again although misinterpreted and confused by man, is a response to the third-ray influence of humanity itself. The three aspects of God's nature are manifested as forms of government. In their essential nature they are all divine; however, man's negative ego has misinterpreted the true nature of all three of them.

The Sixth and Seventh Rays' Influence in the World Today

The sixth ray began to pass out of manifestation in the world in 1625 after a long period of influence. The seventh ray of ceremonial order and magic began to manifest in 1675. The sixth ray is the most powerful ray in manifestation at this time. It is the line of least resistance for most people who constitute the Aryan race.

These great rays affect groups more than they do individuals. Once these groups organize under its influence, a great momentum is created over a long period of time. It is for this reason that a great many people on a mass scale are having a hard time releasing this energy, as it is in the process of going out of manifestation.

The sixth-ray people are the reactionaries, conservatives and fanatics who hold onto the past and inhibit the progress of humanity as it is moving toward the new age. Even though this is the case, they do provide a needed balance and steadying process that is needed in the world at this time.

The seventh ray has been steadily gaining momentum since it came into manifestation. One of the major effects of the seventh-ray energy is to integrate spirit and matter. The sixth ray stops at the astral or emotional plane. The seventh ray has the wonderful effect of grounding and physicalizing things into manifestation.

There are a large number of seventh-ray souls who have incarnated into the world at this time. Their mission is to organize the activities of the age and end the old methods and crystallized outdated attitudes of the sixth ray and the Piscean Age. Part of the world crisis we are experiencing is due to the decreased influx of the sixth-ray energy and the increased flow of the seventh-ray energy.

Humanity is on a kind of bridge between two realities, but not firmly anchored in either. This is also true of the transition between the Piscean Age and the Aquarian Age. The sixth- and seventh-ray energies are, in actuality, clashing. We see this in the political arena and, in actuality, all aspects of life. The sixth ray controls the solar plexus and the seventh ray controls the second chakra. This is why there is so much emotion, idealism and desire mixed all together in the world conflict and transformation.

Every ray has a higher and lower form. It is as if the ray can be used by the higher self or the lower self. The higher expression of the sixth ray was found in Christianity as demonstrated by the Master Jesus. Jesus and the Lord Maitreya set the ideal for the two thousand-year Piscean cycle. The word "ideal" is the key word of the sixth ray.

Djwhal Khul, in his writings, said that there were three great masters who most perfectly manifested the ideal for humanity. One of these, I think, is going to surprise you. The first two are Christ and the Buddha. The third was Hercules, who was the perfect disciple, but not yet the perfect son of God.

Buddha was the perfect initiate. He achieved illumination by perfection in all his attributes of divinity. Christ was the absolute perfect expression of divinity for this cycle. Lord Maitreya's coming again at the beginning of the Aquarian Age will manifest an even higher perfection than manifested two thousand years ago. In these three we have examples of perfection which stand far above the majority of the human race. In all three of them the sixth, seventh and first rays were the controlling factors.

Hercules has a first-ray soul, a second-ray personality and a sixth-ray astral body. Buddha has a second-ray soul, a first-ray personality and a sixth-ray mind. Christ has a second-ray soul, a sixth-ray personality and a first-ray mind.

The lower aspect of the sixth ray is the dogmatic, authoritative religion of the organized fundamentalist and orthodox churches of our time. This manifests within the church as formulated theologies, hatreds, bigotry, separateness, self-righteousness, ego, pomp and luxurious outer appeal. This applies to all religions.

The seventh ray is a little harder to differentiate between the higher and lower aspects than the sixth ray. One way that can be clearly seen is in the difference between the white and black magician. The work of "white magic" is to integrate and synthesize the following aspects:

1. The within and the without;
2. That which is above and that which is below;
3. Spirit and matter;
4. Life and form;
5. Soul and the personality;
6. Soul and its outer expression;
7. The higher worlds of spiritual will, intuition and higher abstract, and that of its lower reflection of mind, emotion and physical beingness;
8. Integrating the head and the heart, or the third chakra and the heart chakra;
9. The etheric and astral planes with the dense physical plane;
10. Intangible subjective reality with outer tangible reality.

The work of the black magician, of course, is just the opposite. Disintegration is its motto and worship of the form side of life its focus. This is one aspect of the lower manifestation of this ray.

Spiritualism was the dominant religion of the old Atlantis, and the seventh ray dominated that civilization, especially during its first half. The fifth ray of "concrete science" (the mind) dominates our Aryan age and we see how science and the mind has dominated our culture, to the eradicating of the soul of things in a great many ways.

The masses of people in the world today are still Atlantean (emotional) and are only emerging to Aryan viewpoint (mind). The future Meruvian root race that is coming into manifestation now is overlapping with the Aryan root race that carries the soul of things. The higher aspect of the seventh ray, according to Djwhal Khul, is most active at this time.

The Nations and Their Rays

As I mentioned earlier, every nation has a personality ray and a soul ray. Most nations of the Earth are identified with their personality ray. The soul ray is only sensed by the aspirants, disciples and initiates of any given nation. One of the main objectives of the new group of world servers is to invoke the soul ray for the nation in which each server lives.

The following diagram from the Alice Bailey book *The Destiny of the Nations* gives the personality and soul rays of some of the most influential nations in this period of history.

Nation	Personality Ray	Soul Ray	National Motto
India	4th ray of harmony through conflict	1st ray of power	I hide the light
China	3rd ray of intelligence	1st ray of power	I indicate the way
Germany	1st ray of power	4th ray of harmony through conflict	I preserve
France	3rd ray of intelligence	5th ray of knowledge	I release the light
Great Britain	1st ray of power	2nd ray of love	I serve
Italy	4th ray of harmony through conflict	6th ray of idealism	I carve the paths
U.S.	6th ray of idealism	2nd ray of love	I light the way
Russia	6th ray of idealism	7th ray of order	I link two ways

Austria	5th ray of knowledge	4th ray of harmony through conflict	I serve the lighted way
Spain	7th ray of order	6th ray of idealism	I disperse the darkness
Brazil	2nd ray of love	4th ray of harmony through conflict	I hide the seed

If you study this diagram, it is amazing how much sense it makes. For instance, Germany is a first-ray personality, which of course has to do with power—and look how Germany misused power in World War II. France is the third ray of intelligence and intellect, which make total sense, the lower aspect being that of arrogance.

Great Britain is a first ray also and that makes total sense. Look at Margaret Thatcher when she was in office and the whole psychology of the British government. Italy is the fourth ray, and look at the great art and sculpting that has been produced there. Do you see how perfect the science of the rays is even in describing countries, let alone incarnated personalities?

The United States is a sixth-ray personality, which is idealism, and is perfect for describing this country. Russia is the same, which makes perfect sense. On the diagram one can see each country's soul ray and have an idea of what each country will be evolving into.

It is also very interesting to study the national motto or affirmation of each country. The United States is, "I light the way." The sixth ray in both the U.S. and Russia has manifested as fanatical adherence to an ideal. India's motto is "I hide the light." This, again, perfectly describes India in terms of how they are so inwardly developed but not outwardly developed.

The seventh-ray soul of the former Soviet Union, or Russia, led her to impose enforced ordered ideal. The United States' second-ray soul guided her to idealism based on love.

Great Britain is the custodian of the wisdom aspect of the second ray. The United States will fulfill this same office in the immediate future. Brazil will then take over this job many thousands of years hence, according to Djwhal Khul.

These three countries, the United States, Great Britain and Brazil, with their second-ray souls, will demonstrate wisdom and right government based on true idealism and love. I, myself, being a second-ray soul and monad, know why I am so comfortable and happy to be living in the United States.

It is no accident that the Lord Maitreya is living in London, England, being a second-ray master. Great Britain represents the aspect of mind, which expresses itself in "intelligent government" based on loving understanding. This is the ideal for this government, although not fulfilled as yet.

The United States represents the intuitive faculty, expressed as illumination. Brazil will represent, in the future, "abstract consciousness," which is a blend of intellect and intuition.

Another interesting aspect to study in dealing with nations is whether they are feminine or masculine. India, France, United States, Russia and Brazil are all feminine nations. China, Germany, Great Britain and Italy are all masculine. If you tune in to these countries, this really fits. Some are more mental, others are more nurturing and mothering.

The Effect of the Incoming Rays

The incoming seventh ray is slowly but surely imposing a new order and rhythm on humankind. When a new ray comes in, at any given time it is felt in a sequential order. The following list gives this sequential order for any new incoming ray:

1. The sensing of an ideal;
2. The formulation of a theory;
3. The growth of public opinion;
4. The imposition of the new and developing pattern upon evolving life;
5. The production of a form based upon that pattern;
6. The stabilized functioning of the life within the new form.

Each ray embodies an idea that can be sensed as an ideal. Every ray produces three major patterns, which are imposed upon the form nature of either man, a nation or a planet. These three major patterns are the emotional pattern, mental pattern and soul pattern.

The following diagram shows the rays that govern humanity as a whole and includes humanity's mind, astral and physical ray.

Soul ray	2nd	Humanity must express love
Personality ray	3rd	Developing intelligence for transmutation into love/wisdom
Mind ray	5th	Scientific achievement
Astral ray	6th	Idealistic achievement
Physical ray	7th	Organization; business

Rays In and Out of Manifestation

This diagram from the Alice Bailey book *Esoteric Psychology* shows the seven rays and the exact dates when the rays came in and out of manifestation.

Ray 1	Not in manifestation
Ray 2	In manifestation since A.D. 1575
Ray 3	In manifestation since A.D. 1425
Ray 4	To come slowly into manifestation around A.D. 2025
Ray 5	In manifestation since A.D. 1775
Ray 6	Passing rapidly out of manifestation, began to pass out in A.D. 1625
Ray 7	In manifestation since A.D. 1675

Major Cities and Their Rays

You might be surprised to understand that every city also has a personality and soul ray. There are five major cities that serve as centers of spiritual transmission. These are London, New York, Tokyo, Geneva and Darjeeling.

Djwhal has said that two more cities will be added in the future to make seven. The following diagram from the Alice Bailey book *The Destiny of the Nations* shows the soul, personality ray and astrological sign governing these five major spiritual centers for distribution of spiritual energy.

City	Soul	Personality	Sign
London	5th Ray	7th Ray	Gemini
New York	2nd Ray	3rd Ray	Cancer
Tokyo	6th Ray	4th Ray	Cancer
Geneva	1st Ray	2nd Ray	Leo
Darjeeling	2nd Ray	5th Ray	Scorpio

The fact that the United Nations Center is in New York and that that city is one of the spiritual centers is no accident. The two future cities that will make the total number of seven, just like the seven chakras, will be in Africa and in Australia.

The centers have some relationship to the fact that we are in the fifth root race. These five cities through which the Hierarchy and Shamballa are working correspond esoterically to the four chakras up the spine and the third-eye center in the body of humanity and of individual man.

Los Angeles, Djwhal Khul has told us, in terms of its psychological age is just now coming out of its teenage years and is moving into the beginning years of maturity. It is a very spiritual city, which its name "City of Angels" indicates. It does not have the same maturity as a city like London, however.

If you look at a lot of what is being taught in Los Angeles on a mass scale I think you can see the truth of this statement. I say this in no way as a criticism, for I happen to like Los Angeles and have benefited greatly from being here. It is interesting to think of the spiritual maturity level of the different cities around the globe.

Seventh-Ray's Effects on the Four Kingdoms

One of the effects of the seventh-ray energy will be to create a closer integration and synthesis of the four kingdoms (human, animal, plant and mineral). Part of humanity's job, which most people on this planet don't realize, is to be a distributing agent of spiritual energy to these lower kingdoms. The seventh ray will steadily refine both human and animal bodies to a more specialized state of development. This will allow the soul to have far better instruments to work through.

Another effect of the seventh ray will be to create a special closeness between the human and animal kingdoms. One other side effect will be the extinction of certain types of animal bodies and very low-grade human bodies. One of the major qualities of the seventh-ray disciple will be that of intense practicality.

The sixth-ray disciple was much more abstract and mystical and had little understanding of the right relationship between spirit and matter. The sixth-ray disciple tended to matter and was only interested in the soul of things. This didn't help the creation of heaven on Earth. This has caused a type of "split personality." The separation between science and religion is just one example of this.

One of the current tasks of the new age lightworker is to heal this separation and to spiritualize matter. The sixth-ray disciple carried his/her work down to the astral plane and stopped. The sixth ray produced the Eastern school of occultism. The seventh ray will produce the Western school of occultism.

Now, one very important point to understand in regard to all the incoming rays is that their effects vary according to the ray type of the disciple involved. Each person has a monadic, soul, personality, mental, emotional and physical ray. These more personal rays and the level of spiritual evolution of the disciple will have a great effect on how the more planetary rays effect the individual.

This small diagram from Alice Bailey's book *The Destiny of the Nations* gives a summation of the rays and the quality of energy they embody:

Ray 1: Force; energy; action; the occultist

Ray 2: Consciousness; expansion; initiation; the true psychic

Ray 3: Adaptation; development; evolution; the magician

Ray 4: Vibration; response; expression; the artist

Ray 5: Mentation; knowledge; science; the scientist

Ray 6: Devotion; abstraction; idealism; the devotee

Ray 7: Incantation; magic; ritual; the ritualist

What Causes the Differences among Disciples?

Djwhal Khul, in the Alice Bailey book *A Treatise on White Magic*, listed the six main reasons that causes disciples to be different and, hence, to also be affected differently by the great planetary rays. These six differences between people are:

1. Their ray type (physical, emotional, mental, personality, soul and monad);
2. Their approach to truth, in terms of whether they follow the mystic or occult path;
3. Whether they are polarized physically, mentally or emotionally;
4. Their level of evolution and initiation status;
5. Their astrological sign;
6. Their race (only because each race has a particular racial thought form).

The First Initiation and the Seventh Ray

The first initiation, esoterically called the birth at Bethlehem, is connected to the seventh ray of ceremonial order and magic. The effect of this ray will be as follows:

1. To bring about the birth of the Christ consciousness among the masses of aspiring human beings on this planet;
2. To set in motion certain relatively new evolutionary processes that will transform humanity into the world disciple and initiate;
3. To bring about good will, which is a reflection of the first-ray energy of will-to-good;
4. To rebalance and readjust romantic relationships;
5. To intensify human creativity and hence bring in the new art forms that will serve as a conditioning factor for humanity as a whole;
6. To reorganize world affairs so as to instigate the new world order of the Christ.

In relationship to the individual, the seventh ray will:

1. Bring upon the mental plane a widespread recognition of the relationship between the soul and the mind;
2. Produce greater order in the emotional body of the disciple thus preparing him/her for the second initiation;
3. Enable the disciple on the physical plane to establish service relationships, to learn beginning white magic and to demonstrate the first stage of truly creative life.

The Second Initiation and the Sixth Ray

The second initiation is connected to Ray Six and has been esoterically called the baptism in the Jordan. The effects of this ray on humanity are as follows:

1. An embryonic realization of the will nature;
2. A magnified conflict between the lower and higher self, which Djwhal Khul has called the conflict between the emotional nature and true realization;
3. The development on the part of humanity to clarify the world atmosphere and the releasing of the energy of good will;
4. The setting of the stage for humanity as a whole to take the first and/or second initiation;
5. The sudden and powerful emergence of the world ideologies;
6. The transformation of the astral plane.

In relationship to the individual initiate, the sixth ray produces the following effects:

1. A vortex is created in which all emotional and ideological reactions of the aspirant are intensified;
2. When the above-mentioned effect subsides, the initiate's alignment raises to an astral/mental attunement;
3. Within the initiate's mental vehicle a crystallization of all thought occurs as well as a fanatical adherence to mass idealism.

The Third Initiation and the Fifth Ray

The third initiation is connected to the fifth ray and is esoterically called the initiation of transfiguration or soul merge. The effects of the fifth ray on humanity are:

1. It is the most potent energy of the planet at this time, because in a previous solar system (we are in the third solar system) it was brought to full maturity.
2. It is the energy that admits humanity into the mysteries of the mind of God; it is the key to the universal mind.
3. This energy is esoterically related to the three buddhas of activity.
4. This energy corresponds to the mental energy of a human being.
5. The quality of this ray is extremely responsive to impressions from the soul and the upper spiritual triad via the antakarana.
6. This energy serves as a light bearer; it responds in time and space to the "light of the logos."
7. This energy transforms divine ideas into human ideals, relating the knowledge and sciences of humanity to these ideals, thus mak-

ing them workable factors in human evolution.

8. The energy of the fifth ray can be regarded as common sense; it receives various energies and synthesis and produces order out of them.

9. This energy is the thought form-making energy of humankind.

10. This ray of concrete science, along with the fact that humanity is in a fifth root race (Aryan age), which is a mental focus, also has greatly accelerated human evolution.

11. There is a close relationship between the second ray of love and the knowledge energy of the fifth ray.

12. The fifth-ray energy produces three major areas of thought, or three prime conditions, wherein the thought form-making energy expresses itself:

    A. Science .... Education .... Medicine
    B. Philosophy ... Ideas .... Ideals
    C. Psychology ... In process of modern development

13. The fifth-ray energy is also responsible for the rapid formation of the great conditioning ideologies of the planet.

14. It is the important factor in making possible the third initiation, or soul merge.

15. In respect to the personality, it works in three ways: transmutes the physical body, the astral body and the mental body.

The Fourth Initiation and the Fourth Ray

The fourth initiation is connected to the fourth ray of harmony through conflict and is esoterically called the initiation of renunciation. The fourth ray is out of incarnation at this time in terms of fourth-ray souls coming onto this planet.

From another angle, however, this ray is always active and present because it is the ray that governs the fourth kingdom (third kingdom is animals; fourth, humanity; fifth, spiritual). Because of this relationship, it is the dominant energy always exerting pressure on the kingdom of humanity.

The pressure began to exert itself primarily toward the end of the fourth root race, which was the Atlantean race. Because of this influence man began to give evidence of a growing sense of responsibility and the power to demonstrate discriminative choice. The effect of this ray on humanity is more of a group effect since no fourth-ray souls are incarnated at this time except in the ranks of the Great White Lodge, which is not a physical incarnation.

The key principle of the fourth ray is that of conflict. It is the conflict between the major pairs of opposites, which manifests most succinctly in the conflict between spirit vs. matter and good vs. evil. In Atlantean times the leaders with their power of free choice chose matter. In the present Aryan age it was this materialism that led to the world wars, which Djwhal says was really a sign of a shifting orientation.

The balance is now swinging over to the side of spirit. This principle of conflict clarifies for the individual and humanity as a whole the choice we all have to make: to renounce glamour, maya, illusion and negative ego, which is the result of attachment to the form side of life. It is only by doing this that a disciple can pass the fourth initiation.

Conflict is always present prior to renunciation. The fourth ray forces us to use our discriminative power of choice. The fourth ray, in a sense, forces us to learn right discrimination, which leads to the higher aspect of the fourth ray of harmony.

The fourth ray makes humanity aware of the duality of the manifested world. This creates a battleground and field of experience, which eventually leads to right choice, right perception and right decision. It is the choice of the Christ consciousness over negative-ego consciousness.

The conflict in the world today has increased because of the following factors as discussed by Djwhal Khul in the Alice Bailey book *The Rays and the Initiations*:

1. The crisis of ideologies;
2. The awakening of humanity to a better understanding;
3. The growth of good will, which leads to the presentation of certain fundamental cleavages that must be bridged by human effort;
4. The partial "sealing of the door where evil dwells";
5. The use of the Great Invocation with its extraordinary and rapid effects, at present unrealized by humanity;
6. The gradual approach of the Hierarchy to a closer and more intimate relation to humanity;
7. The return of the Christ, the Lord Maitreya.

The effect of the fourth ray in conjunction with the second ray, which is also now coming in, is to create right human relationships and the growth of the universal spirit of good will amongst all people. It is this influence that is implementing the return and full coming declaration of the Christ. Each disciple and all groups of disciples should always strive toward a right orientation and a broad point of view, always preserving a calm, dispassionate and loving understanding.

The energy of the fourth ray produces conflict, which leads to inner or outer war, which leads to renunciation, which leads to liberation, which is the result of passing the fourth initiation. The principle of conflict is active in the world today in all nations, religions and organizations. This is leading to the emergence of the new age. The conflict produces a point of crisis, then a point of tension, then a point of emergence. This principle of conflict is, in reality, paving the way for the return and full declaration of the Christ. As the individual disciple learns to harmonize himself through conflict, he sets an example for humanity as a whole.

The Fifth Initiation and the First Ray

The fifth initiation is connected to the first ray and is esoterically called the initiation of revelation. It signifies the power to wield light in the three worlds and to have a revelation as to the next step to be taken upon the way of higher evolution.

The first ray manifests in three progressive stages: first, God is love; second, good will; and third, the will-to-good. These are the three aspects of the first ray. When a master takes the fifth initiation he already knows the first two aspects. It is the third, or will-to-good, that is now realized at the fifth initiation.

The first ray, or Shamballa, energy is not in incarnation at this time in terms of first-ray souls incarnating. The influence of this ray on humanity has been allowed to come in and throw off the effects of the First World War and the fission of the atom that resulted in the creation of the atomic bomb.

The first ray is the will energy and the energy of destruction. Ideally, it is the destruction of the old forms, which allows the new forms to manifest. Another effect of the first-ray energy from Shamballa is that the reasoning faculty within humanity will be stimulated so as to allow humanity as a whole to reach new heights.

In the beginning stages of this development can be found instability of the human mental mechanism and in the human thinking process. At the fourth initiation it is the energy of destruction of the first ray that allows the disciple to destroy all that has held him in the three worlds of human endeavor.

At the fifth initiation the first ray helps the initiate to attain a spiritual orientation that will remain permanent. At the fifth initiation all the initiate's spiritual and material realizations are renounced and, hence, he/she stands free from every aspect of desire.

This being the case, spiritual will has been substituted for desire. This is reinforced by the first ray from Shamballa, which embodies this will energy. This state of consciousness of the initiate/master allows him to receive this influx of energy, which will enable him to see that which is to be revealed and to accept revelation.

The process is one of first the will to self-betterment, which leads to the will to human service, good will and then, finally, to the will-to-good. The newfound master is able to look into the heart of all things. He becomes aware of the Great Central Spiritual Sun and the way of the higher evolution, which leads inevitably to the center of the most high God.

16

Cosmic Ascension Training

The following is more channeled information from the core group and myself in regard to a training we were given by Djwhal Khul, Lord Arcturus and Melchizedek.

Spiritual Training

Ask now to be taken to the Golden Chamber of Melchizedek so you may have a direct experience while reading the following material. It is here that the ritual of connecting with the yod spectrum and the ten lost rays will begin. The ten lost rays were lost after humanity entered the Atlantean root race and the illusion of separation from the physical and etheric aspects of God's creation came into being.

The reconnection with the platinum ray will help in the anchoring and realization of the mayavarupa body, which is the divine blueprint body. It is the energy needed to understand the complete ascension process. It will help to alter our physical atomic structure. The energies coming through the platinum ray facilitate this alteration.

The process, therefore, is one of first, stabilizing the ascension energies in the mental vehicle, and this is done by the completing of the seven levels of initiation. Then it must be further stabilized in the emotional body. There are often many lapses in the emotional body due to negative-ego interpretations, causing negative emotional outbursts.

There is no judgment in this. However, this must be worked on to develop a calm, ongoing inner peace, joy, love and equanimity in all circumstances. The last step is to stabilize this ascension energy in the physical vehicle through the realization of the mayavarupa and monadic blueprint body. The platinum ray fills the zohar body, which activates the realization of the mayavarupa body.

Ascension Activation Number One

Call forth to Melchizedek, Lord Maitreya, Djwhal Khul and Vywamus, and to any other masters you choose to invite in for the complete weaving of the ascension energy into the mental body.

Ascension Activation Number Two

The following day or week, as you prefer, ask that the full ascension energy be woven into the emotional and astral body.

Ascension Activation Number Three

Call to the same masters again and request that the ascension energy now be fully woven into the physical body with the help of the platinum ray and yod spectrum. Request for the full activation of the zohar body and the full anchoring and activation of the mayavarupa body and/or monadic blueprint body.

It must be explained here that this process actually begins with the ascension energies first coming into the spiritual body. I am taking for granted that those reading this book have begun this spiritual-level anchoring. For those of you who are newer to this work, begin with the request for the anchoring of the ascension energies into the spiritual body.

Ascension Activation Number Four

When planetary ascension is completed, the process will move toward the weaving in of all fifty chakras and nine bodies. When that process is complete, then request the weaving of the solar body and solar chakras, galactic body and galactic chakras and, finally, universal body and universal chakras, as I have discussed in previous chapters. Cosmic ascension is a much slower process.

When weaving in the first four bodies, the spiritual-body level is very quick. For the advanced initiates the mental-body-ascension weaving can be very rapid. The emotional-body weaving is slower because this is a weak spot for most. The ultimate ideal is emotional stability and unchanging calmness. The physical level takes the longest to achieve.

The Christ/Buddha-Archetype-Imprinting Activation

The next ascension activation deals with a request to go to Shamballa in meditation. When there, call forth Lord Buddha and Lord Maitreya and request anchoring and activation of the Buddha/Christ-archetype imprinting upon your consciousness and four-body system. Bathe in this energy as long as you are able to retain this focus comfortably.

The Christ/Buddha, Melchizedek Imprinting

In a later or future meditation, request to be taken to the Golden Chamber of Melchizedek and call forth Lord Maitreya, Buddha and Melchizedek. Call forth an imprinting into your consciousness and four-body system of the Christ/Buddha/Melchizedek-archetype imprint. This is the ultimate ideal any soul can strive for on our planet. Request that this be done permanently and this imprint will be coded eternally upon your being. This activation is one step up in advancement to the previous one.

Christ/Buddha/Lord of Sirius/Melchizedek Imprint

If you want to get fancy you can also request the Lord of Sirius imprint. He runs the Great White Lodge on galactic and universal levels. This coding would give one the complete archetypal-imprinting process.

The Lord of Arcturus Wake-up Call

One of the lessons that lightworkers often deal with is fatigue caused from overwork, lack of a good night's sleep and various other reasons. I have discovered a fabulous tool to overcome this that I should bottle and sell for a million dollars.

The next time you wake up feeling exhausted or it is three o'clock in the afternoon and your energy feels depleted, call to the Lord of Arcturus and the Arcturians. Request a 100% light-quotient increase and a complete revitalization and waking up of your physical body. They will hook you up to their computers on the ship and run those energies needed to achieve this result.

This is a thousand times better than a cup of coffee and there are no withdrawal symptoms or poisoning of your liver in the process. The Arcturians are one of God's greatest gifts to humankind. I am their greatest fan and advocate. The Arcturians are like the panacea to all problems.

Invocation of the Yod Spectrum

The following is an invocation that can be used to invoke the yod spectrum:

We now bring in the yod spectrum, through the zohar body, to bond the four-body system into the divine light of the mayavarupa blueprint and totally transform the cellular structure.

We are now bringing through the platinum ray, representing the yod spectrum through Melchizedek, Metatron and the Great Central Sun. We request that God, our infinite Source, grant this dispensation of energy for the highest good. So be it. So it is.

Bring the energy down through the crown chakra to the base chakra, then move the energy left to right, all around in a circle. Then bring it back up and feel the Christ/Buddha coming in through the vehicle and then seal in the direct energies of God through the Christ/Buddha and God most high.

Melchizedek and Metatron stand with us.

Spiritual Mudra Exercise

Connect the index and third fingers together and connect them with the thumb on both hands. Feel the rays of the first and second ray coming together—the power and the love. Feel the yod spectrum channeling through these rays and send it out to the people in your community.

Then feel the first seven rays blend together. Next feel all twelve rays blend together as the yod spectrum channels through all of them. Send this energy out to the planet while still holding your mudra.

Send it across the universe. Experience your body becoming a ray of light. Become the action of the platinum ray. See yourself now sitting in Melchizedek's Golden Chamber receiving the platinum, golden and silver energies. Open your hands now and place them palm upward. Feel the energy fill your hands. Absorb this energy completely on spiritual, mental, emotional and physical levels.

Physically touch your body and channel this energy through your hands into your eyes, face, ears, neck, shoulders, heart, thighs, feet. In particular bring this light emanation into the thymus gland in the heart chakra. Also see this light enhancing your entire monad and all 144 soul extensions that make up your monad group. Feel the presence of your monad with you. Feel yourself fully merged and blended with this presence.

Place your palms together in a cupped position. As you do this, the energy builds and you are storing this energy. The energy of the platinum ray is being cultivated and stored in your field and is now reaching the circuits of your nervous system, along the meridian lines.

Now, place your hands over the thymus gland and heart and feel the platinum ray traveling throughout your nervous and electrical system, stimulating blood, secretions and glands to build the spiritual secretion, the spiritualized glandular substances and the spiritualized cell bodies.

Visualize the circulation of light everywhere in your body. Affirm to yourself silently the regenerative properties of this light: "I now regenerate my entire physical and four-body system structure and build my im-

munity. In the name of God I Am, I restore, I regenerate, I return the consciousness to my perfect divine order, my original blueprint, the body for which I have come into this universe to take hold in the physical and bring to life on the third dimension.

Feel the energies now formulating physically and you might sense an ir-rigation in the body. The oil of the nectar of life is working to massage every point and place and to lubricate, thus bringing in a fluidic flow of divine essence. Now, rub your tongue across the roof of your mouth and your teeth to stimulate the activation of the pineal gland and the flow of the golden nectar. Feel the flow of energy filling the solar plexus and all of the chakras and the entire four-body system. Feel the "oil of God" moistening the cells and entire body matrix.

The Alchemical Marriage

Every person must fully integrate and blend his/her masculine and feminine sides to realize the ascension process fully. "One must be as strong," Yogananda said, "as God-forged steel." The inner self on the mas-culine side must be hard and have steel-like mastery and power so that no disruption can break the flow of the divine current and no shock to the sys-tem cannot be tolerated.

The masculine side must be diamond hard in its purposeful focus on the path, in your knowingness of who you are and what your business is here. Nothing can discount, discourage or make you lose your focus. The hardness is the brilliance. It is not a brittle hardness. The energy is so strong that you might think of yourself as a marblelike being. But the mar-ble is warm and alive and inhabited through the feminine.

The feminine side is completely open and unconditionally loving to the full spectrum of life and sees no prejudice. When prejudice arises, it is im-mediately corrected over and over again until the spectrum of the full being, with no beliefs other than unity in every area of understanding, is complete. When there is a misperception of dominance, dependency, stress, worry, lack of continuity or disunity, it is corrected with complete benevolence, openness and love.

The strength of the masculine and the openness of the feminine are to-tally united and work together in rhythm and harmony. The flame of love, wisdom and power is lit in you fully. You walk the path alone and yet know that you are not alone. You go anywhere, and you know that you are strong, wise, discerning and loving.

This is the full and complete embodiment of the alchemical marriage. We are all doing this together and helping each other. One cannot do this without all of us doing this together; yet each of us holds our own place as a complete individual and walks the path alone. We are simultaneously whole within ourselves and one with the group consciousness. As we walk the path alone, we see everyone else walking the path, and we help and support wherever we can. No one has exactly the same path and yet all paths work together as one.

Feel within yourself now the complete functioning of the masculine and feminine without separation. Feel the entire sense of completion within yourself. The will of God, the love of God; as God is, as you are.

Cosmic-Cleansing Triangulation

Call forth Metatron, Melchizedek and Vywamus to form a triangle around you in the Golden Chamber. The purpose of this next exercise is to go into the deepest parts of ourselves and our genetic and cellular structure from this life and past lives. This will literally break up all the deposits and blockages to truly clear the way for us to move into the mayavarupa blueprint body and to truly become a monad or a mighty I Am Presence.

Visualize yourself as seated in the center of the triangulation of Melchizedek, Metatron and Vywamus. Take a deep breath. Visualize Melchizedek facing you. On the right is Metatron and on the left is Vywamus. Metatron embodies the light aspect of God; Vywamus works with the rewiring of our four bodies; and Melchizedek works with the aspect of wisdom.

The three together facilitate a charge of energy that has an enormous clearing effect. It will begin at your feet and then move up your body. It is a blue electrical energy and you will begin to feel a vibration in your feet. Visualize this moving up the body now, through the chakras and up through the entire body. Feel it now penetrating the whole body. Affirm now that you are ready to let the old genetic and cellular structure fall away. This electrical blue charge is now increasing to break this up, like an unwanted calcium deposit that has been surrounding the cells.

Feel it now coming in from a fourfold focus, coming in from the Source and then through Melchizedek, Metatron and Vywamus. Allow it to feed your being, going into the twelve strands of DNA and every cell of your body. Allow a complete cleansing to now take place, pulling all the unwanted energy into the Earth, where it is cleansed and transmuted into the purity of God.

Now, call forth your 144 soul extensions and ask that they be cleansed by this energy, if by their free choice they would like to partake of these energies. Call in a soft blue light to now calm your system, and bathe in this energy for a little while.

Finally, say the monadic mantra:
I am the monad.
I am the light divine.
I am love.
I am will.
I am fixed design.

The Nine Levels of the Soul Mantra

In all my years of spiritual study the single most powerful mantra I have ever come across is the one brought forth by Djwhal Khul through Alice Bailey. In my opinion it's the mantra of all mantras. It is called the Soul Mantra.

I recommend using it before beginning all spiritual work. It will take you into your spiritual center and core like nothing else you could possibly say or do. As taught by Djwhal Khul it goes:

"I am the soul.
I am the light divine.
I am love.
I am will.
I am fixed design."

This mantra activates your soul, or higher self/oversoul, to go to work and go into action. When Djwhal Khul taught this from 1899 to 1940 even the most advanced lightworkers were generally not beyond the third or fourth initiation, as the evolutionary process was very slowed down. Because of the extraordinary times we live in and the many divine dispensations humanity has been given at this time, humanity has accelerated enormously.

The soul or higher self is the intermediary teacher, serving until the evolving son/daughter of God has progressed to the next level. After the fourth initiation it is no longer appropriate to identify with your soul. One should identify instead with the monad or mighty I Am Presence. Therefore the first line of the mantra has needed to be changed. The new mantra states:

I am the monad.
I am the light divine.
I am love.
I am will.
I am fixed design.

I have personally been working with this new mantra created some years ago after receiving guidance. Recently, as I fully completed my own planetary ascension process and seven levels of initiation, I was guided by Melchizedek to make another identity shift.

After completing your seven levels of initiation and fully stabilizing your 99% light quotient, activating your fifty chakras and nine bodies and integrating and cleansing your 144 soul extensions, it is then time to change your identity as you did at the fourth initiation.

Melchizedek explained this as identifying with one's cosmic monad, instead of one's individual monad. The ultimate cosmic monad, he said, is the understanding that there is, in truth, only one monad and one soul. All individualized monads are really just a part of one infinite monad.

He guided the core group and I to begin seeing ourselves as this infinite monad and no longer as individualized monads. This is a natural progression of the spiritual path and movement into the cosmic ascension process. When you identify with the cosmic monad, all people are seen as contained within self. One's aura expands enormously when it begins taking on a cosmic identity, not just an individual monadic identity. This means identifying with oneself as the cosmic mighty I Am Presence, not just the individualized mighty I Am Presence.

Upon reflection, implementing Melchizedek's guidance requires a leap in consciousness and an understanding that there will be stages in this process of complete cosmic-monadic identification. Melchizedek concurred that it would be too mind-boggling a leap to fully integrate this process if the intermediate steps were not understood.

This then led to the insight that there are eight levels of the soul mantra that I am to bring forth to humanity as part of this cosmic-mapping process. Djwhal Khul brought forth through Alice Bailey that which was perfect for humanity at that time. The next seven monadic mantras will take us the rest of the way home in the ultimate cosmic sense.

Therefore, the third monadic mantra newly revealed to humanity is:

I am the six monads.

I am the light divine.

I am love.

I am will.

I am fixed design.

You might ask, why six monads? Remember that the eighth and ninth dimensions are integrated by six monads being grouped together. This is how the group soul and group monad at the eighth- and ninth-dimensional levels are realized. This is the next level of appropriate identification after one has realized his/her identification with the individual monad, or mighty I Am Presence.

The next monadic mantra is:

I am the solar-monadic grouping.

I am the light divine.

I am love.

I am will.

I am fixed design.

Once the solar level is realized there is another shift in monadic identification to the galactic level; hence:

I am the galactic-monadic grouping.

I am the light divine.

I am love.

I am will.

I am fixed design.

Once the galactic level has been realized in the cosmic ascension process, there will be another identity shift to the universal level. The universal mantra is:

I am the universal-monadic grouping.

I am the light divine.

I am love.

I am will.

I am fixed design.

At the multiuniversal level the first sentence of the monadic mantra is:

I am the multiuniversal-monadic grouping.

When one reaches the top of creation there are twelve cosmic rays, each containing a cosmic monad, or cosmic mighty I Am Presence. Each of us is connected to one of these twelve cosmic monads. If, for example, you are a second-ray cosmic monad, your new monadic mantra would be:

I am the second-ray cosmic monad.

I am the light . . .

In the ultimate sense of God realization and cosmic ascension, the twelve cosmic monads of the Cosmic Council of Twelve are all one monad. Therefore, the final monadic mantra upon progressing to this ultimate level is:

I am the ultimate cosmic monad.

These are the nine rather simplistic stages of consciousness identification to achieve cosmic ascension. To get an experiential sense of what our ultimate identity is you can work with these mantras. Realistically, because we cannot go beyond the seventh initiation while still in physical incarnation, we will never be able to fully experience here what these cosmic identifications really mean. This is somewhat mitigated by the fact that we can nevertheless anchor higher chakras, bodies and dimensions and more soul extensions, allowing us to experience this to a certain degree.

These monadic mantras provide a very important tool for beginning to dissolve the negative ego—the imaginary fences that we have thought to be our true identity. In the ultimate sense we are already the ultimate cosmic monad. There is a part of us that lives at that level already. This might be termed our lord's mystical body and self, or our elohim body and self.

In the ultimate truth this is the only reality and all else is illusion. This is why, as stated in *A Course in Miracles,* "Nothing real can be threatened; nothing unreal exists. Herein lies the peace of God." Even though this is true, the process of evolution that God created is that we must, as *A Course in Miracles* pointed out, "realize this ideal through our demonstration and experience to return home."

This brings us to the discussion of equality. All are equal, for all are God. It is not true, however, that all are equal in terms of the level of realizing this truth. Melchizedek is more God realized than you or I—that is a fact. Again, in the ultimate sense, we are equals. That is why *A Course in Miracles* states that "awe" is only appropriate to God, and not to an elder brother or sister. This is true because God created us all.

When one works with the ascended masters, in the beginning he/she might hold this sense of awe for such beings as Jesus/Sananda, Saint Germain, Kuthumi, Lord Maitreya, Buddha, Djwhal Khul and so on. As you work with them for a while you realize that they are people just like you and I, but they are a little more advanced and hold more light.

Conversing with them is really no different from how one converses with friends and associates on Earth. True, they are a little wiser, but oftentimes they are very funny and like to joke around. I can tell that they like to be accepted just as we do.

It is not much different from the business meetings I have with the core group or other high-level initiates. I share this to demystify the ascended masters and to show you how friendly, available and similar to us they really are. Even Melchizedek, the grand master himself and the highest being in our entire universe, is a very personable and likable fellow. He constantly jokes around and teases us, as do all the masters. When we start getting carried away, he lovingly gets us refocused and down to business.

I never thought I would be saying this, but I feel quite chummy with Melchizedek, and I know he feels the same about me. This is not unique to me, for he can have this type of relationship with anyone. So many of our fantasies and projections about the ascended masters are just not true. The easiest way to see this is to recognize that as we complete our mission and move to the inner plane to complete our service work, we will be the inner-plane ascended masters from whom younger humanity will seek guidance. I am quite surprised at this level of equality that I feel with them.

Even if you are not clairvoyant or clairaudient, every sincere request to any one of the ascended masters will engender an instant response from them on the inner plane. The ascended masters will literally respond to your requests or invocations one hundred percent of the time without fail. Your response might be experienced through vision or hearing or in a thought, an intuition, a dreamstate, a meditation, a sense in your feeling body, an image in your mind, or possibly more energetically.

Each person's connection will be different according to how he/she best accesses spirit. This has a lot to do with how God built you—whether you are more the mystic type or the occult type, as well as your development in past lives. It does not matter how you work with the masters as long as you work *with* them. Everyone will be able to feel them energetically when practicing the ascension techniques presented in my various books. Never forget that it is the *energy* that is the key; it is the energy that creates the transformation. By staying connected to the energy, you stay connected to the masters.

Paradigms of Body Systems

In the beginning stages of the spiritual path, we speak of the four-body system: the physical, astral, mental and spiritual bodies. This is really a misnomer, for it should be called the five-body system: the physical, etheric, astral, mental and spiritual bodies. As one evolves, there is a need to expand this system to include the seven-body system: the physical, astral, mental, buddhic, atmic, monadic and logoic bodies. Each of these bodies correlates with one of the seven planes of the same name.

Once we reach the completion of the seventh initiation there is the need to expand the paradigm further to the twelve-body system, which incorporates the group soul, monad and solar, galactic and universal bodies.

In the future, when we integrate the twelve-body system and our two hundred chakras, we will expand this paradigm again in order to include the Paradise Sons' body, the Elohistic Lord's body and the Lord's mystical body. It isn't appropriate to do this now, for we are not realistically at an evolutionary level to be able to incorporate these.

As we evolve through these different levels, we must be open to letting go of past paradigms and models. This is why many of the books we have studied in the past and have treasured are outdated in many ways. It is important not to stay stuck in the past or in a certain dispensation of teachings—no matter how gifted the channel or telepath was who allowed this information to come through. Use past teachings as a foundation to build upon, but don't stay stuck in them. This instruction applies to every single spiritual organization operating on the earthly plane.

The Planetary and Cosmic Ashrams
and the Dimensions of Reality

God's Ashrams and Dimensions of Reality

Ashram	Dimension of Reality
God's ashram (contains all other ashrams as an aspect of His one ashram)	48 & 49 to infinity
Multiuniversal-level ashram	24 to 48
Golden Chamber of Melchizedek	12 to 24
Great White Lodge ashram of Lord of Sirius (within the ashram there is a solar, galactic and universal level)	9 to 12
Buddha's ashram Shamballa	8 & 9
Lord Maitreya's ashram	7
Ashrams of El Morya, Kuthumi, Paul the Venetian, Serapis Bey, Hilarion, Sananda, St. Germain	6
Djwhal Khul's synthesis ashram	5

Bodies and Dimensional Levels

The following chart shows the twelve-body system and beyond. The dimensions out of which our different bodies operate is a loosely defined model, using the forty-nine dimensions of reality that was given to us by the grand master, Melchizedek. With some of the cosmic bodies, an exact number could not be given because of the vastness of God's infinite omniverse. In this case, a range has been given that provides a perspective and map of our cosmic evolutionary journey.

Chart of Our Bodies and Their Dimensional Levels

Body	Dimension
God's body (also known as the Lord's mystical body)	49 and beyond
Elohistic Lord's body	48
Paradise Sons' body	36 to 48
Multiuniversal body	24 to 36 (incorporating Order of Sonship body)
Universal body	12 to 24
Galactic body	11
Solar body	10
Group-monadic body	8 & 9
Group-soul body	7
Logoic body	6

Monadic body	5
Atmic body	4
Buddhic body	4
Mental body	4
Astral body	4
Etheric body	4
Physical body	3

Second Model for Cosmic Bodies and Dimensions

This second model uses Djwhal Khul's model of the cosmos, combining the seven subplanes of the cosmic physical and the seven cosmic planes and their corresponding bodies.

Cosmic Bodies and Dimensions Chart

Body	Dimensions
God's body	49 and beyond
Cosmic logoic body	42 to 49
Cosmic monadic body	35 to 42
Atmic body	28 to 35
Cosmic buddhic body	21 to 28
Cosmic mental body	14 to 21
Cosmic astral body	8 to 14
Cosmic physical bodies	3 to 7

A. Planetary logoic	D. Planetary buddhic	G. Planetary physical
B. Planetary monadic	E. Planetary mental	
C. Planetary atmic	F. Planetary astral	

The previous two charts could actually be merged. In the second chart it is interesting that the omniverse/universe is divided into sevens: seven cosmic planes, seven subplanes of the cosmic physical, seven subplanes between each cosmic plane. Seven times seven, of course, equals forty-nine, which is the number that Melchizedek gave us separately from Djwhal Khul's channelings through Alice Bailey.

Dimensions, Bodies, Chakras, Initiations and Light Quotient

God's level: dimension 49, 330th chakra, initiations 36 to 49, 100% cosmic light quotient

Multiuniversal level: dimensions 24 to 36, chakras 200 to 250, initiations 24 to 36, 60% cosmic light quotient, multiuniversal body.

Universal level: dimensions 12 to 24, chakras 150 to 200, initiations 12 to

24, 40% cosmic light quotient, universal body or anointed Christ overself body and zohar body.

Galactic level: dimension 11, chakras 100 to 150, initiation 11, 30% cosmic light quotient, galactic body.

Solar level: dimension 10, chakras 50 to 100, initiation 10, 20% cosmic light quotient, solar body.

Planetary level: dimensions 1 to 7, chakras 1 to 50, initiations 1 to 7, 99% planetary light quotient, or 10% cosmic light quotient, nine planetary bodies.

It must be understood that this chart is from the perspective of a lightworker incarnated on Earth. These numbers and this model would change from the perspective of a being like Vywamus who is living in the higher dimensions and looking down. This correlates with the understanding that we are only integrating five or ten percent of the solar, galactic and universal levels and taking those initiations. That is why the perspective and numbers would be different. This is, however, a good working model for all souls living in physical bodies on Earth.

Second Cosmic Model Breakdown of Dimensions, Bodies, Chakras, Initiations and Cosmic Light Quotient

God's level (Lord's mystical body): dimension 49, God's body, cosmic chakras 330, cosmic initiations 352, cosmic light quotient 100%.

Cosmic logoic level: dimensions 42 to 48, cosmic logoic body, cosmic chakras 273 to 329, cosmic initiations 293 to 351, cosmic light quotient 90 to 99%.

Cosmic monadic level: dimensions 35 to 42, cosmic monadic body, cosmic chakras 220 to 273, cosmic initiations 236 to 293, cosmic light quotient 74 to 90%.

Cosmic atmic level: dimensions 28 to 35, cosmic atmic body, cosmic chakras 167 to 220, cosmic initiations 179 to 236, cosmic light quotient 58 to 74%.

Cosmic buddhic level: dimensions 21 to 28, cosmic buddhic body, cosmic chakras 114 to 167, initiations 122 to 179, cosmic light quotient 42 to 58%.

Cosmic mental level: dimensions 14 to 21, cosmic mental body, chakras 61 to 114, initiations 65 to 122, cosmic light quotient 26 to 42%.

Cosmic astral level: dimensions 8 to 14, cosmic astral body, chakras 8 to 61, initiations 8 to 65, cosmic light quotient 10 to 26%.

Cosmic physical level:

    A. Planetary logoic level

    B. Planetary monadic level

    C. Planetary atmic level

    D. Planetary buddhic level

    E. Planetary mental level

    F. Planetary astral level

    G. Planetary physical level

Cosmic physical level: dimensions 1 to 7, seven subbodies of the cosmic physical plane listed above, chakras 1 to 50, initiations 1 to 7, 99% cosmic light quotient and/or 10% cosmic light quotient.

This second cosmic chart mapping the requirements for cosmic evolution was done completely mathematically through the sacred geometric paradigms given by the masters. In this chart I used the 352 levels of the Mahatma to present a slightly different paradigm of the initiation process.

As we see here, planetary and cosmic evolution can be brought down to a very exacting science of integration of dimensions, bodies, chakras, initiations and light quotient. Every person in God's infinite universe will go through this process and compete this process. It is just a matter of time.

We are all eternal and immortal beings. The speed at which you evolve is all up to your commitment to self-discipline, focus, love and service. The idea is to move through this process as efficiently and quickly as possible, while enjoying the process as well. Each level must be completely mastered before you are allowed to enter the next level. These charts can be quite helpful, for they provide a road map home—and also keep us humble, realizing how far we have to go.

The highest being on this planet is his holiness, Lord Sai Baba, who at last count was holding a 31% light quotient. People you run into who claim to be fully God realized are living in total illusion and run by the negative ego.

Planetary mastery and true God realization are light-years apart. No one on this plane can or will ever attain true God realization or cosmic ascension. Even the integration of the first twelve dimensions of reality has rarely even been done before on this earthly plane. In the past it has always been done on the inner plane. It is really only since 1987 or 1988 that this doorway has been opened. We are incredibly blessed to be incarnated at this time.

Sai Baba might be operating from the model and paradigm of a being like Vywamus, Sanat Kumara or Lenduce. As an avatar he has taken initiations beyond the seventh, which only an avatar such as Sai Baba or Lord Maitreya can do. Again, an avatar is totally God-realized at birth and needs no spiritual training or spiritual teacher or books.

Sai Baba could materialize things as a child. Krishna, Jesus and Buddha were not truly avatars in the vein I am speaking of here, for they were still working through the initiation process in their lifetimes and in their bodies. Sai Baba and Lord Maitreya's incarnations at this time in Earth's history are true examples of galactic and universal avatars fully awakened at birth, or in the case of Maitreya, at the time of the materialization of his mayavarupa body.

I bring this up to make the point that an avatar doesn't fit into the models I have presented. For this reason, Sai Baba's light quotient might actually be much higher than 31% in our model. We again are integrating only a fraction of solar, galactic and universal energies on this plane, while still retaining physical vehicles.

Why Advanced Ascended-Master Abilities Are Slow to Develop

One of the most commonly asked questions I receive from lightworkers is, "How come if we are taking these higher levels of initiation, we are not able to manifest the advanced ascended-master abilities?"

It must be understood that we are living in a different time period and dispensation of the ascension process. It is occurring en masse now, where in the past it occurred in just isolated spots in the Himalayas and in the secret mystery schools. The Spiritual Hierarchy and Shamballa has, in a sense, changed the ascension process to allow a great many people of this planet to achieve their seven levels of initiation.

Ascension is being achieved now by a great many lightworkers, however, it is really on a spiritual and possibly a mental level. It has not fully actualized on an emotional level for most, and certainly not fully on a physical level. This acceleration is a great blessing from God, for it has allowed many lightworkers to achieve liberation from the wheel of rebirth while still needing to learn many lessons in terms of full integration.

Much of this has to do with this most accelerated time period in Earth's history. Masters in the past had whole lifetimes to integrate one initiation. Now we lightworkers are doing this in one or two years. This is the main reason the advanced abilities, such as teleportation and dematerialization, are potentialities for a later development.

Even if one has taken his/her sixth and/or seventh initiation, this doesn't mean she has fully activated and actualized every aspect of this. Ascension is a process. If we had a whole lifetime to process one initiation, we would develop these abilities sooner. Since evolution is moving so quickly now, the process is not the same as we have read in some books. According to Melchizedek, given how fast it is moving, we must now integrate up through the twelfth dimension or universal level before the advanced ascended-master abilities will come.

Fifty or one hundred years ago this would have been impossible to achieve even by the most advanced master. Given how fast things are moving now and the new dispensations humankind has received, this is totally within reach of all dedicated lightworkers. Our core group was told that in the leadership positions we are in, if we continue in this pattern we have the potentiality to move from the ninth to the twelfth level in five years, which involves working through our 150 chakras.

Part of this has to do with the fact that we are focusing on this during the exact years of mass ascension for humanity—from 1995 to 2000. In a sense we are all riding a great wave. This is why it is of the utmost importance to be as dedicated, focused and committed as possible during this most extraordinary period in Earth's history.

Advanced ascended-master abilities will come, but before this can happen the ascension energies must be woven, integrated and stabilized within the four-body system to allow this to take place. Be patient. What took Djwhal Khul fourteen years to accomplish we are now doing in one year. He only left the planet fifty years ago and was one of the most advanced initiates on Earth.

The twelfth-dimensional levels ensure that this work be done before such awesome siddhas, or powers, be made manifest. Focus more on spiritual growth, light-quotient building, ascension activations, chakra anchorings, dimensional-body anchoring, soul-extension integration and clearing and leadership and planetary-world service. Then the advanced ascended-master abilities will come as a natural byproduct and unfolding of this work.

Also, the dissolving of the physical form into light has been pushed back to a later stage than in the past because of the speed of evolution. It is only because of a special dispensation from Shamballa that we are even allowed to take the sixth and seventh initiations without perfecting the mental, emotional and physical vehicles.

In the past masters had to take many, many lifetimes perfecting these vehicles before being allowed to take these initiations. It is now literally a million times easier to achieve these initiations than it was before. Because it is so much easier for the masses to achieve ascension and seventh-level-initiation completion, it only makes sense that advanced ascended-master abilities would be pushed back to a much higher stage of advancement. It is still a potentiality for all and all will achieve it in time.

This process begins with developing perfect health in the physical body and mastering such physical aspects as prosperity consciousness and ascended-master demonstration in the real world, as a preliminary step. As we manifest the ascension energies and ascension movement into the third-dimensional world, in terms of service work, it will also simultaneously manifest within our physical bodies.

The grounding of spiritual energies is the key principle of the new age. This relates to the ending of the cycle of the sixth ray on a planetary level and the beginning of the seventh ray on a planetary level. Spirituality in the past two thousand-year cycle has been held in the spiritual, mental, psychic and emotional realms, but was not grounded. This is the great work of the spiritual leadership group and the new group of world servers in the next phase of Earth's history.

This process will lead to the development of all twelve strands of DNA and the fully integrated circuiting of all bodies, not just in the etheric levels, but full circuiting in the physical vehicle as well, forming a unified circuit of energy.

The Seamless Body of Golden Light

Visualize your body as a seamless body of golden light, which in the center holds the platinum ray—diamond bright. Your body is seamless in the sense that it has no divisions at all; it is smooth and perfected.

Call forth to Vywamus and ask that this body now be made fully manifest within you. Feel Vywamus' hands running down this body, molding into you all the characteristics and qualities of divinity that we hold in truth. Ask to sit in the Shamballa seat of ascension and ask Vywamus to sit with you and meld his energies with you for the purpose of perfecting this seamless body of golden and platinum light.

Feel the unity of heart and mind and the entire chakra system. Feel the adjustment Vywamus is making of lower and higher, losing separation and definition of opposites and becoming one. Feel unification throughout your entire being, inner and outer dissolving. Experience the purity and innocence in this new body. Experience the joy of Vywamus, galactic being, playing within your energy field.

Contemplate now, from this Shamballa ascension seat, which is at the ninth-dimensional level, the purpose of the planet. Then blend your consciousness with Lord Maitreya at the eighth-dimensional level as head of the Spiritual Hierarchy, and blend in total oneness and unity with the solar, galactic and universal masters in the Golden Chamber of Melchizedek. Feel the unification just as God, Christ and the Holy Spirit are one. This is the journey of the Mahatma taking all 352 steps back to the godhead.

Call forth now a special dispensation from the Karmic Board. See before you Kwan Yin holding the scales of justice, mercy and compassion. See Buddha, Mother Mary and all the rest of the Karmic Board. Call forth for a special dispensation of karmic balance for your sector and twelve-body system and overall program.

See Sai Baba appear and place a petition of light upon the Karmic Board table to allow this balance within your bodies, planet and universe to be brought into divine order. Call forth for an acceleration of your path of ascension, as Sai Baba, Vywamus, Lord Melchizedek, Lord Buddha, Lord Maitreya, Sanat Kumara, Helios and Vesta, Melchior, the Lord of Sirius from the Great White Lodge and the Karmic Board members stand before you. In essence, you are petitioning balance for the entire monadic 144 soul-extension consciousness.

You are requesting for every theme to be harmonized through you. You are asking to take your place and your puzzlepiece of the great ascension process of humanity and the planet. You are committing yourself to your part of the world-service work of the divine plan and to demonstrate that part in both waking and dreaming consciousness as a unifier. Holding balance and holding your Earth mission as woman, as man, as ascended being—a representative of the Spiritual Hierarchy, a bodhisattva.

Speak and pray privately now in the sanctuary of your own being to the Karmic Board and all the masters gathered, for whatever you need to assist you with this purpose, for the highest good of all concerned. Know finally and completely that what you have requested is upheld and granted forevermore.

Sit now within the inner chamber in the stillness and let all energies of negative ego be dissipated. Let all past mistakes now be completely forgiven. Let any harm that has been done to self or others in this life or any past lives be healed, cleansed, forgiven and now balanced. Let all the patterns, habits, archetypes, subpersonalities and past-life aspects come into harmony with the Christ/Buddha/Melchizedek archetype and pattern.

Feel all archetypes, rays and astrological signs now become divinely integrated into perfect harmony and balance. Feel all of these aspects becoming balanced under the mighty energies of wisdom. Feel the flame of God burning brightly within the core of your being. Feel the violet transmuting flame of Saint Germain and Archangel Zadkiel purifying and burning up all that is not of the light of God.

Before all the masters present, in the inner silence of your own being, instead of praying, this time make your ultimate vows of commitment and service to God, the likes of which you have never made before, in a way and manner that you know you will never allow yourself to break. Make these vows with absolutely steel-like strength and power.

This is the vow that completes your freedom to fully be yourself and as-

sures your success in your planetary and cosmic ascension process. Make the vow and reaffirmation of the "I Am that I am." The vow that, "I am all that I Am!" Now breathe this fully into your being and lock it into place for all eternity.

Peace has come at last. Feel how grounded you now are in this energy. Everything that you have become is now brought into your physical body and is now connected to the Earth. You have brought heaven to Earth and are now the living embodiment of the monad and the mighty I Am Presence on Earth. You are here for no other reason but to serve, which is the vow of the bodhisattva. You are God made manifest on Earth to demonstrate that this is your true identity and share it in unconditional love, complete egolessness and balance in all things.

Open your eyes after completing this meditation. Hold this place and attunement, knowing that you don't have to go into meditation to achieve it. In truth, it has been there all along. Meditation is nothing more than a tool to help you remember who and what you really are, always have been and always will be.

The Arcturian Light Chamber

Anytime you would like to focus upon building your light quotient, you can call to Lord Arcturus and the Arcturians to be taken in your spiritual body to the Arcturian light chamber. It is, in reality, a type of ascension seat. It has a tremendous calming effect and balances the reflexes. It is one of the chambers on Lord Arcturus' mothership. It also seems to have a strong healing effect upon the physical vehicle, as an added benefit.

Lord Michael's Sword of Clarity and Vision

Call forth Archangel Lord Michael and his sword of clarity and truth to cut away all illusion and maya. He is especially good at cutting away the psychic cords of improper bonding patterns we form with other people, and is also extremely helpful in providing protection. Call for Lord Michael and his legions of angels anytime you are in need.

Prana Wind-Clearing Device

This is an Arcturian tool that I have discussed in some of my previous books. I mention it again here because more information has come in about this wonderful technology.

It is a type of fan that is lowered into the third chakra or, more recently, the heart, which blows all the etheric mucus and blocked energies out through the meridians, nadis and arteries. This fan spins from left to right clockwise, at a very high speed. It literally blows prana through our entire genetic code. The compartments within the cells receive this pranic energy and begin to expand. The entire etheric web is receiving pranic energy.

When we first received this tool, it was centered in the solar plexus. Now this fan, or prana-blowing machine, is placed in the heart. It clears out the cells and all pockets within the body and through the etheric web. It blows energy through the nadis (etheric channels), or electrical wires, in our body, actually blowing through everything.

It can be called upon whenever you need it and is there just for the asking, by the grace of Lord Arcturus and the Arcturians. It is like blowing into a reed that had some dust in it and the dust is blown out. This is what the prana wind-clearing machine does to your entire etheric system.

This clearing allows our true genetic code, given to us when we first came into this system, to be opened up and further encoded by new crystals of light. This could be thought of as sacred fire letters, key codes and sacred geometries. This allows the ancient-self and the future-self encodements to become clear, as well as our future overlays.

The idea is that each one of us becomes the bright light of truth that we are. The Arcturians have gone through these lessons already and are a beautiful race of beings that have now come to help humanity follow in their footsteps. There seem to be two types of Arcturians. One type is very tall and majestic, which is the form of the Lord of Arcturus. The other type is also beautiful, yet of a smaller, more Asiatic stature, with great expertise in the technical areas of the mothership.

By the grace of God the Arcturians have provided us with an arsenal of spiritual tools in the prana wind machine, Arcturian light chamber, the golden cylinder, direct light-quotient building, the light synthesis chamber [see *The Complete Ascension Manual*], the mechanism chamber, Arcturian plating system [see *Beyond Ascension*], grid-integration technology and the joy machine.

Do take advantage of these tools and techniques, for they are some of the most advanced in our entire galaxy and even universe. The Arcturians, as I have said many times, are Earth's future self and divine prototype. They are the most wonderful, loving and glorious beings imaginable. Call on them and form a bond of friendship and let them help you on your path of ascension.

This prana wind-clearing device can be made incredibly large to fill a room or auditorium, or miniaturized enough to fit into each one of your chakras. Ask that it be miniaturized into each chakra so it may blow open the compartments of each one. Each chakra has seven levels and three compartments. The innermost compartment is opened up to encompass the present and the past and to release the illusion of the past. This helps to unify heart, will, mind and Source.

As the compartments are opened in each chakra, you will come to a point of stillness within the center of the self—free of all debris, free of all separation, free of all prejudices, free of all false conceptions of the negative ego, leading to pure being.

Let the prana wind-clearing device do all the work it needs to do with you through the mind and brain circuits. This allows for even a greater grid repatterning by Vywamus. It is as if the garden of the self is completely weeded out of all that need not be.

Djwhal Khul said that this device is the one that comes after the core fear-matrix-removal program that I presented in *Beyond Ascension*. It not only clears the final dust and debris from our blueprint but also helps to bring in the new energies. We are all aware of how the winds blow on our planet. Through this Arcturian technology we are experiencing the winds of light coming through our body, with the new energies.

Use and work with the tools I have presented here and in my other books. They are among the most advanced cutting-edge tools for spiritual growth on this planet. They are being presented now in this most extraordinary time period through the grace of Melchizedek, the Lord of Sirius in the Great White Lodge, the Lord of Arcturus, Sanat Kumara, Lord Buddha, Lord Maitreya, Lord Metatron, Archangel Michael, Master Kuthumi, Djwhal Khul, the Ashtar Command, Allah Gobi, the Mahachohan, El Morya, Serapis Bey, Paul the Venetian, Hilarion, Sananda and Saint Germain.

These ascension tools and techniques are truly the "airplane method to God" as Paramahansa Yogananda once so aptly stated. They have never been revealed to the planet before and come as a new dispensation in this fabulous period in Earth's history.

Misconceptions about Ascension

In my work I meet and speak with a great many lightworkers from a wide variety of paths, which I always find very interesting. What I share with you here was told to me by the masters when I questioned them on some of the practices in some of these groups. There are many groups on the planet that are going around giving initiations of various kinds and some groups are even giving ascension initiations.

Understand this very clearly: There is no one on Earth who can give an initiation except Lord Maitreya, Buddha, Sanat Kumara and Melchizedek. Even El Morya, Kuthumi, Djwhal Khul, Sananda and Saint Germain cannot give initiations or ascension.

The chohans of the seven rays give reports to Lord Maitreya, Buddha, Sanat Kumara and Melchizedek as to the disciple's and initiate's readiness, but only these four beings can initiate. If anyone tells you they are actually giving you an initiation, it is illusion and a manifestation of the negative ego.

Melchizedek told me that initiations into his order are, in truth, all self-initiated. Any person asking for initiation into the Order of Melchizedek during meditation will receive it. You do not need any outside person to do this.

There are other groups of people going around the planet, who are very lovely people, but who are claiming to initiate people into ascension after a fifteen-minute ceremony. I asked the masters about this and they told me this was illusion. At this time only Buddha and Melchizedek are giving true ascension initiations.

The confusion here is a semantic one. Ascension is not just being awakened to the fact that one is the eternal self. Ascension is not just awakening. It is when Lord Buddha and/or Lord Melchizedek places his rod of initiation upon your being and fully initiates you into your sixth initiation. It is only when you have taken your sixth initiation that you can legitimately call yourself an ascended master.

These other initiations that are being given are lovely ceremonies, but, in truth, mean nothing. They are nothing more than receiving some level of *shaktipat*, or energy, from a spiritual teacher who is a little more advanced. I have actually asked the initiation level of the spiritual teachers who are giving these initiations and they haven't even taken the sixth initiation themselves. Yet they are going around telling people they have ascended after a short-and-sweet ceremony. There is no harm done and most of these spiritual teachers are very lovely people, but the belief that they are ascending people is complete illusion. If I were going to frame this process in the most positive light I possibly could, which I want to do, I would say they are giving preinitiations.

Fellow disciples and initiates, do not be seduced by the negative ego in this regard and think there is a fifteen-minute ceremony someone is going to give you that gives you ascension. It is illusion and you are being seduced by the ego if you believe it.

I looked through the teachings of these groups and leaders and I will now share with you what the confusion stems from. Number one is that true ascension is more than just awakening. Number two, and most important, is the fact that it is true that each person is the eternal self and the "fall" never really happened. We just think it did.

In this context, on the spiritual level, no one really has to do anything to achieve godhood, for we already are God, always have been and always will be. The confusion and misunderstanding here is that just because this is true on a spiritual level doesn't mean that you have "realized" this within your own soul evolution. This enlightenment is a mental enlightenment, which is good. It is not, however, a complete soul, mind, emotional and physical enlightenment in terms of realizing the truth. It is not enough to just think it. One must demonstrate it on the Earth plane to realize this.

There are seven initiations on this plane that must be realized to complete your ascension on a planetary level. There are 352 initiations that must be completed to achieve cosmic ascension. Just realizing that you are the eternal self and so are all others does almost nothing for you in terms of passing these initiations.

These groups are under the misconception that just awakening to your identity as the eternal self meets the requirement of being an ascended master. Being an ascended master means much more than just having this insight and going through a brief shaktipat ceremony. To call yourself an ascended master before you have legitimately achieved ascension is just a manifestation of glamour, maya and illusion.

In essence, this movement, with no malice intended, has a misunderstanding of what ascension is really. It is not something that can be given willy-nilly to anyone who goes through a two-hour class and a ceremony. It is also more than recognizing your oneness with all things.

To achieve true ascension you have to balance at least 50% of all your karma from your entire soul group. You must have 80 to 83% light quotient in your field. It must be decided by one of the chohans of the rays that you are ready. You must anchor your sixteenth chakra into your crown chakra. And you must fully anchor your soul and monad, or mighty I Am Presence, into your four-body system. This is something that is achieved gradually over time, not because some spiritual teacher says it is so, no matter how well-meaning or loving he/she is. Just because a spiritual teacher is extremely loving doesn't mean the philosophy he is operating out of is totally clear.

The belief that doing spiritual practices, or sadhana, is unnecessary, as many of these groups believe is also a dangerous sign that the negative ego and faulty thinking has taken over the spiritual teacher. To believe that praying, mantras and thinking is a form of separation is also an illusion. If you don't believe what I am saying, study the teachings of Sai Baba, who is the highest spiritual being incarnated on this planet and is a universal avatar.

This brings me to the next point about the term *avatar*. The true definition of avatar is "a person who is God realized at birth." I know of only two avatars on this planet: Sai Baba and Lord Maitreya. To think that all people are at the same level of realization is an illusion. Everyone is the eternal self, but not everyone is at the same level of realizing this truth.

That is why it is illusion to go around giving a talk and telling people they are ascended. Again, I repeat, the people who are in these groups are the nicest people you would ever want to meet, and I would be proud and am proud to call many of them my friends. To call what they are doing ascension is a misunderstanding of what ascension is, from the frame of reference of the ascended masters.

This discussion is not meant as a judgment of anyone, but rather a need to raise the understanding of ascension to a much deeper level. The ego is always looking for a shortcut to feel good about itself. There is nothing wrong with this, but make sure it is based on truth not illusion.

Another misconception in many of these groups is that there is going to be a pole shift toward the year 2000. This is also illusion. It was a possibility fifty years ago, but it is not going to happen now. Humanity and the Earth have gone through such an amazing spiritual transformation the past thirty to forty years that all those past catastrophic predictions Edgar Cayce and many others made are now bypassed, and are happening by grace instead of karma.

There is no judgment or fault for those who have believed in these faulty theories. I have been caught up in most of them myself at one time or another. See truth above all else, not following blindly the teachings of any one spiritual teacher. One of the most important lessons lightworkers on this planet need to develop is spiritual discernment. I have been pointing out here many of the faulty thoughts that these organizations and individuals are currently carrying. However, it is important to understand that there are also a great many truths and wonderful teachings held by these organizations.

It is not necessary to throw out the baby with the bath water. Be discerning and accept what is true and don't use what is not true. It is time for lightworkers to let go of the guru-devotee relationship, for this is now passing away as part of the ending of the Piscean Age. It is now time for all to be empowered and still have spiritual teachers, but not to give power to them.

A philosophy based on the belief that one has no philosophy and there is nothing to do to achieve God realization because one is already God is a dangerous philosophy and is extremely contaminated by the negative ego. It is what one might call a half-truth. Be discerning about this. Spiritual teachers who teach such a thing are well-meaning and are unconscious of their own lack of understanding and integration. Much more spiritual discernment and spiritual discrimination is needed by lightworkers around the planet.

Have the courage to admit your mistakes in this regard, for all is forgiven, and use this as a catalyst to take you to the next step. To remain locked into such a philosophy will hold your true ascension process back. Look at these different organizations as stepping stones leading you to the next unfoldment of your spiritual progression. They are not bad experiences, for no experience in life is bad. Every experience is good, for we learn from everything. Trust your own inner guidance of your soul and mighty I Am Presence to tell you if the groups and teachers you are involved with are teaching you the whole truth.

Do not follow any spiritual teacher blindly, including me. No one can be closer to God than your own heart. Trust your own intuition, discernment and gut feeling about what I am saying and what other spiritual teachers are saying. Do not look for perfect spiritual teachers, for there are none. Look for ones who are as clear as possible. The key word is "integration." Make sure that they have integrated philosophies and teachings and are not just operating out of the spiritual plane as many of the Eastern paths sometimes do.

If you want to know your true initiation level within the seven-levels-of-initiation system and have not been able to find out on your own, then give me a call and I will either help you myself or send you to qualified people who are clear channels for the ascended masters who can tell you. Be brave enough to seek truth rather than a quick fix.

This is a difficult assignment for everyone. I have spent many years being lost in many different teachings and theories. I keep striving for greater and greater levels of clarity, refinement and discernment. The ultimate goal is to be able to see through the entire prism and not through the infinite number of refractions of this prism.

Another misconception of many of these teachings is that the goal of life is to let go of all thought. This is not true. One does not have to let go of all thought to realize spirit. One has to let go of negative-ego thought to realize spirit, not Christ thinking. Eastern religion often tends to be antimind and this is unfortunate. As Sai Baba said, "It is your mind that creates bondage, and your mind that creates liberation." Do not get rid of your mind. Try and release the negative ego and/or separative and fear-based mind.

One of the common things one sees among a great many spiritual teachers is the belief that they are more advanced than they really are. There is no spiritual teacher on this planet, except the rare few such as Sai Baba and Lord Maitreya, who are beyond the seventh initiation out of 352 initiations. Most of the ones who think they are so advanced are not beyond the third to the fifth, as is the case with the groups I am referring to, without mentioning any names.

I am not interested in embarrassing or criticizing people. I am interested in helping the disciples and initiates of this planet release themselves from the illusion of the negative ego. The negative ego can be incredibly tricky and has invaded every aspect of reality including the New Age movement. This is why spiritual discernment is probably the single most important Christ/Buddha quality that needs to be developed.

To believe that one is equal with God is also another delusion of this path and the highest form of egotism. We can be one with God but not equal with God, for He created us; we did not create Him. We are equal with our brothers and sisters in a spiritual sense, but not equal to God.

To think that prayer is separation is also a delusion of the negative ego. Given that no being on this planet other than Sai Baba and Lord Maitreya has evolved more than one-tenth of the total spiritual path and then to call prayer a form of separation is a guise of the negative ego. Prayer is a way of healing separation and narrowing the gap of realization. To not allow oneself prayer because of such a belief is literally to deny the power of God and the ascended masters to help you.

The ascended masters are not allowed to help or answer questions unless you ask. Asking is prayer. Ask and you shall receive. We see here how the negative ego and forces of illusion can poison the belief system of the leaders of very large movements. These leaders actually believe they have completed everything and are operating out of the 352d level, when actually, they are at levels three to five.

Lightworkers basically buy into this ego trip, which is really what it is, by the thousands. Did not the Bible say that there would be many false prophets and false teachings? Just because a person says he/she is a master doesn't make him one. Usually when one needs to state it and puts some fancy name on himself, he isn't. No matter how loving he claims to be or seems to be, one must not by hook, line and sinker accept all that he teaches. And just because a spiritual teacher is loving doesn't mean that he has evolved his mental body or philosophical understanding in the slightest.

So it must be understood that all of us are equals spiritually. However, we are not all equals in terms of the realization of this ideal. Buddha and Melchizedek have a much higher level of realization of God than we do. This is the initiation process. The spiritual groups that I am referring to here have no understanding of this process of realization and how it works.

A common belief is that there is nothing to clear or purify because one is already the eternal soul and the christ. This is true, but it does not mean that you don't have anything to purify. Although you might have claimed this for yourself, it doesn't make it true within your four-body system. You might, for example, be filled with alien implants that have never been cleared. You might be contaminated with negative-ego thinking and are unaware of it. You might have physical toxins in your body. You might have core fear stored in your emotional body.

Believing such a philosophy is living in denial. No matter how strongly you hold to such a belief, it is not going to make it true. People in these groups, under the instruction of the leader believe that one should not work on his/her spiritual path, that she should just allow it to happen. This is also delusion of the negative ego. There is a time to work and a time to play. To truly realize God is a long road with much work involved. To think that there isn't is a faulty understanding. It is true that you don't want to over-work and become too serious on the spiritual path, but to think there is no work at all is ridiculous.

Another faulty belief is the Eastern path of striving toward nothingness. In this path the meditations consist of striving toward no thought and attain-ing nothingness. This is not a teaching of the ascended masters. As the old adage goes, "Argue for your limitations and they are yours." There is noth-ing wrong with an occasional meditation of nothingness, but not all the time, as is prescribed.

A more balanced approach to meditation is having all kinds of medita-tions: light-quotient building meditations, ascension seat meditations, con-versing with the masters on the inner plane meditations, light-activation meditations and meditations using mantras, channeling, automatic writing, matrix removal and clearing techniques. So I ask you, my friends, which would you rather have, "nothing" or a combination of many types of medita-tions?

Be aware that the most advanced spiritual teachers on this planet with the largest followings are filled with all kinds of these types of misconcep-tions. This is true of some spiritual teachers who have actually achieved their ascension. Ascension has nothing to do with automatically having a perfectly clear philosophy.

Another misconception about ascension is that ascension is when the body is turned into light. This is not a good definition, for many have achieved their ascension without this happening. Ascension is full integra-tion and merger with one's soul and monad or mighty I Am Presence within the four-body system.

A more exact definition of ascension is that it is the moment you re-ceive the rod of initiation from Buddha, the Planetary Logos, or Melchize-dek, the Universal Logos. At the time of the sixth initiation one is still not a fully realized ascended master. One might be termed a "kindergarten" as-cended master. Your ascension isn't really complete until you take and fin-ish the seventh initiation, integrating and activating your fifty chakras, building your light quotient to the 99% level and integrating and cleansing your 144 soul extensions.

This is why it is so absurd to see people going around calling them-selves ascended masters when, in truth, they are probably at the third or fourth initiation. The ego has found a way to inflate itself beyond the level the person has actually attained. We have all heard that a little knowledge is a dangerous thing. This is what happens when spiritual teachers of a lower-evolved level become world teachers before they are clear themselves.

These spiritual teachers have well-developed leadership abilities, which is good, but don't have true spiritual clarity and attunement to the masters. This is no different from the religious leaders in our world who think they are the most advanced spiritual leaders on Earth, but who have no understanding of anything I write about in my books or of the ascended masters.

The point of attainment of turning the physical body into light is way beyond ascension in our present phase of history. That will not come until we integrate not the fifth dimension but the twelfth-dimensional level, or universal level. This is what Melchizedek has told us.

It must be clear that people can achieve ascension without turning their bodies into light. Transforming the physical body into light is an advanced ascended-master ability, which not everyone who achieves their ascension will attain. Some will choose to release the physical body at death, but will still have achieved their ascension.

Another misconception of many groups is all that you have to do is "witness" in life. Becoming a witness is good, however, that will not solve all your problems. You have heard the expression, "Ignorance is bliss." There are people who witness, but who have no personal power. Personal power must be attached to witness consciousness. One must find a balance between witness consciousness and mental and physical action. One must deny entrance of any thought that is not of God to enter one's mind. A person can be a witness and still be a victim if he/she takes no action.

This ties in with the next misconception that the higher self is going to do everything through you. This is a misunderstanding due to lack of proper integration of the three minds. Each mind has its part to play. The higher self has its part, the conscious mind with personal power has its part and the subconscious mind must do its part.

To think that the higher self has to do everything through you and you have no part to play yourself on the conscious level, is delusion. Remember the expression, "God helps those who help themselves"? God, your personal power and the power of the subconscious mind are an unbeatable team.

It is good to hold the ultimate spiritual ideal of being the eternal self and being physically immortal and sickness being illusion as well as death. However, one must realize that this does not come about just because one thinks it. One must realize it through the process of initiation, light-quotient building and chakra, body, love and dimensional anchoring and activation. These are the mechanics and requirements that define ascension.

Most definitely hold on to your high mental ideal. Be realistic though as to where you really are in terms of the realization of this process. No person on this planet, no matter who his/her spiritual teacher is or what spiritual path or mystery school he is involved with, can escape the initiation process.

It is a process built into our earthly school by Sanat Kumara and the ascended masters. Claiming to be at a certain level doesn't make it so. Don't be deluded by other people's egos and those who make false claims about themselves and give spiritual boons they cannot deliver. Don't be misled by lower-level teachings that don't clearly present what ascension is.

One other misconception is the understanding of the waves of ascension. There are not just three waves of ascension. We are currently on such a rapid pace that there are close to three waves of ascension a year during the years 1995 to the year 2000, which is the window of mass ascension for this planet.

The first wave occurred in May, Wesak 1995. By Wesak 1996 two more waves of mass ascension followed. There will be waves of ascension occurring after the year 2000 at an accelerated rate through to 2012 (end of the Mayan Calendar) continuing on into the golden age and then beginning to taper off around the year 2028.

People will be ascending continually, however, until all on the planet have achieved this ultimate spiritual goal. It must also be emphasized that true liberation from the wheel of rebirth does not occur until one takes at least the beginning of his/her seventh initiation. Many who are claiming to be ascended masters, in truth, have not ascended and have not broken free from the wheel of rebirth.

One wave is not better than the next, for all evolve at their own divine timing. This is not a race or a competition. Lightworkers need to become more informed as to what ascension really is so as to not get caught up in simplistic misinterpretations.

One must also realize that with ascension, one is not dealing with his/her higher self any longer. At the fourth initiation one changes spiritual teachers and no longer works with the higher self, or soul, but instead works with the monad and mighty I Am Presence.

Merger with the higher self occurs at the third initiation and that is why this initiation is called the soul merge. Ascension is monadic or mighty I Am Presence merger and again, is not complete until all seven levels of initiation are completed and the 99% light quotient is achieved. When you attain this level you are then only one-tenth done with your spiritual path.

This is why some of the claims certain spiritual teachers are making are so absurd. In reality even after fully realizing our ascension, we are only *beginning* our true spiritual path.

The one super thing about these groups is that even though there is enormous misunderstanding and misconceptions about the path of ascension, it has served a very positive purpose. It has gotten people interested in and focused on ascension. The next step is to clarify and refine that which has been built.

Command and Vow to Live in Harmony

Djwhal Khul has suggested in training that he has given that each person make a personal vow and commandment to self, to God, to the ascended masters and to humanity. At the very core of your being make a commandment and vow to live in harmony, love and peace at all times, rather than fear, conflict and attack.

This vow and commandment must become the absolute rule of your life without any deviation. One must vow to keep one's mind steady in the light at all times. This vow and commandment must be backed with the full force of first-ray energy (the will of God). It must also be backed with the full force of the spiritual-warrior archetype and first ray power and destructive archetype (Shiva energy).

Once this vow is made, all choice or duality in your life ends. God, love, forgiveness, peace and harmony is all that exists, for this vow keeps your mind focused on this with ultimate vigilance from this day and moment forward. Indulgence of the negative ego and the path of conflict is no longer a potentiality allowed to manifest. Making this psycho-spiritual commitment is essential in working with the Arcturian and ascended-master tools.

If this psycho-spiritual vow is not made, in essence, choosing God instead of the negative ego, then the negative-ego mind will just build up all the negative energy all over again. You will be dealing with symptoms, not causes. The cause of our reality is our mind.

Make this ultimate vow now of peace and harmony. Remove all choice from your life. Nothing will accelerate your spiritual path and process of ascension any more than making this vow and commitment. It will also make your life much easier, for in making this one choice, all choices have, in truth, already been made.

The Externalization of the Hierarchy

Djwhal Khul told us recently that in a few years that which we think of as the Spiritual Hierarchy in the inner plane will actually be made fully manifest and externalized on this earthly plane. There will be no more division and separation between inner and outer or between the fourth kingdom (humanity) and the fifth dimension (Spiritual Hierarchy).

This is coming about as the third dimension is now being raised into the fifth dimension. The Earth has taken her sixth initiation and humanity is now for the first time taking its ascension en masse, where millions of lightworkers will have attained some phase of their ascension process. Mass ascensions in the past were for only a very small number of people. This is the first time in Earth's history that millions are ascending and continuing to remain on Earth and serving as bodhisattvas, taking the vow of spiritual service as liberated beings.

It is time for lightworkers to understand that *we* are the externalization of the hierarchy made manifest now. The core group's and my job is literally to externalize Djwhal Khul's, Lord Maitreya's and Melchizedek's ashram on Earth as it exists on the inner plane. This is why all this knowledge, information and light is now pouring forth.

Before now this was not really possible because Earth and humanity were not evolved enough. The Earth and humanity are taking a quantum leap to heal this separation between not only us and the Spiritual Hierarchy and ascended masters, but also between the extraterrestrial groups such as the Arcturians, Ashtar Command, Pleiadians and many christed extraterrestrial civilizations.

In our lifetime we will see this externalization come about in a more open way. Can you see the vision of what the golden age of this planet is now moving toward at lightning speed? This is the great work of all the lightworkers on Earth: to become the fully realized externalization of the Spiritual Hierarchy and to heal this illusionary and unnecessary separation.

The difference between us and the Spiritual Hierarchy and ascended masters is slowly beginning to fade away. As we realize this more we will begin taking over the positions in the Spiritual Government en masse as many of these beings move into their cosmic evolution in other places in God's universe. It is time for every person to now take hold of the rod of power, the rod of leadership and the rod of love in this regard.

One example of this is how the core group and I have been given the job to take over Djwhal Khul's inner-plane ashram in the year 2012. Even though we will be given this job at that time, we will still be on Earth. The full rod of power will be passed to us at that time and we will be running Djwhal Khul's inner-plane ashram on Earth. The fact is that we are really doing this already. However, the full mantle of responsibility and baton will then be passed. The second-ray department of the Spiritual Government will be literally externalized on Earth.

This is why I ask for the help of the lightworkers by coming to the Wesak celebrations and sharing the books with their students and friends. In this way lightworkers can join as team members in Djwhal Khul's, Maitreya's and Melchizedek's ashrams on Earth.

Each one of us has a puzzlepiece and team member part to play. All of us are members of Lord Maitreya's and Lord Melchizedek's ashrams, for, in truth, there is only one ashram in the universe—God's ashram. Lord Maitreya is in charge of all the seven-ray ashrams, which make up his one ashram. Melchizedek is in charge of all the ashrams in the entire universe, not just our planet.

There is no separation between the ashrams of El Morya, Kuthumi and Djwhal Khul, Paul the Venetian, Serapis Bey, Hilarion, Sananda and Saint Germain. This is important. I emphasize again, the seven ashrams of these chohans are the *one* ashram of Lord Maitreya.

These seven and Lord Maitreya's are the one ashram of the Buddha. Buddha's ashram is part of the ashram of our Solar Logos, Helios and Vesta, which in turn is part of Melchior and the Lord of Sirius Galactic ashram, which is part of the ashram of Melchizedek. They are all one. There is no ego or separation between ashrams. Any competition or separation between these seven great ashrams of the Christ and the seven chohans, which all disciples and initiates fall under, is absurd and such thinking is the height of egotism.

We are all on the same team. I put forth the clarion call to you, my brothers and sisters of the one ashram of the Christ and Melchizedek, to help and do your puzzlepiece, whatever it might be. The work cannot be completed without your help. This clarion call comes from Djwhal Khul, Lord Maitreya and Lord Melchizedek.

I was recently talking to a friend who has been helping me with the Wesak celebration and said to her quite spontaneously in regard to my appreciation to her for her help that she was not, in truth, helping me, for there is no "me." I have no life or thought or breath other than doing the job God and the masters have given to me (although it is not that I don't have friends or go to the movies and so on). In helping "me" you are helping Djwhal Khul, who has no thought but to serve Lord Maitreya and the Buddha, who have no thought other than serving the Lord of Sirius and Melchizedek. Do you see how this works?

I recently had a dream where in the dream someone asked my name and I said, "Djwhal Khul." It is not that I try to be like Djwhal, for I don't. I try to perfectly manifest my own mighty I Am Presence and monad. In doing this Djwhal Khul is the pattern that I reflect without even trying to do so.

I still have a very strong sense of self and the I Am, but it is merged simultaneously and completely with the work of the masters and the spiritual job responsibilities I have been given. My identity is also merged with the core group in this work.

Being given this leadership responsibility in the second-ray ashram, which deals with the education of the planet, I am calling upon you as my brothers, sisters, friends and associates to help me get these books and teachings out. I ask for this help from the blended consciousness of Djwhal Khul, Lord Maitreya and Melchizedek. Please also tell everyone about the Wesak celebrations to be held every year on the full Moon in May. I feel that these celebrations are extremely important, for they provide a meeting place for all the externalized masters of the Spiritual Hierarchy from around the globe to meet and share and be rejuvenated. It is also an opportunity to work as one team regardless of one's affiliation with a spiritual teacher, ashram, mystery school, religion or spiritual teaching.

The Issue of Using External Channels

When I use the term "external channel," what I mean is someone who is channeling other than his/her own channel and inner guidance. The guidance I give you here might surprise you.

There is a common belief among some lightworkers who say you should only rely on your own channel and inner guidance. I don't agree with this. That belief is too independent. On the other side of the coin, many, many lightworkers are too dependent upon one or many external channels and don't trust their own inner guidance. The ideal is interdependence and this has its reflection in the issue of external channels.

Let's begin with the understanding that there is not a channel or medium who has ever channeled who is not doing it through his/her own personality and his own information banks on some level. This even applies to the greats such as Edgar Cayce, Alice Bailey and Godfre Ray King. This is the nature of channeling. It is always somewhat colored by the personality, information banks, past lives, ray configuration, mission and so on of the channel.

Some channels are much clearer and more advanced than others. Much of the channeling in this world, over 90% is astral- and mental-plane channeling and has not even touched the spiritual plane. This is why lightworkers need to be very discerning. There is an interesting phenomenon among lightworkers that I have noticed. If you say it's channeled, they believe it and if it is not, they are likely not to believe it.

This is faulty thinking. There is so much confusion of this issue of channeling. Just because someone tells you he/she is channeling the ascended masters doesn't mean he really is. I don't care if he has written twenty books that he says are channeled by the ascended masters. In my opinion, lightworkers are often way too gullible.

The ascended masters might indeed come through at times, but the information might be contaminated by personality, negative ego and other distortions by as much as 50 to 75 percent. Lightworkers must learn not to give their power to channels as is so often done.

I am going to give two examples here, and normally I never do this, for I don't want to come across as judging or critical of others. I also don't want to embarrass other lightworkers who are often very sincere, beautiful people who have some distortion in their channel and program. I am going to make an exception to this rule because this issue is so very important.

The first example is the work of Elizabeth Claire Prophet. The masters have guided me to stay away from her work, even though she is one of the most well-known ascended-master channels. I am not saying that all her work is bad, for it isn't. I have looked through her material and gained a few points. I think most lightworkers recognize though that something is not right with her program. She is channeling the masters, yet I think there is an enormous contamination going on.

The second example is the I Am America Map, which you have probably seen. Here again this is supposed to have come from the ascended masters, yet I think it is extremely distorted and faulty information. That map might have been a possibility fifty years ago, but it is total illusion now. I mean this as no judgment, but I have checked this out very completely with the masters.

I bring these examples up to point a word of caution in regard to channeling of all kinds, even those channels who claim to and/or do channel the ascended masters. I am sure they are helping many people, for distortions don't discount their whole spiritual path.

Sometimes astral or mental beings claim they are ascended masters and take on their names and the channel doesn't realize it. Sometimes the person is channeling his/her own subconscious mind and thinks it is a master. Other times she is channeling a thought form and not a real being. There are millions of lightworkers on this planet whose normal everyday talking is far more advanced than ninety-eight percent of the channels on this planet.

Now, on the other side of the coin is the point of view that one should only get guidance from inside oneself, that every person is an island unto him or herself. This is dangerous also because everyone receives inner guidance through his/her own "lens," so to speak. One should obviously trust oneself above all else, as Shakespeare eloquently stated: "Above all else to thine own self be true."

Even though this is clearly the case when dealing with channeling, it is very important to be interdependent and sometimes check things out with other channels of a diverse background. When one is channeling sometimes some very strange information can come through and confirmation is needed from other sources. This is part of group consciousness. If a person believes he/she should never get guidance from anyone but from him/herself, then he should also never read a spiritual book.

What do you think books like the *Keys of Enoch, A Course in Miracles,*

The Urantia Book, The "I AM" Discourses and the works of Alice Bailey and Edgar Cayce, material from the Theosophical books and the Tibetan Foundation and even the Bible are? These are all channelings by other people.

People often channel information they read in books that their personality thinks is true, which I believe is the case with the I Am Map. It is wonderful to read and study the channelings of others in books that people write, including this one. After we hear or read the information, we need to check it out with our own inner guidance, channel, intuition and spiritual discernment. No one person channels the whole prism, so to speak.

I personally find it exciting to see life through the lenses of other masters and channels instead of just my own personal ascension lineage and ray configuration. It must be made clear again that just because it is in a channeled spiritual book doesn't make it true; these works could be contaminated.

What causes the contamination? This can be caused by negative ego, the personality, the channel's philosophy, negative emotions, past lives, power, greed, fame, fatigue, moodiness, past books he/she has read, limited information banks in his subconscious mind from past lives on a given subject, interference, astral entities, negative implants and negative elementals, lack of psychological clarity, level of initiation, whether he is operating out of the master a, b or c grid and most of all, his belief system! Other causes are the channel's ray configuration, monad and soul, improper integration of the twelve major archetypes, his/her astrological configuration, electromagnetic interference, even physical health problems, to name a few.

Any one or all of these affect channels. I hope this makes lightworkers a little more discerning in the future. My guidance to you is never give your power away to an external channel. Even though I say this, I also say that one shouldn't throw the baby out with the bath water. Even people who are channels themselves need feedback and confirmation at times.

Ninety-eight percent of the world's population is not clairaudient and cannot communicate directly with the masters. For those of you who would like information about yourself, such as your initiation level, ray configuration or light-quotient level and you would like help, there is absolutely nothing wrong with seeking advice from a qualified channel.

This is the key: finding a qualified channel. Without trying to sound egotistical, I would like to offer my services in helping you to find a qualified one. Most of this work can be done over the phone, so geographic location is not a consideration. If you would like help in this regard, I would be happy to be of service. Finding one good external channel is better than having a thousand readings from mediocre channels. A channel is only as good as the level of evolution of his/her own soul, mental body, emotional body and overall psychological clarity.

So as you can see, I am pointing out both the dangers of channeling and the benefits. The key is to not overdepend on external channels as a great many lightworkers do and to not isolate yourself or underdepend either. Even when using external channels, which is not really that different from reading a book or going to a lecture, be discerning and take what is of value and cast that which is not away.

Another most interesting phenomena in the New Age spiritual movement is how the great channels of the past such as Edgar Cayce, Godfre Ray King and Madam Blavatsky have been immortalized by their followers. They actually believe that there are no other channels or telepaths of any value since the incarnation of these teachers. The absurdity of this is beyond belief.

In truth, this is what traditional religion has also done by stating that the only teachings that are true are those of Jesus, Mohammed, Moses, Buddha or Krishna. What this does, whether we are speaking of traditional religion or the New Age movement, is keeps people locked into a specific time period in the past. Their consciousness is locked in 1942, 1930, 1890, the year zero or 500 B.C. To think that there is only one prophet of God or only one channel of God is ridiculous and such beliefs should be let go of quickly without judgment.

God is incarnated in every human being, every animal, every plant and every rock. God is always evolving and bettering Him/Herself. Don't stay locked into some past teaching. I am not saying you shouldn't study completely these past teachings, for I am the greatest advocate of this.

I love the Alice Bailey books, theosophy and the Tibetan Foundation. However, even this information is constantly evolving and becoming updated. This is what I have been presenting in this book and my other books. Djwhal Khul prophesied in the Alice Bailey books that there would be a third dispensation of ascended-master teachings toward the end of the century following the theosophical movement of Madam Blavatsky and Alice Bailey.

In closing, regarding using an external channel, when you need help in this manner don't be afraid to ask for advice. Find a good channel. Still be discerning and don't become overdependent on the channel. We are all interdependent beings and asking for help in this regard is not different from any other service you offer lightworkers. We are here to help each other, not be islands unto ourselves. Taking advantage of a good external channel, or psychic for that matter, is not different from reading a good book or going to a good lecture. Integrate it from the perspective of not giving your power away and it can be a wonderful tool, asset and catalyst for spiritual growth.

Helios and Vesta's Solar Chamber

This is the great chamber of Helios and Vesta. It is a brilliant golden-orange color. The Arcturians also work closely with and in conjunction to this chamber. Melchizedek will pour down the golden light through Melchior, the Galactic Logos, and then to Helios, the Solar Logos.

These energies are calibrated and stepped down to a frequency that we are able to handle. Through the etheric web, the grid pattern, thousands of miniature golden-orange balls of light begin descending. They begin to roll through our etheric web. We are literally filled with the atomic structure of the Central Sun, which is Helios' chamber.

See your entire etheric web, which has been cleared out by the prana wind-clearing device, light up with golden-orange Christmas treelike lights. When this energy is built up at the intersections, which are the chakras, it becomes very, very bright. We literally become like the brightest sun. We are holding the energy of the Solar Logos.

There is also a geometric formation that can be delineated here. This geometric formation has to do with the degree of light radiance each initiate holds in his/her grid. These geometric formations are formed out of circles, triangles, ellipses, rectangles, star forms. Each person's shining grid of light is built of such geometric formations within the building blocks of the atomic structure. The building blocks of light are forming our amino acid structure, our protein chain, nerve system and blood system. Every system in our body is penetrated and permeated by these structures with the intelligence of these encodements. Experience the seven suns of the self being lit up and joining as one great sun, one brilliant solar sun. This light is visible, tangible and palpable. Anchor it and feel your feet on the Earth. Be balanced in this solar light.

Atomic Structure Increase

At each stage of your initiation process and full movement into the integration of your twelve-body system and two hundred-chakra-system integration, your atomic structure is slowly but surely being increased. This must be done in a gradual, step-by-step process. Whatever level of initiation you are at now, request to Melchizedek, Metatron, Melchior, Helios, Buddha, Lord Maitreya and the master governing your particular ashram affiliation at this time for a special divine dispensation of an increase in your atomic structure to take you to the next step, in your evolution and in your world-service work.

At each stage of your initiation processing and dimensional-integration work, request this atomic-structure increase. Through a gradual process, step by step, block by block, you are building your lightbody through planetary and then cosmic levels of the ascension process.

My Favorite Clearing Tools

I thought it would benefit my readers to share with them the tools I have found to keep my fields and psyche clear and my physical body in good working condition and balance.

1. Calling for direct light-quotient building from the Arcturians while simultaneously calling for a healing and strengthening in areas of my physical body that need support. This can be done by calling to the Arcturians for a one hundred percent light-quotient increase and then a healing and strengthening of organs, glands, immune system, digestive system or whatever the specific assistance might be.

   If, for example, you have a bladder infection, you would say, "I call forth a one hundred percent light-quotient increase, and please heal and strengthen the bladder." Every time you do this the request might change, depending upon your needs.

   I find this particular tool to be one I use during most of the day while writing, working and running errands. It is energizing and strengthening to the physical body, plus it builds the light quotient. My work stamina is much longer also. I personally tend to run the Arcturian energy most of the day. At night while relaxing I work with the ascension seats and some of the other technologies if I need added clearing.

2. The Arcturian light chamber, which again is an ascension seat on the Arcturian mothership.

3. The prana wind-clearing device.

4. The golden cylinder-clearing device of the Arcturians.

5. Axiatonal alignment: This is a tool that I use a couple times a day to balance all my meridians and attune my meridian system to the lanetary and universal meridian system. It has a strengthening effect on the physical vehicle also.

6. Going to the synthesis ashram of Djwhal Khul and calling for the matrix-removal program, for core fear and imbalanced-energy clearing, as described in my book *Beyond Ascension*.

7. Using the crystal light technology of the Arcturians and Melchizedek, which is described in the last section of this book.

8. Utilizing the ascended masters and the angels of healing. Anytime you or someone you know has any physical health problems or emotional problems, call in these beings to balance the energies. They are an absolute godsend.

9. Sitting in the ascension seats, as listed earlier in this book. In the evenings when I relax, I like to just sit in them for long periods of time while watching TV, talking with a friend on the phone, walking or doing various chores around the house.
10. Once a week I do a more in-depth meditation using a lot of the other activation tools, but since completing my own ascension, I don't feel a need or desire to do all the activations that I used to in the past.

My main spiritual practice, or sadhana, now is my service work. In addition, all day long I run some kind of spiritual energy either through the Arcturians or the ascension seats, or light-quotient building, so I really don't need to formally meditate, for in reality I am always meditating.

As I am doing my various service jobs involved with writing books, putting on the Wesak celebration, working with students, networking, selling books and running Djwhal Khul's, Lord Maitreya's and Melchizedek's ashrams, I am automatically running through me all the spiritual energy I need. This is the key: making your whole life an ongoing meditation.

Once you complete your ascension you won't need to do as much of the ascension-activation work you need to do now. Cosmic ascension is a much slower process. No more initiations can be taken and there is a peace of mind that comes from reaching the top of the mountain, so to speak. There are more mountains to climb in regard to cosmic ascension; however, there is a tremendous peace of mind that comes from completing the "planetary ascension" mountain.

Never forget that your most important spiritual practice is love, followed by service. This is what the masters are most interested in seeing in their initiates. When you are serving, you are running the spiritual current through your system.

Another thing you will find after you complete your seven levels of initiation is that focusing on spiritual growth or your own personal evolution is much less a priority. World-service work becomes your all-consuming desire and focus. After you have reached the top of this mountain to focus on personal spiritual growth feels almost selfish, in a negative sense. It is almost like it is okay to do that before completion of the initiation levels, but after you reach this level, your focus should be completely on world service and leadership.

Cosmic evolution at our level is very slowed down and the masters really expect you to now put yourself out there and serve. The training wheels are off; you are now officially an ascended master. The ascended masters on the inner plane are not preoccupied with their own personal evolution. They are completely consumed in service work.

Cosmic evolution kind of takes care of itself once you reach this level. I will not say I do nothing in this regard, but almost nothing compared to what I was doing before. Being completely consumed in my service and leadership work is taking me exactly where I need to go without having to spend very much time thinking about or focusing on it.

Another thing that lightworkers must understand is that once you get into the higher levels of initiation, you become part of a wave, so to speak, with other souls at your level. As long as you basically stay on track, you remain in this wave. Whatever wave group you are in, all get the same spiritual benefits from the masters. The masters focus more on groups of people than individuals. Your level of spiritual attainment will automatically put you in a wave. As you mature in this process, you begin to trust this wave you are spiritually surfing, so to speak, which allows you to focus less upon yourself and more upon helping others.

Once you achieve the sixth and seventh initiations, the inner-plane ascended masters are in a sense beginning to kick you out of the womb and are less and less interested in your spiritual progression and more and more interested in how you can help in the ashramic work and completion of the divine plan.

If you want to have a really good relationship with the ascended masters, then make yourself valuable to them through your service work. In the higher planes they don't focus on spiritual growth in the same way they do here. Instead they focus on service and spiritual leadership.

Cosmic Ascension Battleplan

In the early stages of my ascension process I would call in everything "good" and "appropriate." However, as I matured in this process and completed my own ascension, I realized that all these cosmic energies weren't realistically being integrated. For example, currently in my path I have completed my seven levels of initiation, fifty-chakra anchoring and activation, ninety-nine percent light quotient, nine-body anchoring and activation and 144 soul-extension cleansing and integration.

I have also begun the solar-braiding work and am beginning to integrate the solar body and solar chakras 50 through 100. Realistically, I am in the beginning stage of integrating the solar level, having completed the planetary level. Now in my meditations I can call in the galactic bodies, universal bodies, cosmic bodies, 330 chakras and cosmic monad and so on. But the fact is, I cannot possibly integrate all the things I am calling in.

Being a little more mature in the process, I am no longer calling in all these things that I can't possibly integrate anyway. I am focusing on the level I am at and not trying to skip steps. I am not sorry I called for all those things in the past, for it was fun and got the masters' attention.

Now I am just focusing on the solar level. I spend more time in the

Golden Chamber of Helios and Vesta and make more requests on solar-activational work and not on all this other "cosmic stuff." This is something you, my readers, might also consider as a more efficient use of your energies. An occasional cosmic blowout is good, appropriate and fun. However, part of the spiritual understanding is being efficient.

There is also the danger of blowing your system out with too much cosmic energy that your system is not really ready to handle. A lot of this cosmic energy is not really given anyway (even if you ask for it), for the masters realize how unrealistic it is.

They might overlay you on some level, but they can't really get in until the solar wiring and integration is complete, then the galactic wiring and integration is complete and then the universal wiring and integration is complete. This is something to consider as you move into your sixth and seventh initiations.

The following list includes some of the activations I am personally working on myself with the core group. There are so many activations I have presented in my books that even I can get overwhelmed. I am one for always prioritizing and refining my work down to the key ones I need to do; more is not necessarily better. These activations are the ones I am currently working with as a priority to integrate the solar level. This list does change at times and is not written in stone.

1. Integrating and cleansing my 144 soul extensions;
2. Working with the golden chamber ascension seat, Arcturian light chamber ascension seat on the Arcturian mothership, Lord of Sirius' ascension seat in the Great White Lodge;
3. Working in the golden core of Helios and Vesta for solar bridging and solar-integration work;
4. Platinum ray and yod spectrum anchoring;
5. Downpouring of appropriate fire letters, key codes and sacred geometries to take us to the next step;
6. Light-quotient increase;
7. Inviting my 144 soul extensions to join us in meditation, if they would like to, with their freewill choice;
8. Vywamus' help in rewiring work;
9. Axiatonal alignment on planetary and cosmic levels;
10. Buddha/Christ/Melchizedek-archetypal anchoring and imprinting of energy;
11. Deeper penetration of the energies of the Mahatma;
12. Weaving the ascension fabric into physical, emotional, mental, spiritual and solar bodies;
13. Anchoring and activation of twelve bodies and chakras 50 to 100, especially the solar body;

14. Permanent integration of the anointed Christ overself body, zohar body and overself body;
15. All the clearing tools mentioned in the section titled "My Favorite Clearing Tools," as needed;
16. World-service work sending light to people, groups of people, cities or countries, as needed;
17. Raising of the atomic structure to the solar sun level;
18. Anchoring of light packets of information from the Treasury of Light (tablets of creation, Torah, or cosmic ten commandments, elohim scriptures, cosmic book of knowledge, golden book of Melchizedek, Metatron scriptures);
19. Anchoring of the seventy-two sacred names of Metatron;
20. Anchoring and activation of the decadelta light encodements of the ten superscripts of the divine mind;
21. Deeper opening of the cosmic Tree of Life and the ten cosmic sephiroth and the hidden sephiroth of Daath;
22. Request to the masters to do the next piece of work needed to take us to the next step of our personal spiritual evolutionary process.

Again I want to say that these activations are not the be all or end all of spiritual growth, but they are the ones I am personally working on now. One must gear his/her spiritual program to her own level of realization or initiation. I would suggest to go through all the ascension activations and meditations listed in this book. Use your intuition to make a list and a battleplan of the ones your monad and mighty I Am Presence want you to work on. Your intuition will tell you exactly what to do.

My battleplan is constantly changing at different phases of my life. Once I work with this one for a while, I will probably change, add and subtract to keep it fresh and exciting. The list I have given above is a good list for those who have completed the seven levels of initiations and have integrated the nine bodies and fifty chakras. This is my current battleplan to integrate the solar level.

I usually only do this once a week with the core group. Then I just delve back into my service work. All reading this book are welcome to use this activational meditation. However, I would recommend fashioning your own from all the tools I have given you that perfectly focuses on the next level, initiation and octave you are desiring to incorporate.

It must also be understood that sometimes running a single activation is better than calling in fifty activations. For example, just sitting in the Golden Chamber of Melchizedek's ascension seat for a couple of hours and doing nothing else can have profound results. Or simply running the Arcturian light-quotient energy for a long period of time or working with Metatron's light-quotient building can be highly effective.

More is not always better. As I told you, I run the energies twenty-four hours a day, seven days a week. However, most of the time I run a single energy at a time for about two or three hours. Then I will switch. My current favorites for daily running are the Arcturian light-quotient building, the Golden Chamber of Melchizedek, the Lord of Sirius Great White Lodge ascension seat or the Arcturian light chamber ascension seat.

These are the ones I use when I am feeling strong. When my physical body or energy systems are out of whack or when I am feeling a little contaminated with negative energy, I go to the cleansing tools list, or the ascended masters and the angels of healing and so on.

In reality, I am always working on myself. I am always switching around so I never get bored. I don't need to spend a focused time meditating, for I am always meditating. I am never lonely, for besides having friends, the ascended masters are literally always with me, which is extremely comforting and healing.

Setting up a program like this will have an enormous healing effect on all your bodies, including the physical. It will also give you the feeling that you are making good spiritual progress, for you are. Request every night before bed to go to one of the ascension seats or master's ashrams and retreats so you will take advantage of your sleep time for spiritual growth and you will sleep better. Doing all these things will also make yourself known to the ascended masters, as you will work with them consciously and this will hook you into an appropriate spiritual wave.

Part of the beauty of working with all these tools and ascension-activation techniques is that you don't have to be clairvoyant, clairaudient and clairsentient to use them. Everyone, and I mean everyone, will be able to feel the energy flow or spiritual current that comes from using any one or any combination of these techniques.

The energy is the most important thing. The energy is what does the activation work. Everyone can be connected to the ascended masters and cosmic beings through the energy. That is all you need.

In the past only those who were clairvoyant and clairaudient voice channels had access and even they did not have access to what I am speaking about in these books. Much of it has been opened up only since 1987 and the Harmonic Convergence. Working with these tools in my books and with the ascended masters in general is by far the fastest path on this planet to achieve ascension and self-realization. So share them with your friends and students. Spread them around the globe and let's work as a team to make this planet in the same prototypical light as the shining star of Arcturus.

17

Eighteen Great Cosmic Clearings

The following is some of the most important information in this entire book to achieve planetary and cosmic ascension. For this reason I have placed it at the very end of the book.

These eighteen areas of consciousness must all be cleared and purified to achieve self-realization. This can be done by asking the masters to help you. The spiritual path is amazingly simple because anything you want to achieve or attain is there for the asking.

In this book are the ultimate keys for accelerating your evolution. This has never been given forth to humanity in such an easy-to-understand, practical manner. These simple requests and invocations can literally save you many lifetimes and eons of spiritual work. The masters are willing to do these things for you, but you must ask.

This book was written to be your cosmic map and handbook. Go through each exercise one by one. The transformation you go through will be truly transfiguring, my friends.

Humanity for many millions of years has not known what to ask for, or who to ask. This list tells you what clearings to ask for. Among the masters to ask for assistance, I recommend Djwhal Khul, Lord Maitreya, Melchizedek, Lord Buddha, other masters of your choice and the Angels of Healing.

1. Genetic-Line Clearing

Call to the masters and request that they clear your entire genetic line. Your genetic line is connected to your genetics in this lifetime and all your previous lifetimes, tracing your physical body's heritage.

Just ask and the masters will do this for you. How they do it is not completely clear, but that is not important. This is the first stage of planetary and cosmic purification and cleansing. It can be done in meditation, lying down or at night while you sleep.

I asked Melchizedek where the core group and I were in this process. He said we had cleared ninety percent of our genetic-line karma. I then asked if he would just clear the rest for us. He replied that he would be happy to oblige. I wondered if we should do a formal meditation or not. Melchizedek said he would do it while we slept. As fully completed seventh-degree initiates I think that the only reason this had not been completed before is that we had not asked.

2. Past-Life Clearing

According to Djwhal Khul most people have had 200 to 250 past lives. Multiply this number by twelve if you want to include your eleven other soul extensions to get the total number of incarnations of the entire oversoul. If you want the total number of incarnations of your monad, multiply the number of past lives by 144.

This clearing process is specifically focused on your personal incarnational history. Call forth the masters and request that all your past lives be cleared since your very first past life on Earth. This is one of the requirements for planetary ascension. I asked Melchizedek if we had cleared this level. He said we had, which I found interesting because I had never officially invoked this before. It was cleared as part of the initiation process.

If you want to get real fancy, you can also request to have your future and parallel lives cleared and cleansed.

3. Soul-Extension Clearing

The next clearing process, spoken of in a previous chapter, is the purification and integration first of the eleven other soul extensions of your oversoul and then of the 144 soul extensions from your monad. This process then continues at the eighth level to the twelve oversoul leaders of the six monads or seventy-two soul extensions in your group soul. Next, at the ninth level, the monadic grouping of 864 soul extensions is cleared and integrated. At the tenth level the extensions at the solar, galactic and then universal levels are cleared. At these levels the numbers are vast and nearly impossible to figure out.

Do not ask for these higher levels of eighth, ninth, solar, galactic and universal levels until you first clear your soul and then your monad. As an intuitive guess, you can figure on integrating and clearing one soul extension a week. The core group and I have nearly completed the cleansing and integrating of our 144 soul extensions. The higher levels can't be started until you finish this level first.

4. Archetypal Clearing

Next request from the masters a clearing and cleansing of the twelve major archetypes and all minor archetypes. When this is complete, request an imprinting into the core of your being of all Christ, Buddha and Melchizedek archetypes on a permanent basis. If the conscious mind does not completely understand this material there is the danger of building the negative-ego archetypes back, even though the masters have cleared them. The masters will clear them energetically; you must clear them in your conscious- and subconscious-thinking process.

5. Cosmic-Cellular Clearing

This cosmic-cellular clearing was spoken of earlier in the book. It combines the energies of Melchizedek, Metatron and Vywamus and is intended to clean out your cells, or cellular structure, at the deepest possible level.

Again, it is interesting that many of these aspects are cleared in an overlapping manner. I had never spent much time focusing on this aspect in my meditations or invoking it specifically. Yet when I asked about this level, Melchizedek said it was ninety-eight percent clear for the three of us. It is good, however, to go through all the exercises at least once to make sure it has been cleared.

My motto is better safe than sorry. I would rather overdo it a little bit than underdo it. Some of the more advanced clearings on the cosmic level will take hundreds, if not thousands of meditations to fully clear.

6. Generalized Karma Clearing

The next great cleansing to invoke is for a massive generalized karma clearing. As many know, you need to balance 51% of your karma to achieve ascension. Even after achieving your ascension the process continues and you want to strive toward balancing all your karma.

This begins with your personal karma from all your past lives, then karma from all your eleven soul extensions from your oversoul. After that the balancing of all the karma from your 144 monadic-soul extensions occurs.

The masters can help you in this process. It will take a whole lifetime of meditating to clear everything; however, it is a noble goal to strive for. Just the process of integrating and cleansing our 144 soul extensions is clearing our core group of karma up to around 75%. Using the rest of these tools makes a goal of getting up into the high 90s a distinct possibility for all devoted and dedicated initiates.

7. Physical-Body Clearing

This clearing is not for your genetic line, but rather just your present physical body. Call forth to the masters, the Lord of Arcturus and the Arcturians for the complete cleansing and purification of your physical vehicle. Request that all disease be completely removed including all negative bacteria, viruses, fungus, cancer, tumors and genetic weakness. Request full permanent imprinting of the divine monadic-blueprint body and mayavarupa body to reign forever supreme.

8. Emotional Desire and Astral-Body Clearing

This cleansing invocation is for your present astral body. Ask that all negative emotions, lower-self desire, astral entities and negative psychic energies of all forms and all kinds that are not of the Christ/Buddha archetype be removed. Immediately call for this in the name of the Christ, the Buddha and Melchizedek. When your physical and astral bodies are clear, then move to the mental body.

9. Mental-Body Clearing

Call forth to the masters again and request a complete clearing of your mental body in this lifetime. Ask that all negative ego and imbalanced thought forms be removed and banished from your consciousness forever. Request that all remaining thought forms left in your conscious, subconscious and superconscious minds be only of the Christ/Buddha/Melchizedek archetype.

10. Etheric-Body Cleansing

Request of the masters a complete clearing and repair of your etheric body. Ask that all etheric mucus be immediately removed and that your etheric body be restored to its original divine blueprint.

11. Core Fear Clearing

This next clearing is connected to the astral-body clearing. However, it is so important that I have given it a category of its own.

There are only two emotions in life: love and fear. This could also be termed Christ consciousness and negative-ego consciousness. Call forth to the masters to anchor the core fear-matrix-removal program and request that you want all your core fear removed from this life, all your past lives and all your soul and monadic extensions.

During one weekend workshop focusing on this topic the masters told us they removed 45% of our core fear from our entire lifetime. This clearing process might take a great many meditations. If you are aware of a specific fear, ask that it be pulled out as you become aware of it. After the clearing ask to be filled with core love.

12. Implants and Elementals

Call forth to the masters that all negative extraterrestrial implants and negative elementals be removed. Call forth the golden cylinder from Lord Arcturus and the Arcturians and the matrix-removal program from Djwhal Khul and Vywamus to help in this process. When this is complete, ask Archangel Lord Michael and Vywamus to place a golden dome of protection around you on a permanent basis.

13. Twelve-Body Clearing

This clearing process is an extension of the five-body clearing that has already been done. Request that all twelve bodies, which includes the bodies up through the solar, galactic and universal levels, be completely cleared by the grace of Melchizedek, Metatron and Archangel Michael.

14. Fifty-Chakras Clearing

First request of the masters that your seven chakras be completely cleared of all energies that are not of the Christ. When this is complete then request that all fifty chakras leading up through the ninth dimension of reality be cleared and cleansed by the Grace of Melchizedek, Metatron and Michael.

15. Clearing Negative-Ray Influences

Every person on this planet is under the influence of the seven great rays. Each person's monad, soul, personality, mind, emotions and body come under the influence of one of these rays. Each ray has a higher and lower expression, as does each astrological sign.

Call forth to the masters and request a cleansing and purification of all lower uses and expressions of these ray influences. Call forth the seven ray masters, El Morya, Kuthumi and Djwhal Khul, Paul the Venetian, Serapis Bey, Hilarion, Sananda and Saint Germain, to help in this work. These masters are especially adept at this work, for they are the chohans or lords of these rays. The masters will clear you energetically in this regard.

However, your conscious and subconscious mind must understand this work also, for there is a danger of recontamination. Therefore, I recommend you study this more in-depth.

16. Clearing Negative Astrological Influences

Call forth to the masters again and request a complete clearing and purification of all negative astrological influences. Each astrological sign, house and planet has a higher and lower expression. Ask the masters to cleanse all lower expressions of these signs. Then ask them to anchor and imprint upon the core of your being the higher divine expression of these signs that God would have you manifest. At the end call forth an activation of the twelve heavenly houses for the highest possible ascension acceleration.

17. Monadic Clearing

For this next activation call forth Melchizedek, Metatron, Vywamus, Lord Buddha and Djwhal Khul. Call forth a cleansing of your entire monad. This invocation is much greater than just cleansing the 144 soul extensions. It is for the complete cleansing of all aspects of monadic existence.

Melchizedek said that this is one of the more cosmic ascension clearings and will take awhile to complete. Here you are taking on clearing your entire monad, not just your oversoul or just your self as one soul of twelve from your oversoul. The more you evolve, the greater responsibility you are taking for cosmic cleansing. This is a meditation you can do many times.

18. Super Cosmic-Clearing Invocation

This last super cosmic-clearing invocation was saved specifically until the end of this chapter and book. This activational clearing invokes a clearing of misaligned choices made long before your first visitation on Earth. It goes all the way back to your original covenant with God at the beginning of your creation, at the highest cosmic planes.

Since your first creation you have had free choice. This cosmic cleansing clears all choices from the beginning of your existence. Melchizedek says it also clears your original divine blueprint. This activation is really only appropriate when you are beginning your cosmic ascension process. You may invoke it before, however, the real work won't begin until the planetary ascension prep work is done.

He also said that this is such a vast and immense clearing that it should be done only in a group. The core group and I were told that we were not to invoke this by ourselves individually. We were allowed to do it in our group meditations.

One of the benefits to the 1200 to 2500 people who come to the Wesak celebration in Mount Shasta each year is that we have been given permission to do this activation and cleansing for the entire group. It is only because of the large group that this has been allowed.

For this activation call forth Melchizedek, Metatron, Archangel Michael, Buddha, Vywamus and Thoth/Hermes. The energies we are dealing with here are so vast and immense that it takes a group-body vehicle of a very high level of magnitude and vibration to handle them.

This clearing also clears our incarnations on other planets, in other solar systems, galaxies and universes. This is not something that can be cleared in one sitting. It would take a lifetime of meditating, for we are speaking here of clearing all 352 levels back to the godhead.

This might be called the ultimate cosmic ascension-clearing process (not planetary). Melchizedek said that this clearing also helps to clear the core field to allow the full impregnation of the mayavarupa, or divine blueprint body. It is not just for oneself, but is for the entire monadic-group consciousness.

The monad, remember, is much larger than each one of us as individuals. We are, in truth, just facets of this greater being that is the monad or mighty I Am Presence. This invocation is clearing the monad's or mighty I Am Presence's existence back to its original creation as an individualized spark of God.

On an individual level it helps energetically to know and understand our place and mission on Earth from the highest cosmic understanding. Buddha and his past life as Thoth/Hermes is instrumental in orchestrating this clearing for the advanced initiates on this planet. Vywamus is also helping with this work as an essential key. He is the higher aspect of Sanat Kumara, who is currently overlighting the Buddha as Planetary Logos, as Sanat Kumara has taken his next step in his cosmic evolution.

This super cosmic clearing really involves all the other seventeen clearings already invoked and much more, to say the least. Melchizedek said that at Wesak we would literally be clearing hundreds and potentially thousands of monads. All other clearings have been focused on more planetary ascension levels and clearing from your first stepping onto the Earth's planetary mystery school, which might be as far back as 18.5 million years.

This clearing is from one's original conception and creation in spirit as a monadic consciousness. I think you can see then how profound this clearing actually is. The super cosmic-clearing process is literally preparing and clearing the pathway back to one's original point of spiritual origin.

The Ultimate Divine Dispensation

Call forth to Melchizedek, Metatron, Archangel Michael, Lord Maitreya and Djwhal Khul for a divine dispensation to have the clearing work from the processes in this chapter to occur every night while you sleep for the coming months leading up to the next Wesak in the full moon in Taurus, when all initiations are given.

By calling forth a divine dispensation such as this the work is done automatically without having to consciously ask for it. This saves an enormous amount of time and energy. Personally I am big on efficiency of energy and all shortcuts to God realization. What lightworkers must realize is that God has given us everything. As stated in the lesson book of *A Course in Miracles*, "My salvation is up to me."

Your salvation is not up to God, for He has already given you His kingdom. In truth, you are already the christ. You already are and have everything. It is only our personal choice to identify with negative ego, separation and fear-based consciousness rather than Christ consciousness that prevents salvation, bliss, inner peace, abundance and happiness.

God and the masters are willing to answer any heartfelt request or divine dispensation as long as your heart is pure and your motivations are sincere. The only requirement that God places upon you (which is the golden key to supreme ascension acceleration) is that you must ask.

In this book I have laid out in a most practical easy-to-understand manner what to ask for. All you have to do to give salvation to yourself is really quite simple:

1. Take the time to meditate.
2. Ask for the help you need, and then receive it.
3. Practice the ascension techniques I have provided.
4. Practice the presence of God and being an ascended master in your daily life.
5. Make the supreme commitment to be vigilant for God and His kingdom, choosing Christ consciousness rather than negative-ego consciousness.
6. Dedicate your life completely to service of humanity in a balanced manner. God and the masters will deny nothing to a sincere heart.

Conclusion and Summation

I am here to tell you from personal experience that ascension and liberation is much easier to realize than any of us have previously imagined. By the grace of the ascended masters they will do a lot of the work for you on the inner plane in meditation and while you sleep. They will do this if you will ask. They are prevented by divine law from helping without your simple requests. Request their help and they will give you the kingdom.

Once you achieve your planetary ascension, which you all will, you can begin working on your cosmic ascension. That will be a much longer process. Knowing you have achieved liberation from the wheel of rebirth and feeling your close connection with your soul, your monad and the ascended masters will all be a great comfort to you. Also having learned to think with your Christ mind rather than with your negative-ego mind will free you from the bondage of your own creation. This will allow you to live in this world as an ascended being and a bodhisattva, a liberated being who remains on Earth to be of service to his/her brothers and sisters. This is the destiny of us all.

Before too long we will return to the inner planes and continue our service work on more expanded levels of consciousness. We will have transcended the need to return to physical existence and will continue evolving and serving until we ultimately achieve our cosmic ascension as well. Then we will become cosmic bodhisattvas, whose work will not be complete until all our brothers and sisters have achieved cosmic ascension as well.

It is only then that God's plan will be complete. Take comfort that the hardest part of our journey through our hundreds of incarnations is now over. The light at the end of the tunnel is near. Victory is now inevitable. The keys and the map to the kingdom are now ours. We are all blessed beyond our wildest imagination to be incarnated at this time in Earth's history.

What previously took four billion years is now being accomplished in forty years. All you have to do is with full commitment and personal power get onto this planetary rocketship. The force is with us and all we have to do is choose to be with the force. There is no faster spiritual path in this world than working with the ascended masters and the ascension movement.

As a fellow brother on the path I beseech you to take advantage of this golden opportunity that has been provided in this lifetime. Let us transform this world together and bring an end to suffering, glamour, maya and illusion. Let us all work together arm in arm, shoulder to shoulder, to transform the consciousness of humanity from a third- and fourth-dimensional consciousness to a fifth-, sixth- and seventh-dimensional consciousness.

Let us together make the Earth into a shining star and a truly heavenly planet to visit. There is much hard work to do to accomplish this; however, there is much love and joy in the fellowship. The goal we all seek for humanity and the Earth is inevitable. All people on Earth are God and nothing can stop the evolutionary process. The Dark Brotherhood can create minor problems; however, illusion cannot win over truth. Ego cannot defeat God. We all have a most noble and sometimes difficult mission on Earth. But if God be with us, who or what can be against us?

We can do all things with Christ/Buddha/Melchizedek/God who strengthens us. God, the ascended masters, our personal power and the power of the subconscious mind are an unbeatable team. The complete transformation of planet Earth and humanity while being a not-fully realized ascended planet is the stuff of which legends are made. Let us all work together to make this little speck of a planet in the outer reaches of the Milky Way galaxy a speck that all of creation takes note of because of the courage, strength, love, devotion and commitment to service of the great and noble beings who live here. Let us all now take on the mantle of leadership in this regard and be unceasing in our efforts until it is time to pass the baton on to the next generation ascension wave. Let us make our generation the pivotal turning point in this process and in this regard. Namasté.

Personal Summation of Cosmic Ascension Process

My beloved readers, during the writing of this book at times I have shared some of my personal relationship with the material. The funny thing about writing a book is that by the time the book is written, edited, a publisher found, the book reedited and finally professionally published, much of what has been written on a personal level has become outdated. On a personal level things continue to evolve, not only with myself but with everybody and with life itself.

So three years after this book was written I had the choice whether to take out all the personal sharing and/or have to reedit the book for a third time, which I really didn't want to do since I'd already written nine new books and am now more interested in spending my time bringing through new material. I consulted with the inner-plane ascended masters on this point and what they suggested is that I just add this final summation and addendum on a personal level to share with my readers the evolution of my process up to this point. Of course, what I'm writing right now will be completely outdated on a personal level in two to three years' time, not in terms of the theoretical material of this book but in terms of my personal evolutionary relationship to the material.

So as to the personal update, as of writing this book I have taken the twelfth initiation. The beginning of the tenth initiation is the beginning of true cosmic ascension. I was initially told by Metatron it would take two to three years to complete this movement from the tenth to eleventh initiation. As it turned out it only took one full year. I took my tenth initiation at Wesak 1996 and my eleventh at Wesak 1997. This was quite amazing to me in a humble kind of sense because the movement from the tenth to the eleventh initiation requires one to anchor and activate chakras 50 through 100. The first ten initiations involve the anchoring and activation of the first fifty chakras.

Once one moves into the realm of cosmic ascension, instead of anchoring seven chakras per initiation one must anchor and activate fifty chakras to realize that initiation. The first ten initiations require the integration and cleansing of one's 144 soul extensions. The movement from the tenth to the eleventh initiation requires the integration and cleansing of ten thousand soul extensions from one's monadic-soul grouping (mentioned earlier in this book). So, my beloved readers, you can see why I was humbly amazed to be given the grace to do this in one year's time from the 1996 Wesak to the 1997 Wesak. Cosmic initiations are much more vast in scope than planetary initiations one through ten.

The amazing thing about this process was that most of the work went on in the inner plane and was the product of the grace of the cosmic and planetary masters with whom I work. Yogananda said that the self-realization fellowship was the airplane method to God. Beloved readers, if self-realization fellowship is the airplane method to God, working with the cosmic and planetary ascended masters is the rocket ship to God. The amazing thing about this movement from the tenth to the eleventh initiation in one year, which was my first cosmic initiation, was that I barely even meditated. I spent most of the year completely immersed in my service work of writing books, being the director and coordinator of Wesak, running the Melchizedek Synthesis Light Ashram and Academy and keeping up with the enormous amount of correspondence and phone calls. My life was my meditation. I was not really even focusing on spiritual growth as I had in the past because I was too busy. This is the grace of working with the cosmic and planetary ascended masters and I cannot emphasize this point enough.

This grace was exemplified even further when the following year I moved from the eleventh to the twelfth cosmic initiation in only eight months. This is the anchoring and activation of chakras 100 to 150 and the integration and cleansing of one hundred thousand soul extensions, as well as the needed light quotient. Again I spent most of the year focusing on service work and the inner-plane cosmic and planetary masters agreed to push me forward in my progression basically because of my commitment to service and to realizing integrated ascension.

The completion of my twelfth initiation and the beginning of the thirteenth initiation is scheduled for approximately September 1998 on the current timetable the masters have me running on. This initiation involves the anchoring and activation of chakras 150 to 200, as well as the integration and cleansing of one million soul extensions in one's monadic-soul group, as well as the needed cosmic light quotient to pass this initiation. I want to be clear here that when I speak of the twelfth initiation I am not speaking of the twelfth initiation in the same vein that I spoke of it in my first book, *The Complete Ascension Manual*.

In that book I spoke of the system of twelve initiations being equivalent to the completion of the seven levels of initiation. In that system initiations seven through twelve were subinitiations of the true and major initiations one through seven. I am not speaking of subinitiations here; I'm speaking of the major initiations. After the seven initiations are fully completed, which is liberation from the wheel of rebirth, then initiations eight and nine can be taken to complete planetary ascension. Once planetary ascension is completed, if ready, the cosmic ascension process can begin. The tenth initiation is the beginning of the solar level, the eleventh initiation, the beginning of the galactic level and the twelfth initiation, the beginning of the universal level.

These initiations have never before been taken on this planet, until this time. The only exception to this is his holiness, Lord Sai Baba, who is an incarnated avatar born at a level far beyond this. He was born at a fully realized universal level. Being an avatar he is in a class by himself and no one on the planet is even close to his level of evolution. He is the most advanced spiritual being on this planet and the most advanced incarnated being in the history of Earth's evolution. So when I say no one has taken these cosmic initiations before until this recent time period, he is the only exception to this rule. He is an incarnated avatar. When I use the term "avatar" I mean he was God realized at birth.

This term is loosely used in New Age circles. It must be understood that Jesus, Buddha, Mohammed, Moses, Babaji, Yogananda, Ramakrishna, Saint Germain, El Morya, Kuthumi and the rest of the masters you can think of were not avatars. They were very advanced beings who came in at very high levels of initiation but were not avatars. They came in at a planetary level and through hard work and good deeds realized their initiation process and ascension in the same manner we are now doing, except it was harder to achieve this during the times in which they lived. We are blessed to live in a period of Earth's history where things are a hundred thousand times more speeded up than when these masters lived. They also achieved their initiations in a more integrated and balanced way than many are doing at this time in Earth's history. Where these masters came into incarnation at a planetary level, Sai Baba came in not at a planetary level, not at a solar level, not at a galactic level, but incarnated already having achieved all his initiations up to the universal level. This is why he is considered an avatar in the truest sense of the term.

The last thing I want to say here, having realized the twelfth initiation, is that it must be understood that initiations deal with spiritual development and not necessarily psychological and physical earthly development. Initiations have more to do with the amount of light and frequency one carries. I now feel strongly guided and compelled to give a warning to lightworkers. Just because one achieves his/her planetary initiations and has even begun her cosmic initiations, does not mean she is fully God realized. To become fully God realized one must achieve what I am now calling integrated ascension.

I have a number of students under my care and many friends who have taken higher levels of initiation. What is very disturbing to the inner-plane ascended masters and myself is the enormous lack of proper psychological integration into many of these lightworkers and spiritual leaders on Earth. They might have taken higher levels of initiation, however, they have not learned to control their negative ego. They have not learned to master their emotional and desire body and the subconscious mind. They have not learned to properly parent their inner child. They have not learned to properly balance the four-body system. They have not learned to fully become causes of their own reality. They have not learned to master and properly integrate the mental body. They often do not properly take care of their physical vehicle. They often have not learned the lessons of proper earthly integration.

If one does not learn and master these lessons, he/she will not be allowed to take her cosmic initiations and she will have to reincarnate on the astral and mental plane after this incarnation, even if she is beyond the seventh initiation. The ideal is not to achieve ascension but rather to achieve *integrated* ascension. This issue of lightworkers not being properly integrated and not properly integrating the seven levels of initiation into their four lower bodies is of enormous concern to the cosmic and planetary ascended masters. What is happening is that lightworkers are taking the initiations, however, only on the spiritual level. In the past masters had whole lifetimes to integrate one initiation. Now initiates are taking these initiations in two to three years and proper integration is not occurring.

Lightworkers need to spend more time focusing on the psychological level of God realization. There are three levels that need to be mastered to truly achieve God realization: the spiritual, the psychological and the physical. Each must be mastered distinctly on its own level. It is essential that all lightworkers pay their rent, so to speak, on all levels and not just the spiritual level. It is my humble prayer that these words serve as a helpful guiding light in the process of your full realization of your planetary and cosmic ascension.

Namasté.

A Channeled Message from the Mahatma

I pervade all 352 levels of existence; at every stage and every step of the way there am I. Do you, my children, pervade the universe at every level, but you know it not, or if you know it, you know it but in vague, dreamy intellectual understanding. In the case of more highly evolved souls and/or monads, you know it as the very touch of heaven itself.

It can be said that all self-realized cosmic masters, which you will all one day become, will awaken to this pervasive aspect of your being and in cojoining with the godhead itself will know you are so joined with the universe in total, the multiuniversal level, the christed universal level and beyond that place that words come from, but that which no word can describe.

I am the path and the journey's end. I am the top of the 352d level of the godhead and all levels from the first to the last leading upward to God Itself. I ask you in reading this to set aside your instinct to comprehend me with the mind and instead with your monadic alignment allow me to be revealed to your highest spiritual minds, and even that revelation of itself will be incomplete. As it is more my intent that you know me by my vibration and the highest of me, allow yourselves to seek to know me thus. Using these revelatory words as seed words, come further and further, deeper and deeper into my beingness.

This point I would like you to know, my beloveds who dwell within my very self: The journey upward, the journey of ascension takes one higher and higher—but "higher and higher" is a phrase used metaphorically. It rather takes you deeper and deeper into the vastness of your own God-self, which is all. One day upon your cosmic journey home you will awaken to the fact that you too, my little "Mahatma-selves," are also the 352 levels of God.

Diverse and many are the ways the universe reveals itself. What I wish to make known is, why then do you know me as the Mahatma, Melchizedek as Melchizedek, Metatron as Metatron, when at a certain point all in the universe and universes merge into the *one*? This one embraces every level, every being, mineral, plant, animal, human, elemental, devic, angelic and so many more in the vastness of worlds upon worlds that to name them would do no justice to the infinite.

I Am one and yet that one is many. I am a vast group body, which is one and yet that group body of oneness is unique in function, in purpose, in service of God. All the vast array of cosmic masters, logos, supralogos, archangels and again the more limited cosmic and planetary masters and beings (from my point of view, oh children of the one, limited not from your point of view) all have a unique position and group position within the vastness of the one. Just as upon Earth you might be part of a body, let us simply say a student body, functioning with one goal and one purpose, yet each individual being likewise, unique in purpose and individuality, so it is in the vastness of the cosmic expanses.

Each follows a divine purpose, planetary, solar, galactic, universal and multiuniversal, outward, inward, deeper and more inclusive than you can ever imagine from your vantage point, yet unique nontheless. Therefore, know that it is my unique purpose and I Am group though I Am, we are one in purpose to pervade and care for all the realms and levels of your existence. Mahatma is the great stairway, the many levels and the pinnacle of those levels. I (though we are group), our unity is of such a nature that we function as a whole and to say "we" would but put division in that which is one, and therefore we say "I." I am with you upon every step of that journey, for again I Am Mahatma, all levels of that journey and the journey's end. That is my function. I ask you not to try and comprehend that function except by meditation and intuition. Some great beings watch over and pervade over the evolution of a world and its cycle.

Certain masters, as you well know, have certain ashrams. There is a point where all melds into the whole and yet distinct and individual is the work and purpose within that whole.

As you travel deeper and vaster and "higher," as you call it, you become more and more attuned to the vastness of who I Am and begin to know this through frequencies and vibrational shifts. Yet you need not wait to know me, for I, being at one with every step of those levels, pervade the whole. I can be called upon *now*, at this moment on whatever rung of the ladder you are upon, and come to you, I will, for I Am already there. And uplift your frequencies I will, for that is the nature of the stairway to godhead, to increase all that needs to be increased to further the journey "upward" until you reach the heights that let you know and in actuality be the all-pervasive *whole*.

But I say again, being the many levels itself is a unique mission, a "cosmic job." Do not try to grasp the fullness of this job upon the reading, but simply to attune with the highest and deepest frequencies of my beingness. This will elevate you so that more can be revealed and made known unto you.

The further you expand through the levels of my being, the greater and more expansive you become. The greater and more expansive you become, the greater of access I am to you in the revelation of my totality, although you must be aware that there is a limit, a ring-pass-not of just how much of my total self that can ever be brought forth upon the Earth plane of matter. And yet it is far greater than many of you suspect or that has hitherto been accessible and attainable. So hear well that it is my very purpose and my prayer request, if you will, that you will daily call upon me to overlight you. You see, although I pervade everywhere and am in truth the synthesis of all things, it is through the accessing of more and more of the greater aspects of myself that I can most efficiently and effectively do my work through you. This is what I seek to achieve and why I have of recently made myself known to you in the fashion I have.

So much of your world still functions in great divisions. The obvious ones of race, creed and color hardly need mentioning, yet I mention them so that you—and particularly you lightworkers who have grown far beyond this point and might overlook the obvious—can look again at this issue and take fully into your awareness how deep the level of separation still is on your Earth. Or inversely, you can look at how utterly superficially pervasive fragmentation and separation still abound on this, your hallowed world. It is with the energy of synthesis that I seek to help you overcome this and that I inversely seek out your help, oh noble ones of light and wisdom. For the bulk of humanity there still abides a great chasm between the four lower bodies, the soul and certainly the monad. Many of you reading these pages, although you have achieved great levels of light realization and actualization, still likewise struggle with the total synthesis of the four lower bodies, despite the fact that you are soul or monadically merged.

It seems odd, but it is a fact and the full installation, activation and actualization of your greater lightbodies awaits you. Please know, dear ones of my self, that I am working diligently with you, the trailblazing lightworkers of the world, who are requesting and effectuating a synthesis of those bodies. The deeper you venture into the core of my being, the more light you become and the greater and greater your personal process of integration and synthesis. As it so occurs within you, so it occurs within your world and this on every level and plane of existence on your world and beyond. There must be this integration and synthesis, for as I have stated, all is one great whole and the actualization of your personal synthesis will bring you and your world, one by one and group by group into *synthesis itself.*

So it is as I have said, my group purpose as the avatar of synthesis is to help you bring this about and ask again that you call upon me. I restate that although I pervade all 352 levels and am everywhere, so too I seek to bring you to those higher levels, which are in actuality more inclusive, more synthesized levels of myself. This I can only do by working through and within you and this I can and will do if you but simply request it. I am already functioning thus within those of you who have made this request and to you

I am most grateful. To you I also say that you may continually ask for deeper penetration of myself and I will actualize this moving at a safe pace through your light-expanding system, and for this deeper penetration I await your call. Call thus and with de*light* I shall so come unto you with expansion of light, love and in the bringing forth within you a more vital realization of these deeper levels of synthesis that I embody.

Your ultimate potential, each one of you, is infinite, and stage by stage I seek to bring each of you into greater realization of the levels of our *being in unison*. So let us then proceed as the whole we are, dear children of myself, my "little Mahatmas" who are now unfolding into the vastness of synthesized being. simply call upon me to incorporate, activate and bring to full realization and manifestation the synthesis you are, as monads incarnate, functioning in all your bodies in ever-greater frequencies, ever-greater harmony, ever-greater *at-onement* of yourself and your soul's potential, your monadic potential, your expanding greater group purpose as monads synthesizing into the whole, the *one*, traversing the 352 levels of the godhead that is Mahatma: That I Am and because that I Am so thou art.

Yet remember, I Am where you are now even as I am the apex to which you journey. I ask that you call upon me only that I may work more deeply with you in your expansion and I ask that you keep constant remembrance of the truth that I am where you are now even so as I await your arrival into the total expansion into the godhead. With you now I Am and where you are headed, there I await your arrival.

Pay heed and do your right work upon every step of your journey, for remember I Am the very steps of that journey. I Am Mahatma and I bless you all.

A Message from Archangel Michael

I am Archangel Michael and I come to you, my beloved children. I speak to, through and within the hearts and minds of all who open unto me and my purpose. This time of acceleration is quite demanding on you, my beloveds, and so I come to offer you my love, my wisdom, my strength and indeed my protection. There is an interesting phenomenon occurring that I wish to make you, dear readers, aware of. Many, many of you are growing in strength, even as you are growing in your capacity to love unconditionally, even as you are expanding your light quotient and growing and expanding telepathically. Your sensitivities are extending vertically, from the dense physical vehicle, up into the higher realms, where divine wisdom is being imparted to you, where the angelic kingdom and line of evolution, the planetary and cosmic masters and those beloved friends and fellow initiates on the inner plane can be seen, felt, heard and known.

Likewise are your telepathic abilities extending horizontally from one to another. This is of course to your great advantage and a sign of your development and advancement of your ascension process. Yet this, if not carefully monitored, can also leave you vulnerable to incoming patterns of thoughts and emotions that you are so very often not aware of, but that impedes upon your minds and nervous systems in general.

Let me explain, and know that in my explaining I am guiding you toward self-protection and an awareness of how I might be of service to you along these lines. To begin with, in the normal course of evolution you can see that it is through the development of the nervous system that consciousness itself develops and kingdoms are transcended from one to the other in ordered succession. The mineral feels but little; the vegetable senses more. In the animal kingdoms the nervous system truly begins to take shape and in the more evolved and domesticated animals true emotions are felt. Then we have man in his varying degrees of sensitivity—from the savage, almost animalistic man to the young baby soul to average humanity to the disciples and initiates I am presently addressing. For you, dear ones, are your sensitivities great indeed, as your very nervous system is in a constant state of refinement that you may all the more easily be in telepathic rapport with those of us on the inner planes and more quickly achieve liberation and ascension.

You therefore grow increasingly more sensitive to the subtler aspects of yourself, your brothers and sisters, those with whom you work both on the inner and outer planes and the ascended planetary and cosmic masters (the last two categories requiring extreme sensitivity). Because of this you are open in a way that those who are less evolved, less expansive and less sensitized are not open, and it is vital that you learn how to close off at the appropriate times and how to protect yourselves. One of the best ways to do this is to ask for help, since your process often necessitates your being open channels to write, to heal and to commune. Please know that this is my prime function and purpose and that if you but call I will surround you with my blue-flame sword of protection and stand as a barrier between you and any and all unwanted or misqualified energy.

Beloveds, let me give you a specific, or potentially specific, example. All of you who are lightworkers are connected with a specific group of beings with whom you work. Most of you who are lightworkers also do some sort of work in the world, certainly you have some interaction even if just at the market. All of you who are lightworkers are extremely open to the inner realms of light and to activities occurring on the inner planes in general. You are protected by the very nature of your own light-and-love selves and yet, as I have said, are also vulnerable. For example, if a member(s) of the group with whom you serve is having a bit of a "time of it" as most of you are turning this phase of rapid transition and you tune into your group consciously during meditation, or even unconsciously simply by being telepathically linked with that group, some leakage of another's struggles is bound to come into your auric field. There is nothing really wrong with this, as it is all part of the process of learning how to function in ever-greater group formation and goes with the territory of the ascension process. Yet it is a problem that can be easily overcome by invoking protection, and this I offer in abundance, dear hearts, for this is my particular puzzlepiece.

In this way, with your invocation I will surround you by my protective sword, encircle you with the fire of its strength and power and block you from being sensitive to any disturbances. With this protection can you more easily proceed with your purpose, function and sensitivities.

Along other lines, the deliberate harshness with which the world at large functions can and often does cut like a knife and we of the higher realms know this. Call upon me and my sword then, which is far stronger than the knife and I will cut loose and junk that which has been thrown your way and taken into your sensitive auric field. Also know this, my beloveds, and that is that I ask you to ask me for my constant protection upon the inner realms. There will be a time, I promise you, when your strengths will supersede your sensitivities, but for almost all of you that time is not now. Let me stand as a wall before you and any and all psychic debris that clutters the lower astral and lower mental realms and can make its way into any area of psychic vulnerability that you might still have.

What I am saying in essence is, I am here for you and want nothing more than to serve you. The path onward and upward increases sensitivity by virtue of the very nature of that path and it is my divine calling, my divine job to blaze my sword in strength and protection of all pilgrims upon that path, if you but ask. Ask much from me, dear ones, for I have much to give. I will serve as your protector, and you need protection as your nervous systems become ever more rarefied. I will also teach you how to protect yourselves, for as you call to me, tune in to me and let me serve you, so too will you learn from me. Buffer not bewilderment from your sensitivities, for that refinement is essential to your development. However, do not continue needless suffering when I am here awaiting the call to protect, for that is my essence, my service, my joy. To love, serve and protect is what I am and who I am.

With love, your Archangel Michael.

Channeled Concluding Message from Archangel Metatron

Welcome into the sphere of light. Those of you who have traversed these pages of *Cosmic Ascension* have done more than mere reading. What you have done is connect your physical brains via the lower- and higher-mind aspect of yourselves with a deep and abiding illumination. What we have done (by "we" I mean the planetary and cosmic masters working with you) is help and guide you through this vast encounter with these teachings and help to open the kingdoms within you. We did this with the hope that each one of you finds that sacred place within yourself where the truth of cosmic revelation, the truth, love and wisdom within the words revealed upon these pages and within yourself might resonate as one.

What I have done and do now and every time you attune thusly to the higher cosmic nature of reality is to gift you with my light that you may bathe in light substance itself, drinking in the light, becoming the light and therefore within the light, having the deepest realization of truth shine forth from within you and as you. I am the archangel of light itself, which you would liken unto a fire, a fire that burns but does not consume, the *zohat*, the cosmic fire. Then I would be for you the caretaker ever mindful to keep that light-fire ablaze.

With my light do I alight you and help to bring all godly aspects of who you are to the highest they can possibly vibrate at any given time. Therefore, am I the illumination for your all-encompassing and unconditional love, your ever-expanding wisdom, your growing God power (the power of the will to good) and the illumination of all that your ascension process shall unfold.

As it is with all the cosmic masters who span and enfold the vastness, deepness and fullness of the one, ever am I at one with you, even as I am myself one who in ages and eons past has taken my specific post in upholding the puzzlepiece that is called light. Therefore, am I within you and am I transcendent of you, available to aid you with the radiance of my being. Even as I seek to communicate with you, what I should rather do upon this book's closing and make available to you whenever you read these pages or ponder upon these vast subjects is to light your way in the understanding and comprehension of truth itself. It has been well said that he who has nothing to hide fears not the light. I wish that you all know that you indeed have nothing to hide, nor could you ever in actuality hide, for light pervades the universe and what you should ever seek is to transcend and transmute that from which you would run and hide.

All stands revealed, oh flames of my heart, fire of my fire, hearts of my heart, for light revealeth all and there is nothing to fear from that which brings forth illumination. We of the cosmic realms, we who are the embodiments of that which you seek to unfold within yourselves are ever at hand to love and guide you upon your own planetary and cosmic journey of ascension. Light seeks to do naught out to further alight, more intensely bring to light that which is hidden—and this is my function.

Therefore, the gift I give is one of illumination. It springs from both the fountain of silence and the fountain of the words you have now studied and taken into yourselves via the mind. I then call you into meditation at the conclusion of this most blessed book of these most sacred mysteries revealed under the title of *Cosmic Ascension*. Each reading will take you further into the comprehending, as will each pondering upon that which is written. Yet unless you drink of the light contained therein, the wisdom, love and truth contained therein will do naught but remain at the outer edges of your mind.

It is in the interest and spirit of integrating these truths and revelations into the core of your very selves that I now gently guide you into meditation. Close the book, except for these last few pages and close the faculty of third- or even fourth-dimensional thinking. If you can, tape this meditation for use so that there be naught but a quiet and direct voice guiding you through the silence.

Take a deep breath and upon the exhale expel the very thinking process itself. Say to yourself: I who am of the light have read and pondered upon the light and now seek to blend and merge with that light I Am. Lord Metatron embodies light and will now, upon my request and in the stillness void of chatter, merge me thus with the light I Am and bring illumination into every part of myself.

All that I wish to know will and is being revealed to me as I breathe in the very breath of light substance. I allow every cell of all my bodies to thus increase in brilliance and know through direct contact that which I have invoked through study and pondering. Just as there is an inbreath and an outbreath, so there is the period of study, pondering and contemplation and the period of assimilating what I have contemplated. As light I open to the greater light; I fuse the spark with the flame and am naught but illumination. Thus in the silence I sit and let the truth of light reveal itself to me.

Then sit in the quiet stillness of unity between the spark and the flame, the flame and the cosmic fire, allowing the inner light to fuse with the light most brilliant. Allow wisdom to take hold within you and know I am there overlighting this process. Do this after each study period and more and more light will be shed upon the wisdom/love/light you have pondered upon by allowing yourself this period of meditation (and it need not be long, although sit longer if you are pulled to). You are guaranteed to assimilate truth on every level of your being in a complete and integrated fashion. That which you have but thought upon you will become, and thus in the light of illumination will all things stand revealed.

Then end your meditation with these words: *Let light and love and power descend unto me in fullness ever as I ascend unto it in fullness. Om, om, om.*

Then in quietness go about your next task, knowing a greater and wondrous illumination is taking place within you. Thus it is that the wisdom of the word revealed through these pages, as you study them again and again, and the wisdom born of the silence merge as one light within you, bringing to light, at the appropriate hour, all that you hunger to know.

In light I am, in love I serve, in truth I am revealed, Archangel Metatron.

Bibliography

Bailey, Alice A. *Discipleship in the New Age*, Vols. I and II, New York: Lucis Publishing Co., 1944, 1955.

———. *The Destiny of the Nations*, New York: Lucis Publishing Co., 1449.

———. *Ponder on This*, New York: Lucis Publishing Co., 1971.

———. *Serving Humanity*, New York: Lucis Publishing Co., 1972.

A Special Thank You

I would like to give a special thank you to Zandria Louise Fossa for her wonderful help in putting my books on computer and helping out with many of the computer graphics. Her dedication and devotion in this area has allowed me to continue my creative flow of writing new books, rather than getting bogged down in the time-consuming details of authorship.

Other Books by
Joshua David Stone, Ph.D.

The Ascended Masters Light the Way
A Beginner's Guide to Ascension
Beyond Ascension
The Complete Ascension Manual
Hidden Mysteries
How to Teach Ascension Classes
Manual for Planetary Leadership
Revelations of Sai Baba and the Ascended Masters
Soul Psychology

About the Author

Joshua David Stone has a Ph.D. in transpersonal psychology and is also a licensed marriage, family and child counselor in Los Angeles, California. On a spiritual level he anchors what is called the Melchizedek Synthesis Ashram, which is an integrated inner- and outer-plane ashram representing all paths to God. Serving as a spokesperson for the planetary ascension movement, Stone's spiritual lineage is directly linked to Djwhal Khul, Kuthumi, Lord Maitreya, Lord Melchizedek and the Mahatma. He also feels a close connection with the divine Mother, Metatron, Lord Buddha, as well as a deep devotion to Sathya Sai Baba.

Author's address:

Joshua David Stone
5252 Coldwater Canyon Ave., #112
Van Nuys, CA 91401
Tel. (818) 769-1181
Fax (818) 762-1782

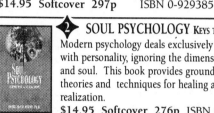

⬥7 A BEGINNER'S GUIDE
TO THE PATH OF ASCENSION

This volume covers the basics of ascension clearly and completely, from the spiritual hierarchy to the angels and star beings, in Dr. Stone's easy-to-read style. From his background in psychology he offers a unique perspective on such issues as karma, the transcendence of the negative ego, the power of the spoken word and the psychology of ascension.

$14.95   Softcover 166p   ISBN 1-891824-02-3

⬥8 GOLDEN KEYS TO ASCENSION AND HEALING
REVELATIONS OF SAI BABA
AND THE ASCENDED MASTERS

This book represents the wisdom of the ascended masters condensed into concise keys that serve as a spiritual guide. These 420 golden keys present the multitude of methods, techniques, affirmations, prayers and insights Dr. Stone has gleaned from his own background in psychology and life conditions and his thorough research of all the ancient and contemporary classics that speak of the path to God realization.

$14.95 Softcover 206p   ISBN 1-891824-03-1

⬥9 MANUAL FOR PLANETARY LEADERSHIP

Here at last is an indispensible book that has been urgently needed in these uncertain times. This book lays out, in an orderly and clear fashion the guidelines for leadership in the world and in one's own life. It serves as a reference manual for moral and spiritual living and offers a vision of a world where strong love and the highest aspirations of humanity triumph.

$14.95 Softcover 284p   ISBN 1-891824-05-8

⬥10 YOUR ASCENSION MISSION
EMBRACING YOUR PUZZLE PIECE

This book shows how each person's puzzle piece is just as vital and necessary as any other. Fourteen chapters explain in detail all aspects of living the fullest expression of your unique individuality.

$14.95 Softcover 248p   ISBN 1-891824-09-0

⬥11 REVELATIONS OF A MELCHIZEDEK INITIATE

Dr. Stone's spiritual autobiography, beginning with his ascension initiation and progression into the 12th initiation, is filled with insight, tools and information. It will lift you into wondrous planetary and cosmic realms.

$14.95 Softcover   ISBN 1-891824-10-4

⬥12 HOW TO TEACH ASCENSION CLASSES

This book serves as an ideal foundation for teaching ascension classes and presenting workshops. The inner-plane ascended masters have guided Dr. Stone to write this book, using his Easy-to-Read-Encyclopedia of the Spiritual Path as a foundation. It covers an entire one- to two-year program of classes.

$14.95 Softcover 136p   ISBN 1-891824-15-5

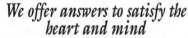

Former U.S. Naval Intelligence Briefing Team Member reveals information kept secret by our government since the 1940s. UFOs, the J.F.K. assassination, the Secret Government, the war on drugs and more by the world's leading expert on UFOs.

Behold A Pale Horse

About the Author

Bill Cooper, former United States Naval Intelligence Briefing Team member, reveals information that remains hidden from the public eye. This information has been kept in top-secret government files since the 1940s.

In 1988 Bill decided to "talk" due to events then taking place worldwide. Since Bill has been "talking," he has correctly predicted the lowering of the Iron Curtain, the fall of the Berlin Wall and the invasion of Panama, all of record well before the events occurred. His information comes from top-secret documents that he read while with the Intelligence Briefing Team and from over 17 years of thorough research.

by
William Cooper

$25⁰⁰

Softcover 500p
ISBN 0-929385-22-5

Excerpt from pg. 94

"I read while in Naval Intelligence that at least once a year, maybe more, two nuclear submarines meet beneath the polar icecap and mate together at an airlock. Representatives of the Soviet Union meet with the Policy Committee of the Bilderberg Group. The Russians are given the script for their next performance. Items on the agenda include the combined efforts in the secret space program governing Alternative 3. I now have in my possession official NASA photographs of a moon base in the crater Copernicus."

Table of Contents

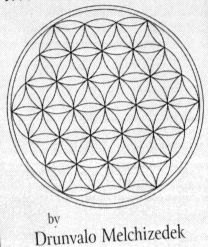